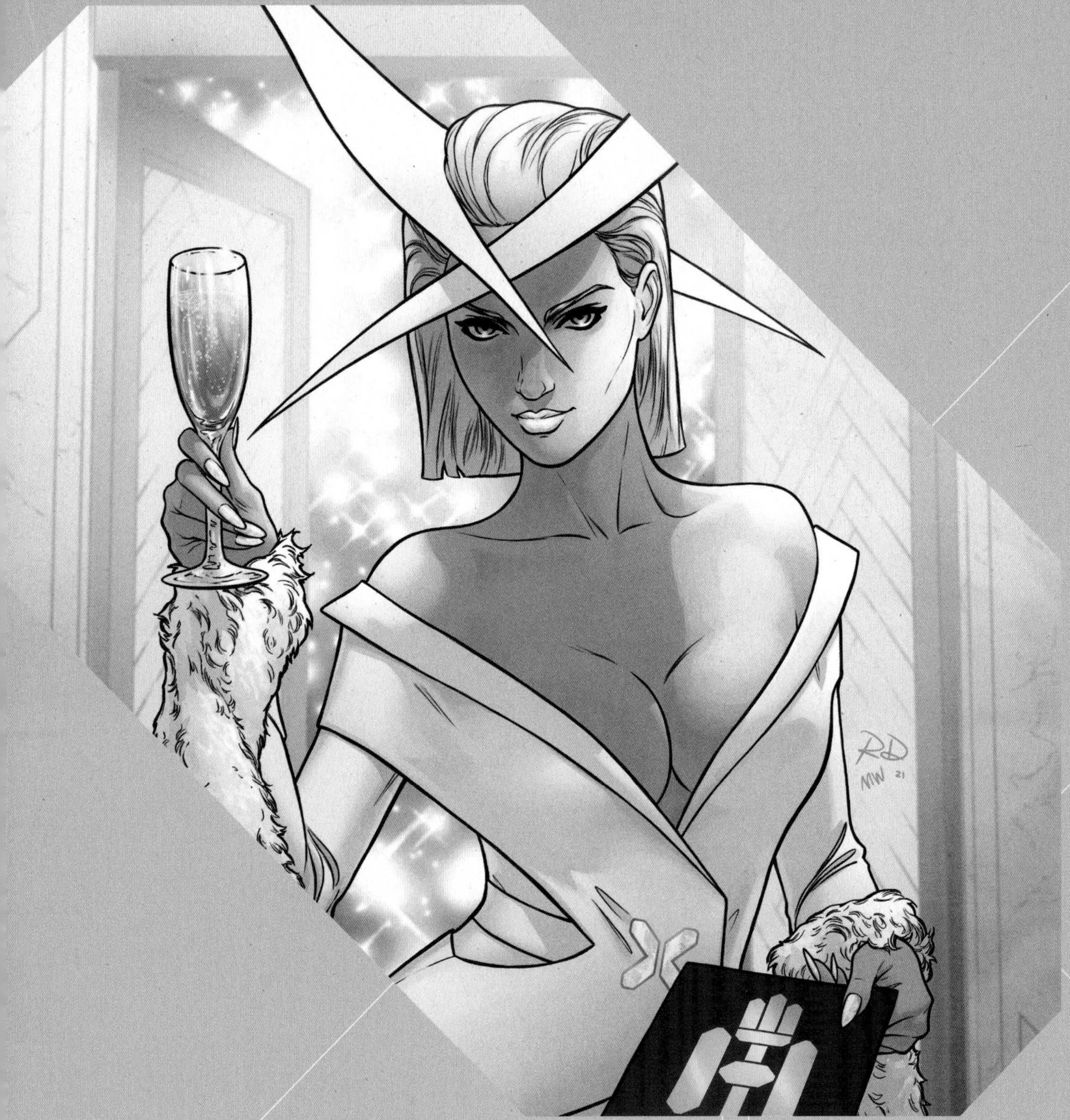

REIGN OF X VOL. 12. Contains material originally published in magazine form as MARAUDERS (2019) #21, X-FORCE (2019) #20, HELLIONS (2020) #12, EXCALIBUR (2019) #21 and X-MEN (2019) #21. First printing 2022. ISBN 978-1-302-94498-8. Published by MARVEL WORLDWIDE, INC., a subsidiary of MARVEL ENTERTAINMENT, LLC. OFFICE OF PUBLICATION: 1290 Avenue of the Americas, New York, NY 10104. © 2022 MARVEL No similarity between any of the names, characters, persons, and/or institutions in this book with those of any living or dead person or institution is intended, and any such similarity which may exist is purely coincidental. **Printed in the Canada.** KEVIN FEIGE, Chief Creative Officer; DAN BUCKLEY, President, Marvel Entertainment; JOE QUESADA, EVP & Creative Director; DAVID BOGART, Associate Publisher & SVP of Talent Affairs; TOM BREVOORT, VP, Executive Editor; NICK LOWE, Executive Editor, VP of Content, Digital Publishing; DAVID GABRIEL, VP of Print & Digital Publishing; MARK ANNUNZIATO, VP of Planning & Forecasting; JEFF YOUNGQUIST, VP of Production & Special Projects; ALEX MORALES, Director of Publishing Operations; DAN EDINGTON, Director of Editorial Operations; RICKEY PURDIN, Director of Talent Relations; JENNIFER GRÜNWALD, Director of Production & Special Projects; SUSAN CRESPI, Production Manager; STAN LEE, Chairman Emeritus. For information regarding advertising in Marvel Comics or on Marvel.com, please contact Vit DeBellis, Custom Solutions & Integrated Advertising Manager, at vdebellis@marvel.com. For Marvel subscription inquiries, please call 888-511-5480. **Manufactured between 4/29/2022 and 5/31/2022 by SOLISCO PRINTERS, SCOTT, QC, CANADA.**

10 9 8 7 6 5 4 3 2 1

REIGN OF X

Volume 12

X-Men created by Stan Lee & Jack Kirby

Writers:	Gerry Duggan, Benjamin Percy, Zeb Wells, Tini Howard & Jonathan Hickman
Artists:	Matteo Lolli, Joshua Cassara, Stephen Segovia, Marcus To, Nick Dragotta, Russell Dauterman, Lucas Werneck & Sara Pichelli
Color Artists:	Edgar Delgado, Guru-eFX, David Curiel, Erick Arciniega, Frank Martin, Matthew Wilson, Sunny Gho & Nolan Woodard
Letterers:	VC's Cory Petit, Joe Caramagna, Ariana Maher & Clayton Cowles
Cover Art:	Russell Dauterman & Matthew Wilson; Joshua Cassara & Dean White; Stephen Segovia & Rain Beredo; Mahmud Asrar & Matthew Wilson; and Leinil Francis Yu & Sunny Gho
Head of X:	Jonathan Hickman
Design:	Tom Muller
Assistant Editor:	Lauren Amaro
Associate Editor:	Annalise Bissa
Editor:	Jordan D. White
Collection Cover Art:	Russell Dauterman & Matthew Wilson
Collection Editor:	Jennifer Grünwald
Assistant Editor:	Daniel Kirchhoffer
Assistant Managing Editor:	Maia Loy
Associate Manager, Talent Relations:	Lisa Montalbano
VP Production & Special Projects:	Jeff Youngquist
SVP Print, Sales & Marketing:	David Gabriel
Editor in Chief:	C.B. Cebulski

[reign_of_x]

[kra_]
[koa_]

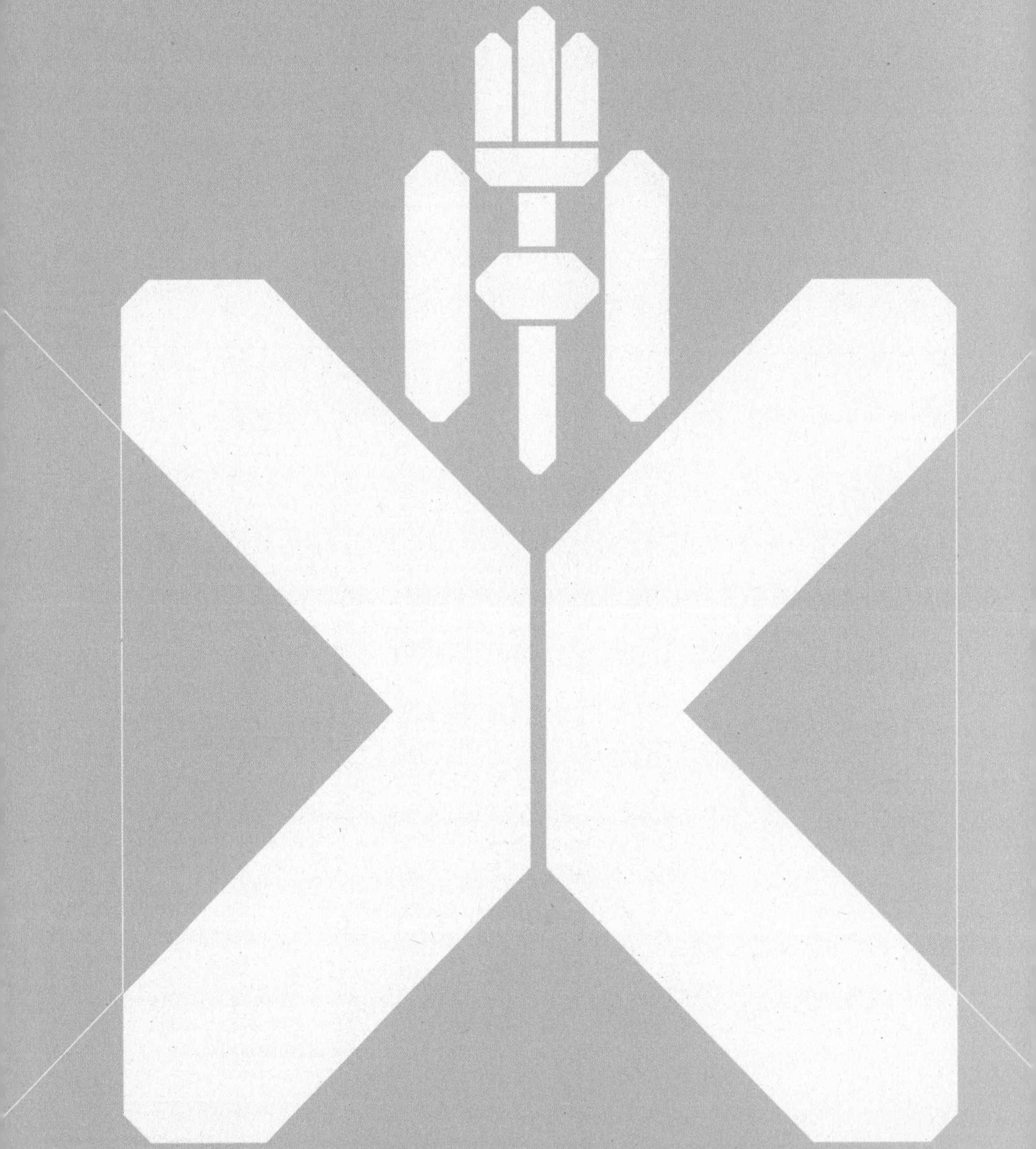

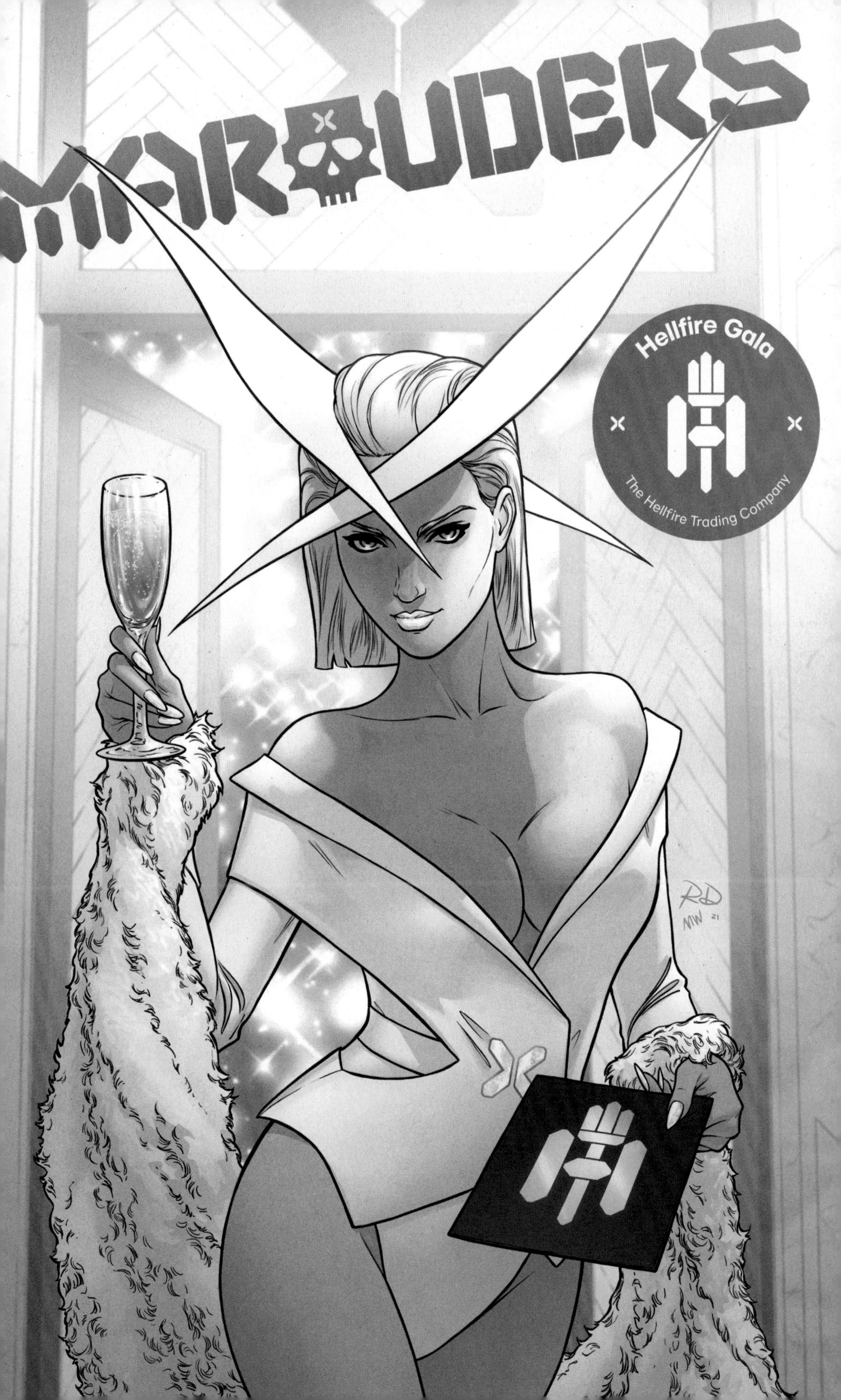
MARAUDERS
Hellfire Gala
The Hellfire Trading Company

YOU ARE CORDIALLY INVITED
TO THE

Hellfire Gala

The Hellfire Trading Company

ON THE EVENING OF THE SUMMER SOLSTICE

Host Emma Frost invites you to
celebrate mutant culture and to
strengthen Krakoa's friendship
with the nations of man.

GATES OPEN 7PM GMT

COCKTAIL HOUR

TELEPATHIC CONCERT

DINNER

**INTRODUCTION OF THE NEW X-MEN,
HEROES OF KRAKOA**

CELEBRATION & DANCING

**CLOSING REMARKS FROM THIS
YEAR'S HOST: EMMA FROST**

FIREWORKS DISPLAY

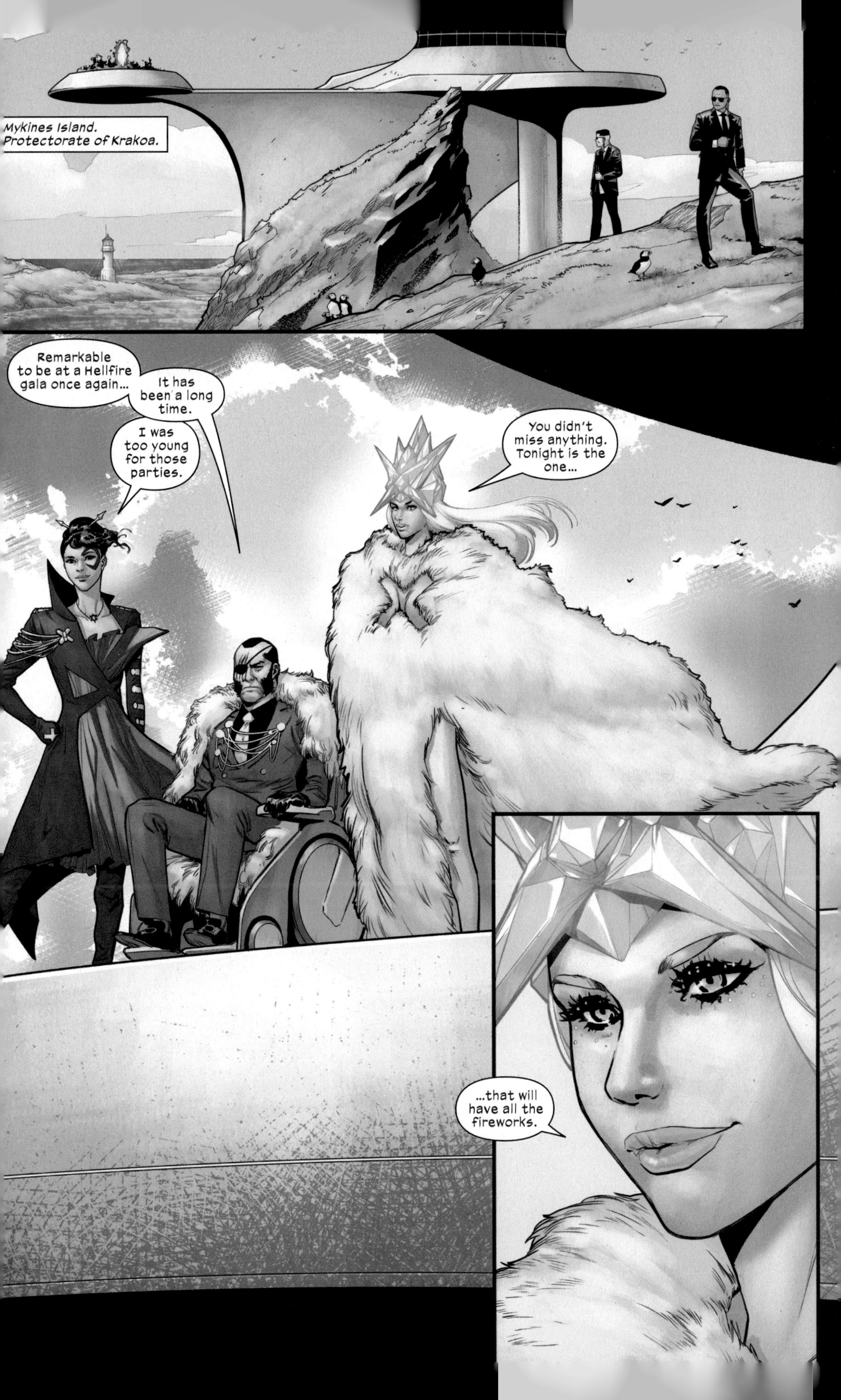

Mykines Island.
Protectorate of Krakoa.
Remarkable to be at a Hellfire gala once again...
It has been a long time.
I was too young for those parties.
You didn't miss anything. Tonight is the one...
...that will have all the fireworks.

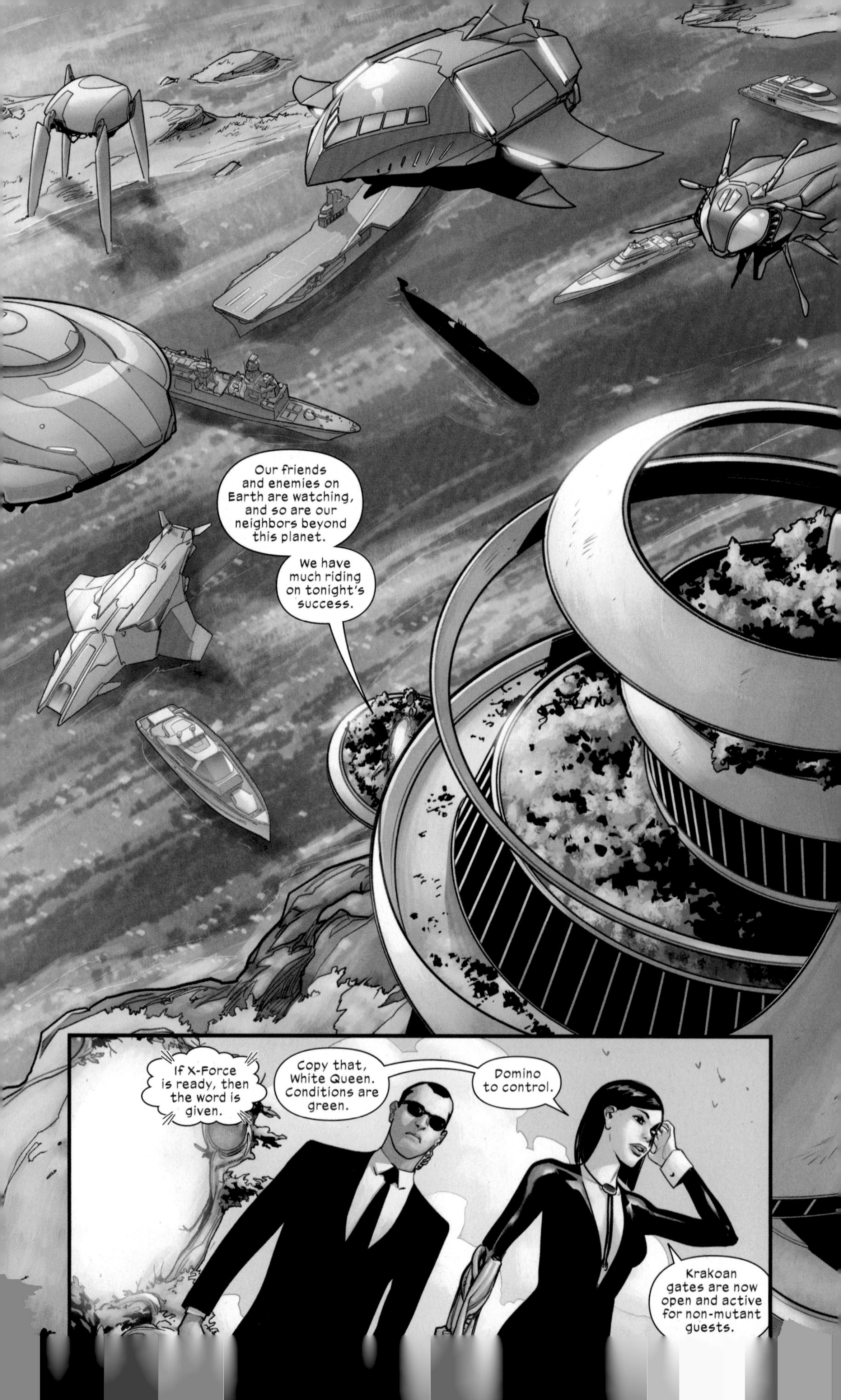

Our friends and enemies on Earth are watching, and so are our neighbors beyond this planet.
We have much riding on tonight's success.
If X-Force is ready, then the word is given.
Copy that, White Queen. Conditions are green.
Domino to control.
Krakoan gates are now open and active for non-mutant guests.

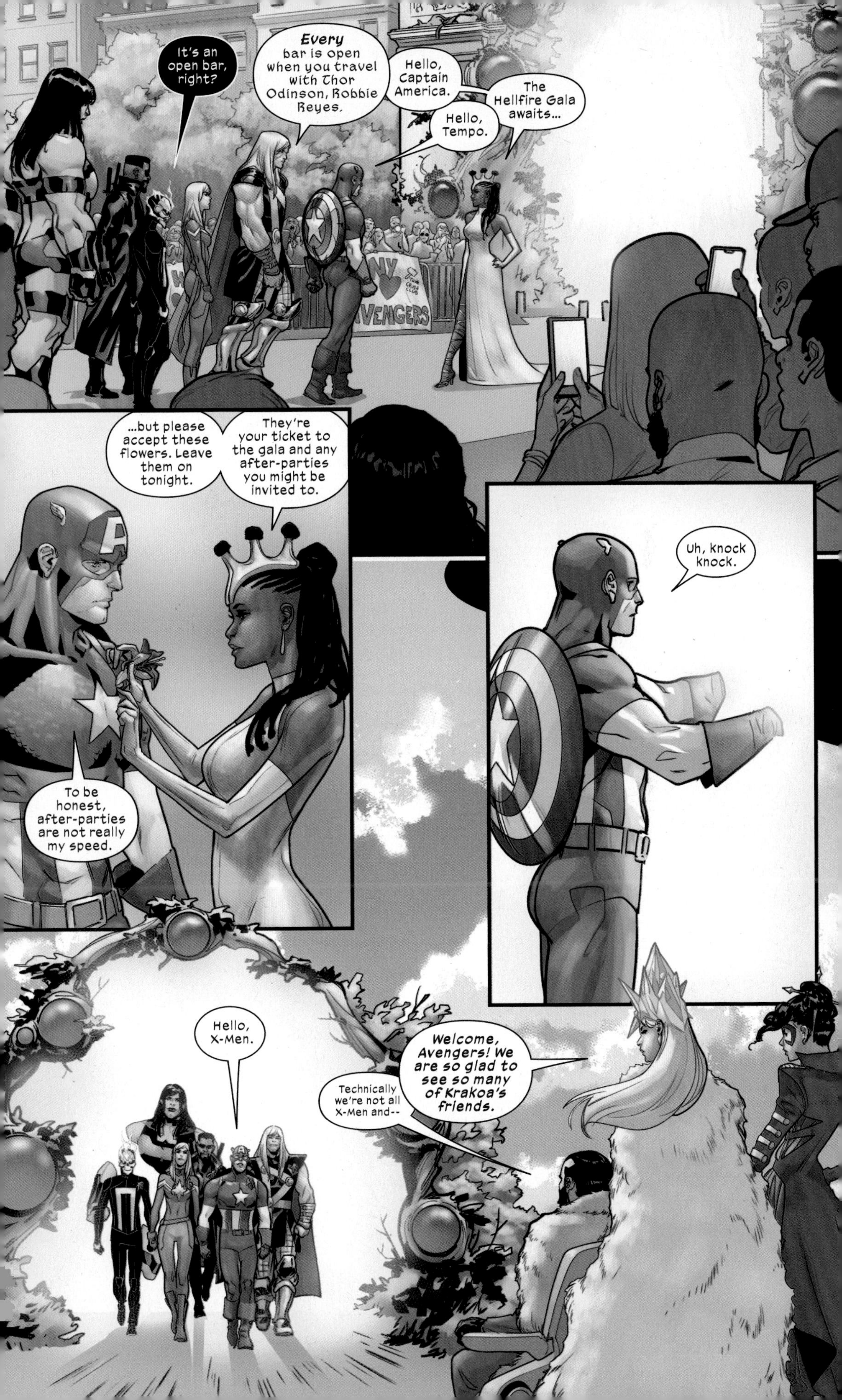
It's an open bar, right?
Every bar is open when you travel with Thor Odinson, Robbie Reyes.
Hello, Captain America.
Hello, Tempo.
The Hellfire Gala awaits...
NY ♥ AVENGERS
...but please accept these flowers. Leave them on tonight.
They're your ticket to the gala and any after-parties you might be invited to.
To be honest, after-parties are not really my speed.
Uh, knock knock.
Hello, X-Men.
Welcome, Avengers! We are so glad to see so many of Krakoa's friends.
Technically we're not all X-Men and--

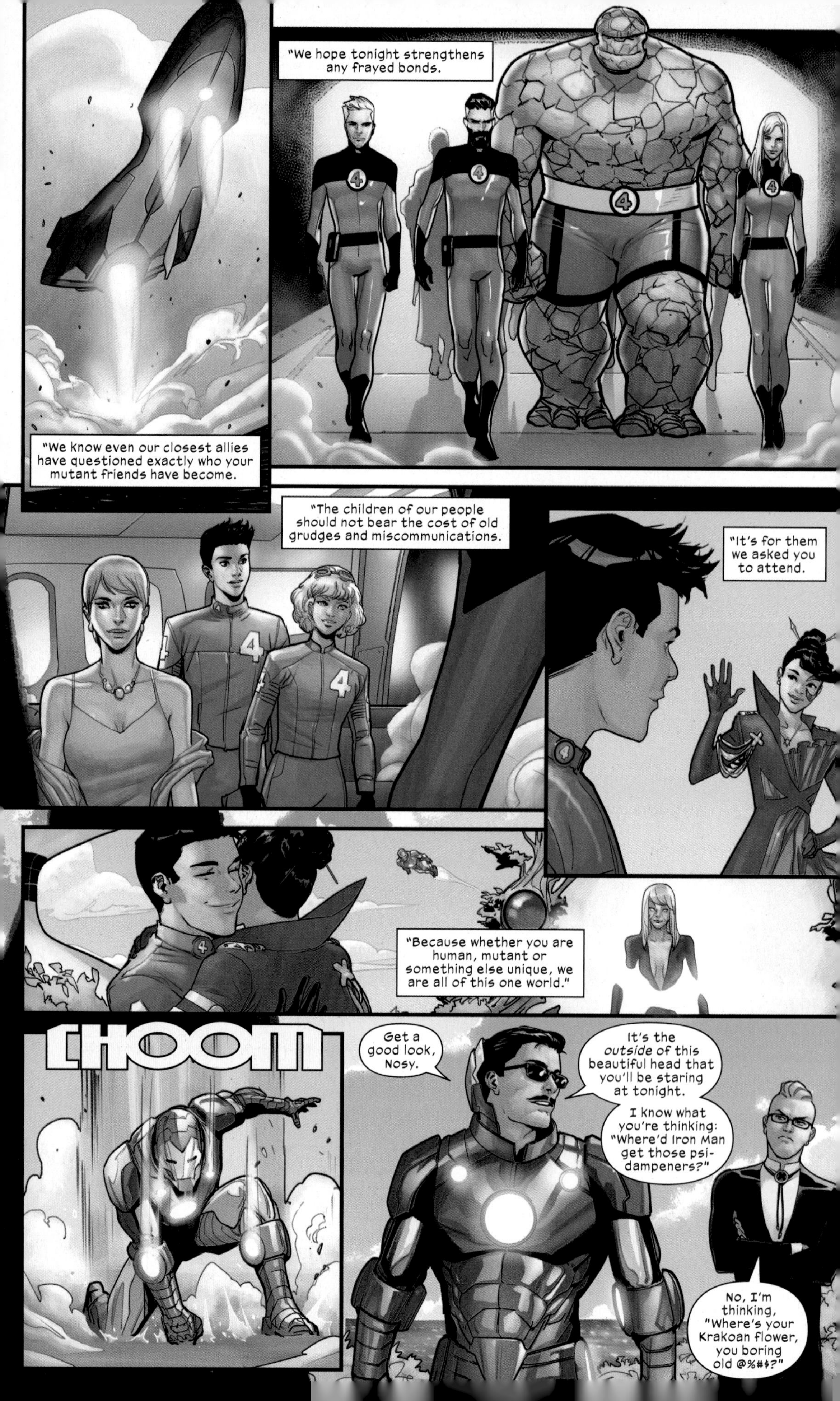
"We know even our closest allies have questioned exactly who your mutant friends have become.
"We hope tonight strengthens any frayed bonds.
"The children of our people should not bear the cost of old grudges and miscommunications.
"It's for them we asked you to attend.
"Because whether you are human, mutant or something else unique, we are all of this one world."
CHOOM
Get a good look, Nosy.
It's the *outside* of this beautiful head that you'll be staring at tonight.
I know what you're thinking: "Where'd Iron Man get those psi-dampeners?"
No, I'm thinking, "Where's your Krakoan flower, you boring old @%#$?"

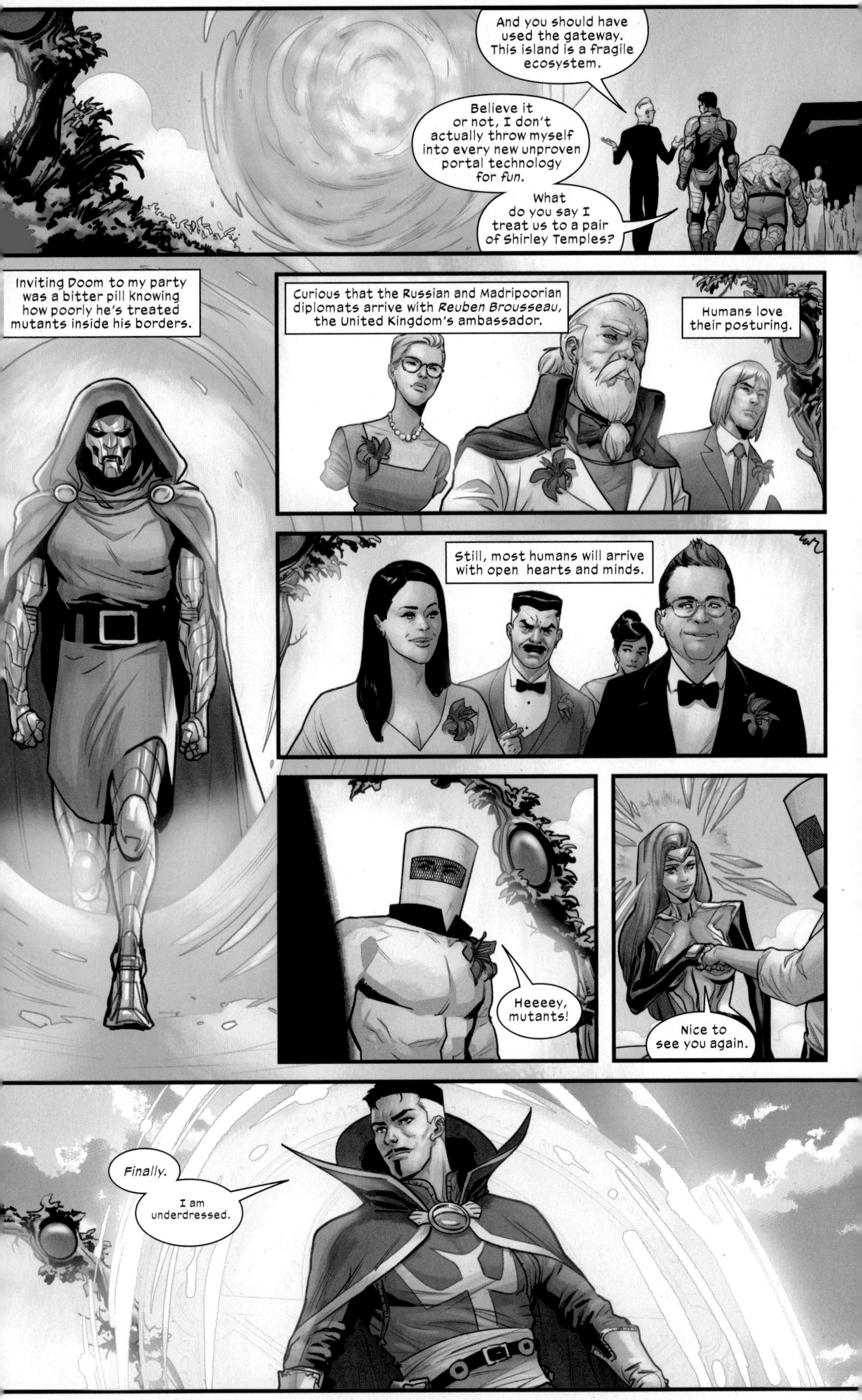
And you should have used the gateway. This island is a fragile ecosystem.
Believe it or not, I don't actually throw myself into every new unproven portal technology for *fun.*
What do you say I treat us to a pair of Shirley Temples?
Inviting Doom to my party was a bitter pill knowing how poorly he's treated mutants inside his borders.
Curious that the Russian and Madripoorian diplomats arrive with *Reuben Brousseau,* the United Kingdom's ambassador.
Humans love their posturing.
Still, most humans will arrive with open hearts and minds.
Heeeey, mutants!
Nice to see you again.
Finally.
I am underdressed.

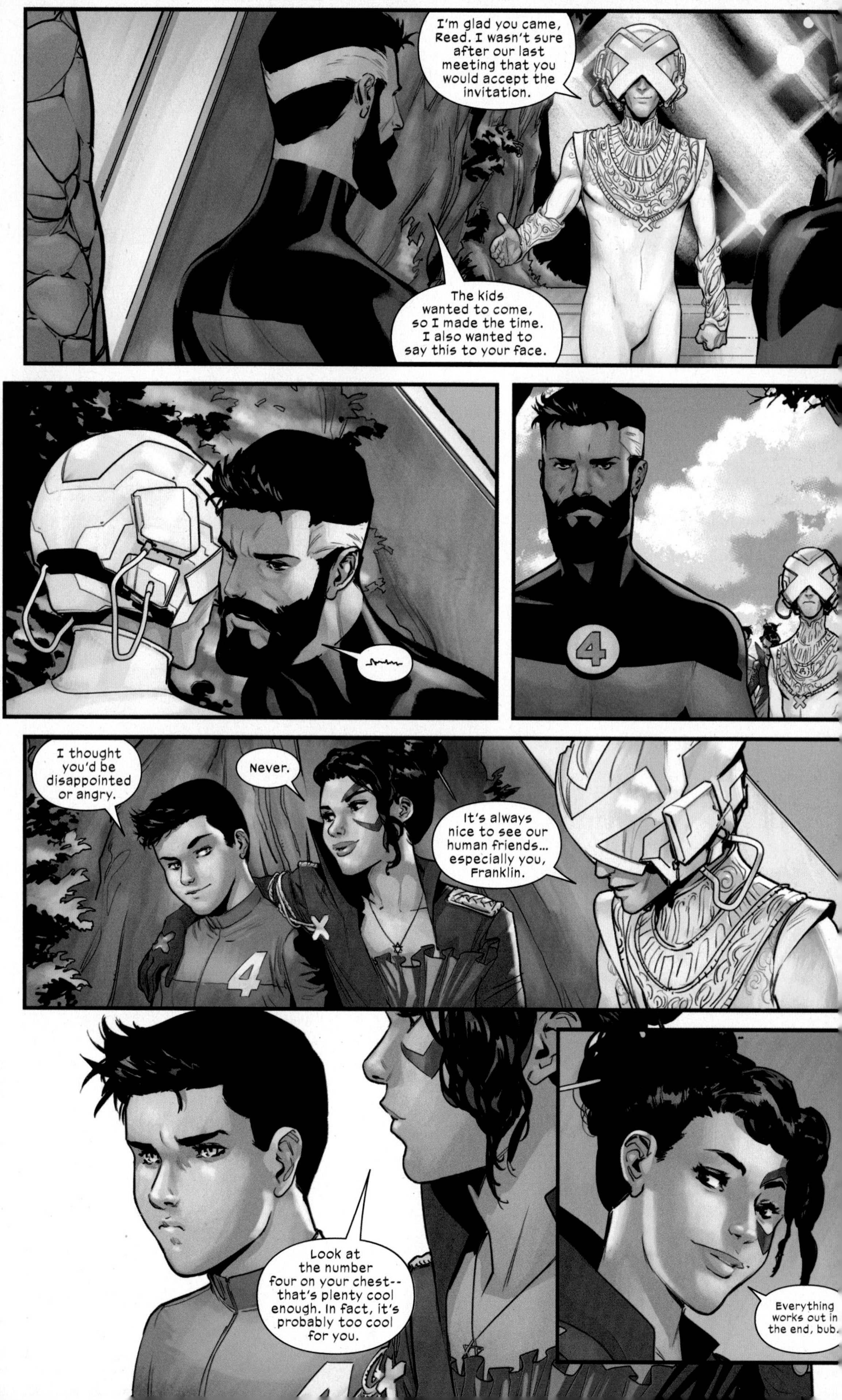

I'm glad you came, Reed. I wasn't sure after our last meeting that you would accept the invitation.
The kids wanted to come, so I made the time. I also wanted to say this to your face.
I thought you'd be disappointed or angry.
Never.
It's always nice to see our human friends... especially you, Franklin.
Look at the number four on your chest--that's plenty cool enough. In fact, it's probably too cool for you.
Everything works out in the end, bub.

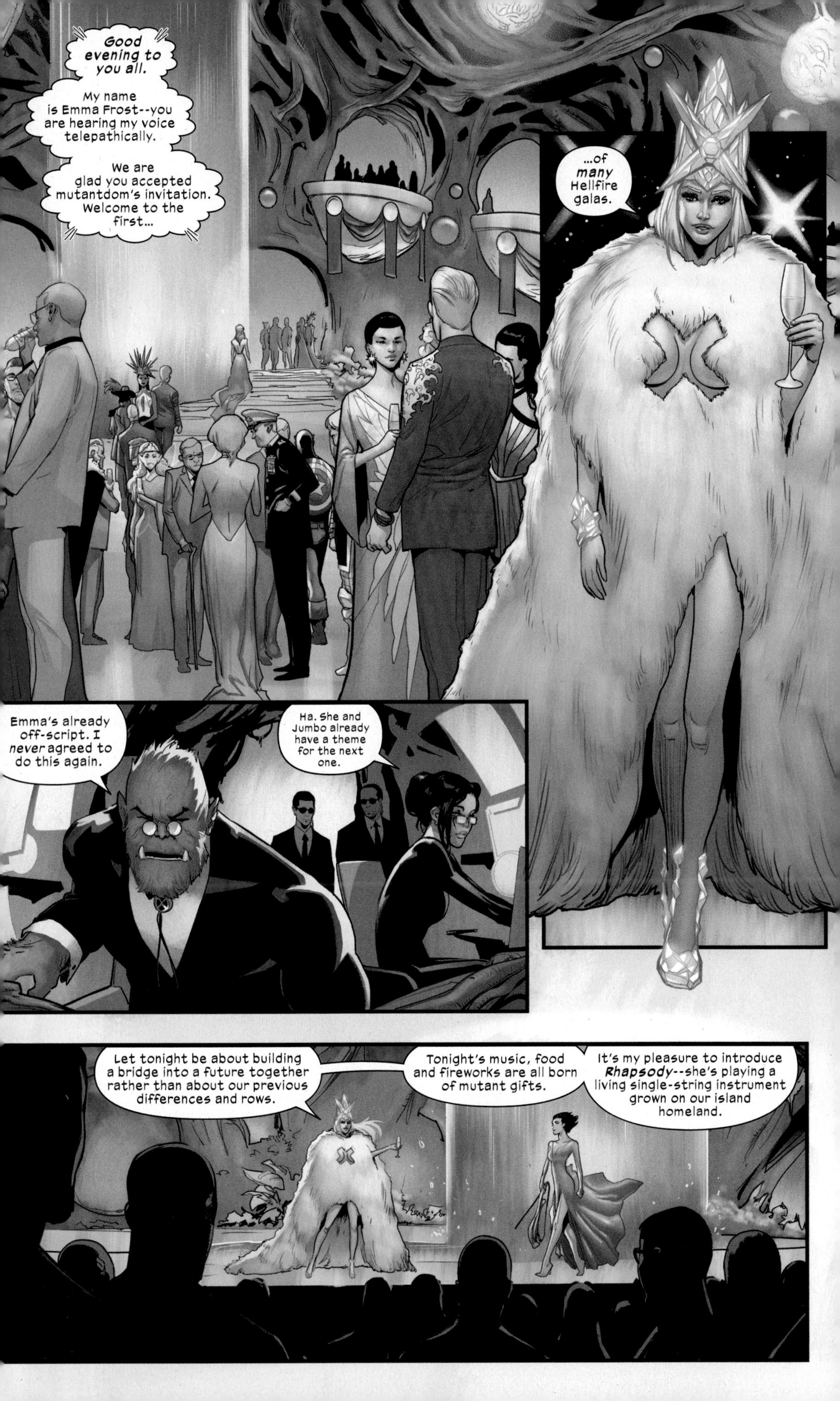

Good evening to you all.
My name is Emma Frost--you are hearing my voice telepathically.
We are glad you accepted mutantdom's invitation. Welcome to the first...
...of *many* Hellfire galas.
Emma's already off-script. I *never* agreed to do this again.
Ha. She and Jumbo already have a theme for the next one.
Let tonight be about building a bridge into a future together rather than about our previous differences and rows.
Tonight's music, food and fireworks are all born of mutant gifts.
It's my pleasure to introduce *Rhapsody*--she's playing a living single-string instrument grown on our island homeland.

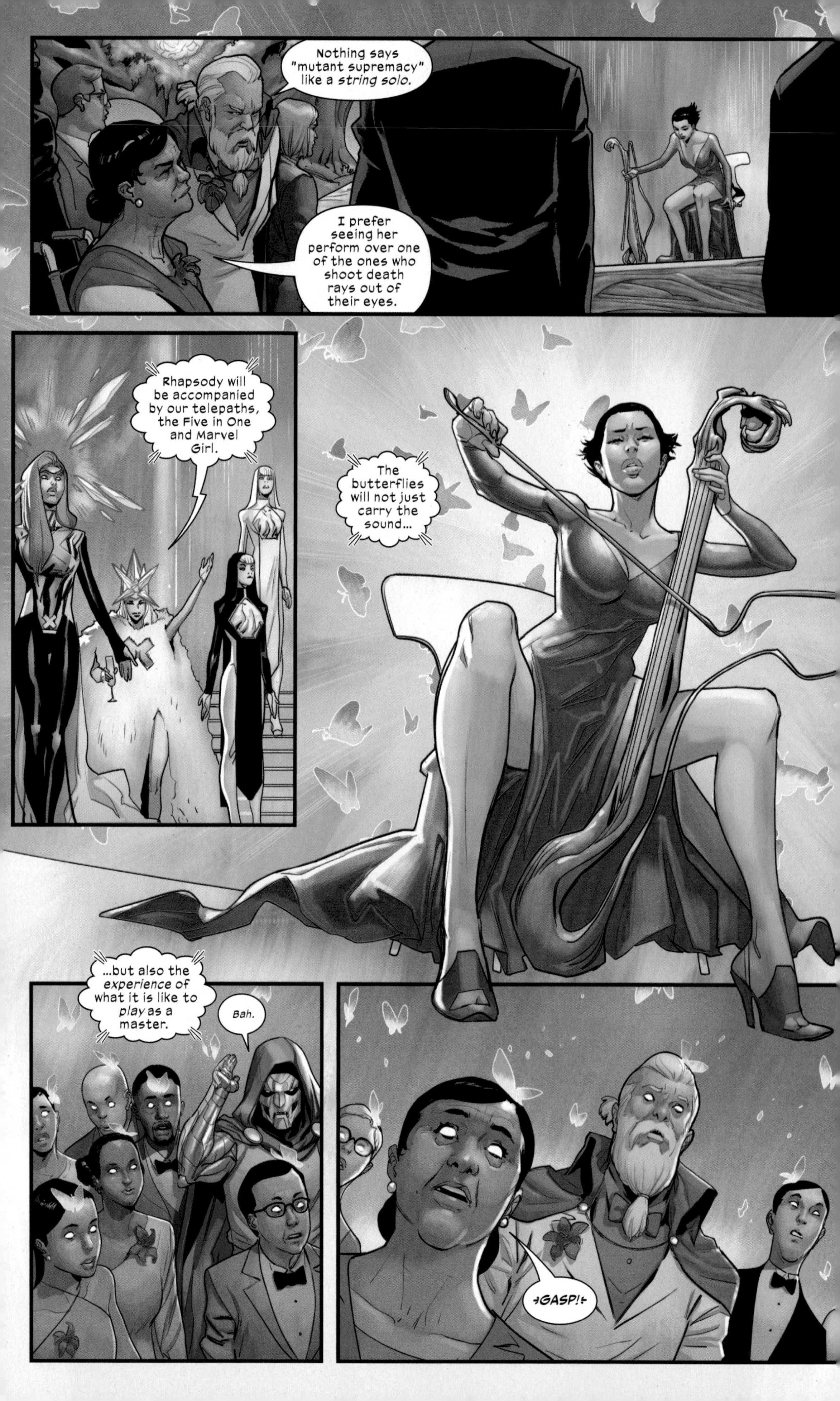

Nothing says "mutant supremacy" like a *string solo.*
I prefer seeing her perform over one of the ones who shoot death rays out of their eyes.
Rhapsody will be accompanied by our telepaths, the Five in One and Marvel Girl.
The butterflies will not just carry the sound...
...but also the *experience* of what it is like to *play* as a master.
Bah.
GASP!

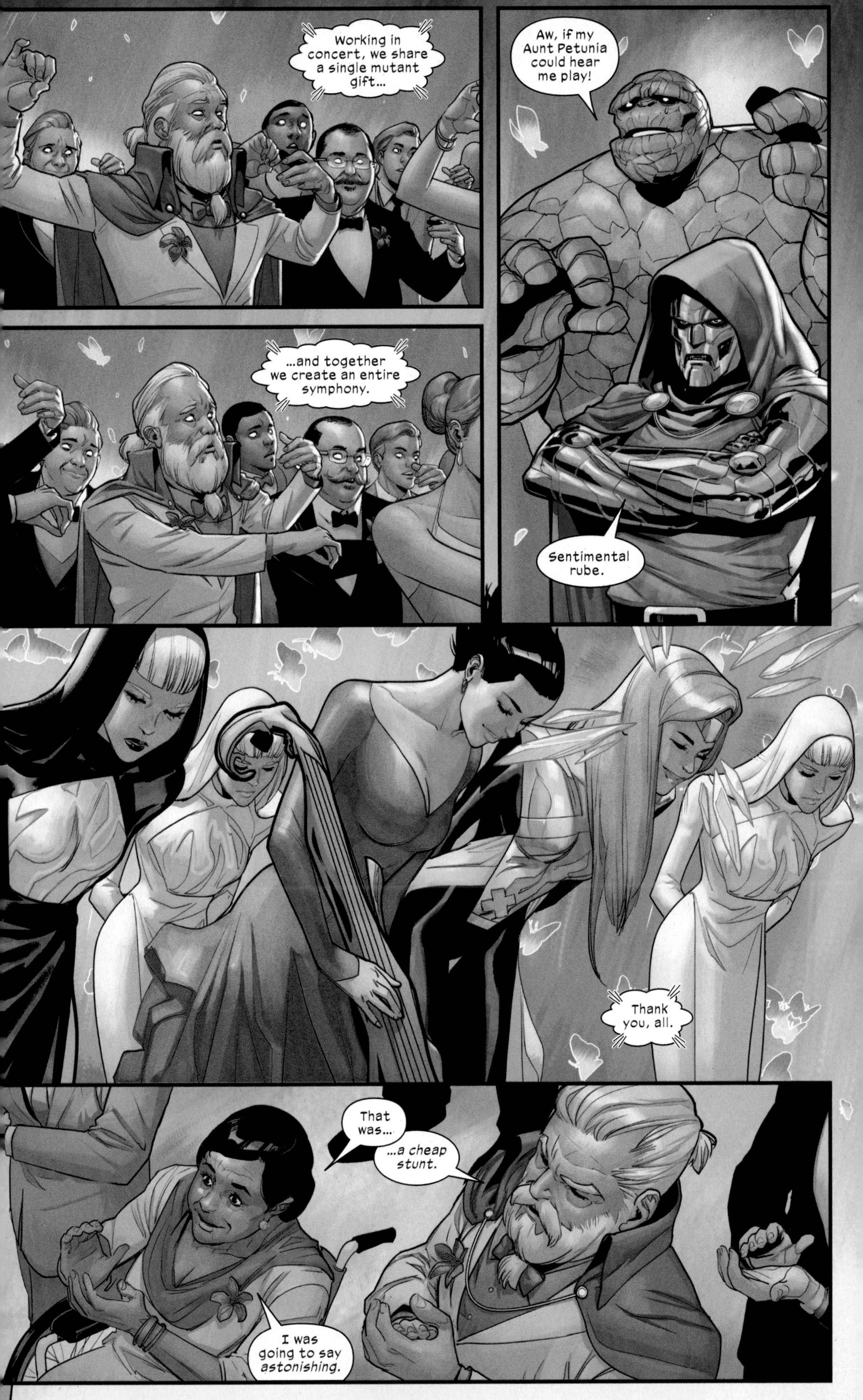

Working in concert, we share a single mutant gift...
...and together we create an entire symphony.
Aw, if my Aunt Petunia could hear me play!
Sentimental rube.
Thank you, all.
That was...
...a cheap stunt.
I was going to say *astonishing.*

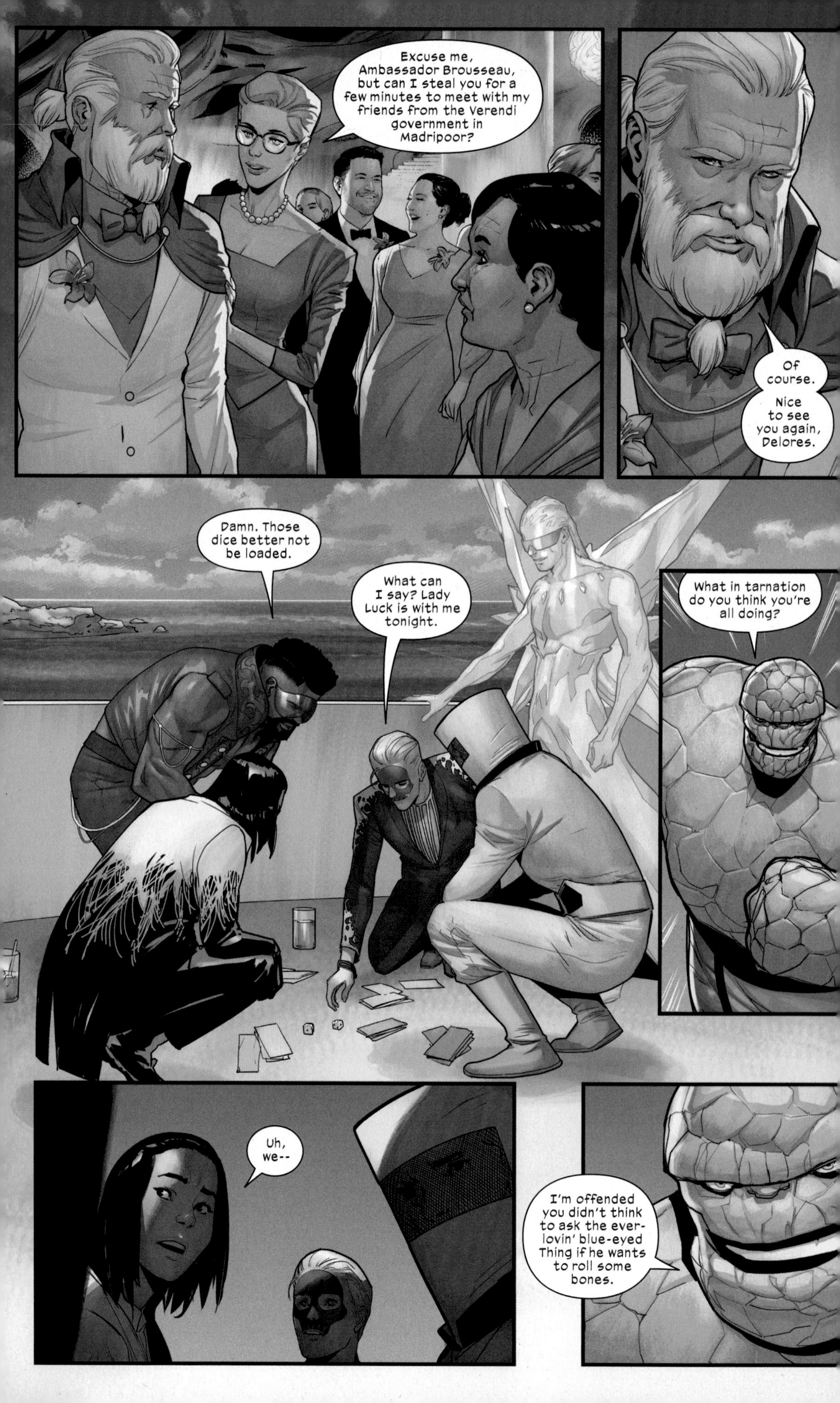
Excuse me, Ambassador Brousseau, but can I steal you for a few minutes to meet with my friends from the Verendi government in Madripoor?
Of course.
Nice to see you again, Delores.
Damn. Those dice better not be loaded.
What can I say? Lady Luck is with me tonight.
What in tarnation do you think you're all doing?
Uh, we--
I'm offended you didn't think to ask the ever-lovin' blue-eyed Thing if he wants to roll some bones.

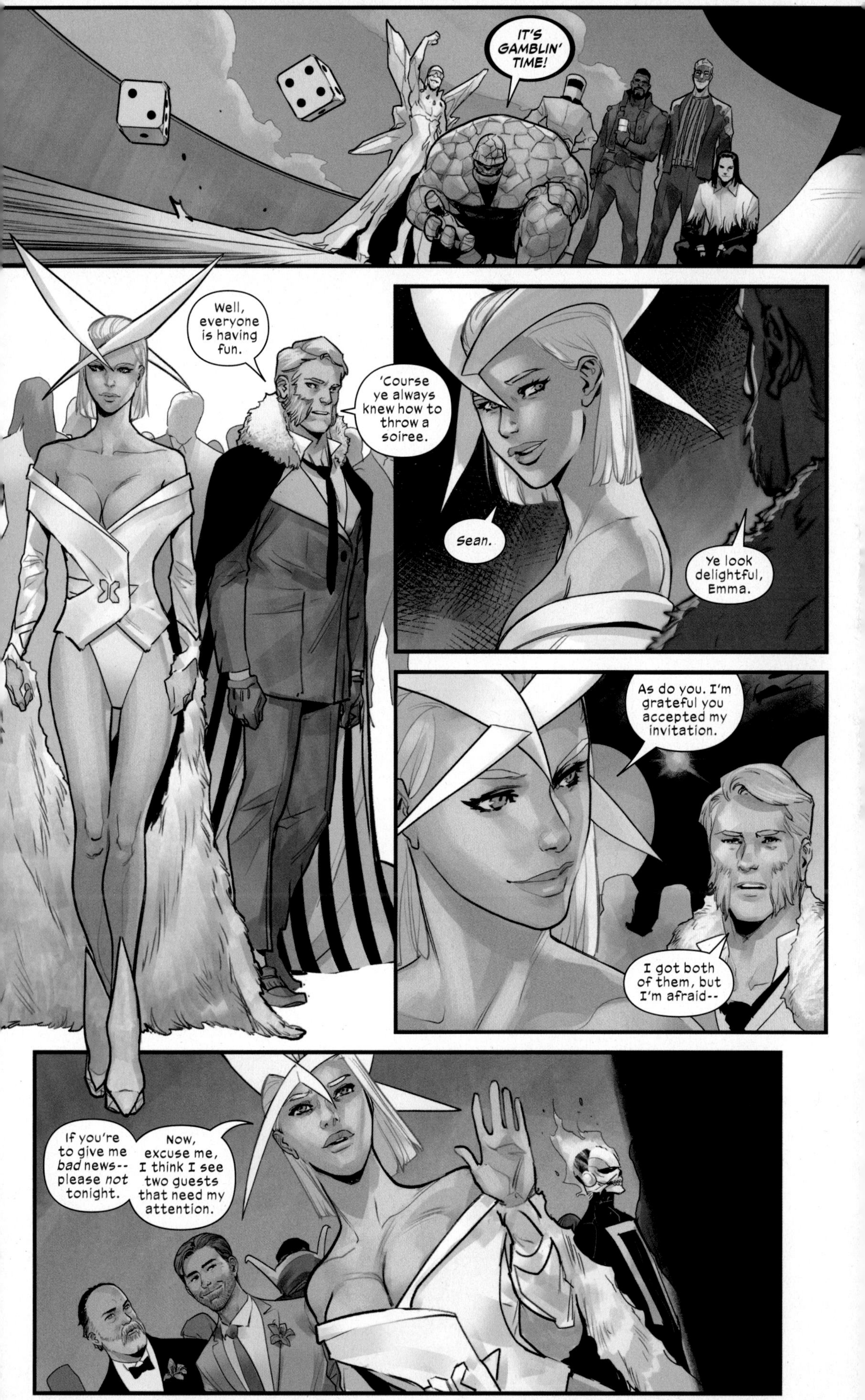
IT'S GAMBLIN' TIME!
Well, everyone is having fun.
'Course ye always knew how to throw a soiree.
Sean.
Ye look delightful, Emma.
As do you. I'm grateful you accepted my invitation.
I got both of them, but I'm afraid--
If you're to give me *bad* news-- please *not* tonight.
Now, excuse me, I think I see two guests that need my attention.

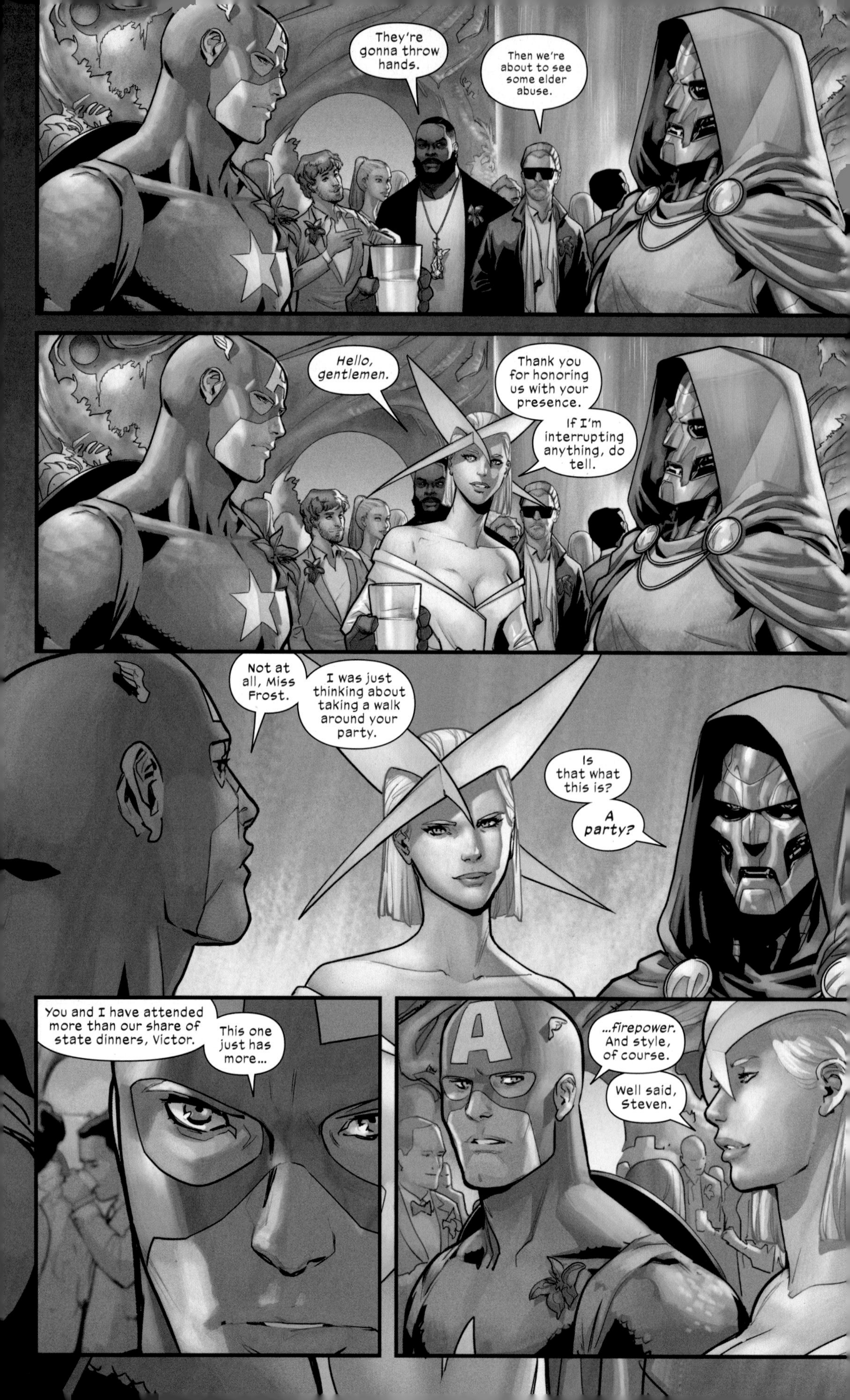
They're gonna throw hands.
Then we're about to see some elder abuse.
Hello, gentlemen.
Thank you for honoring us with your presence.
If I'm interrupting anything, do tell.
Not at all, Miss Frost.
I was just thinking about taking a walk around your party.
Is that what this is?
A party?
You and I have attended more than our share of state dinners, Victor.
This one just has more...
...firepower. And style, of course.
Well said, Steven.

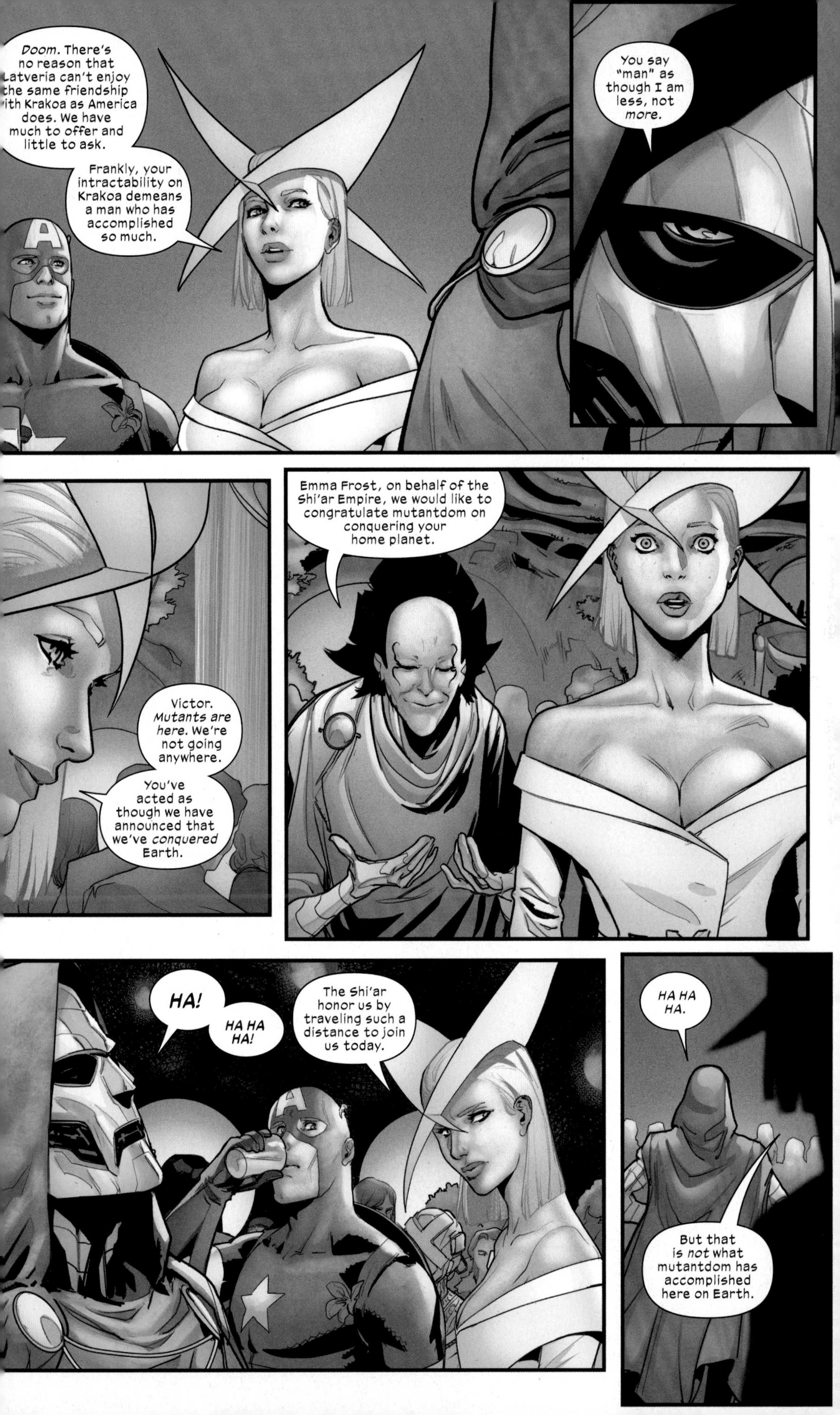
Doom. There's no reason that Latveria can't enjoy the same friendship with Krakoa as America does. We have much to offer and little to ask.
Frankly, your intractability on Krakoa demeans a man who has accomplished so much.
You say "man" as though I am less, not more.
Victor. Mutants are here. We're not going anywhere.
You've acted as though we have announced that we've conquered Earth.
Emma Frost, on behalf of the Shi'ar Empire, we would like to congratulate mutantdom on conquering your home planet.
HA!
HA HA HA!
The Shi'ar honor us by traveling such a distance to join us today.
HA HA HA.
But that is not what mutantdom has accomplished here on Earth.

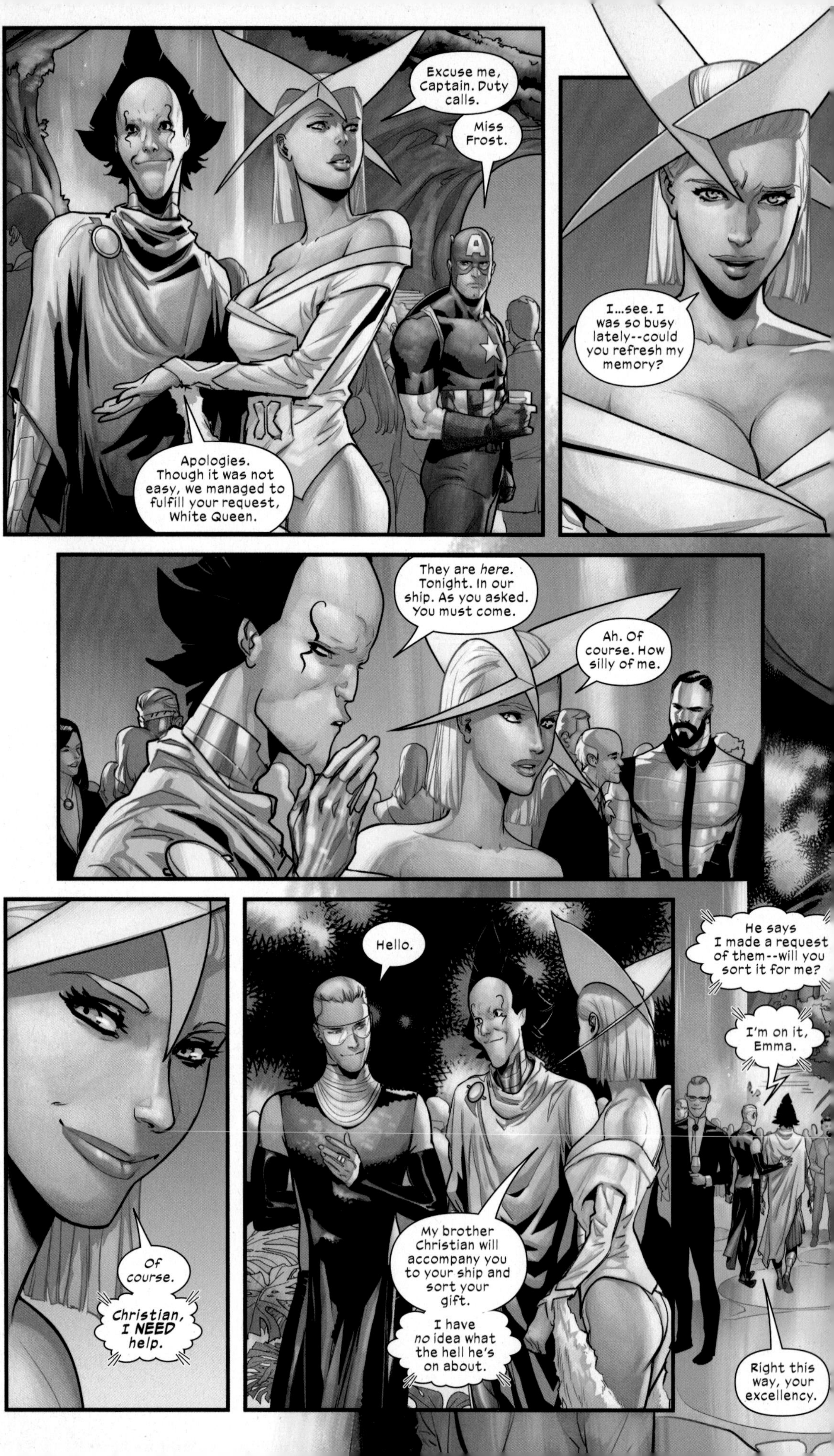

Excuse me, Captain. Duty calls.
Miss Frost.
Apologies. Though it was not easy, we managed to fulfill your request, White Queen.
I...see. I was so busy lately--could you refresh my memory?
They are *here.* Tonight. In our ship. As you asked. You must come.
Ah. Of course. How silly of me.
Of course.
Christian, **I NEED** help.
Hello.
My brother Christian will accompany you to your ship and sort your gift.
I have *no* idea what the hell he's on about.
He says I made a request of them--will you sort it for me?
I'm on it, Emma.
Right this way, your excellency.

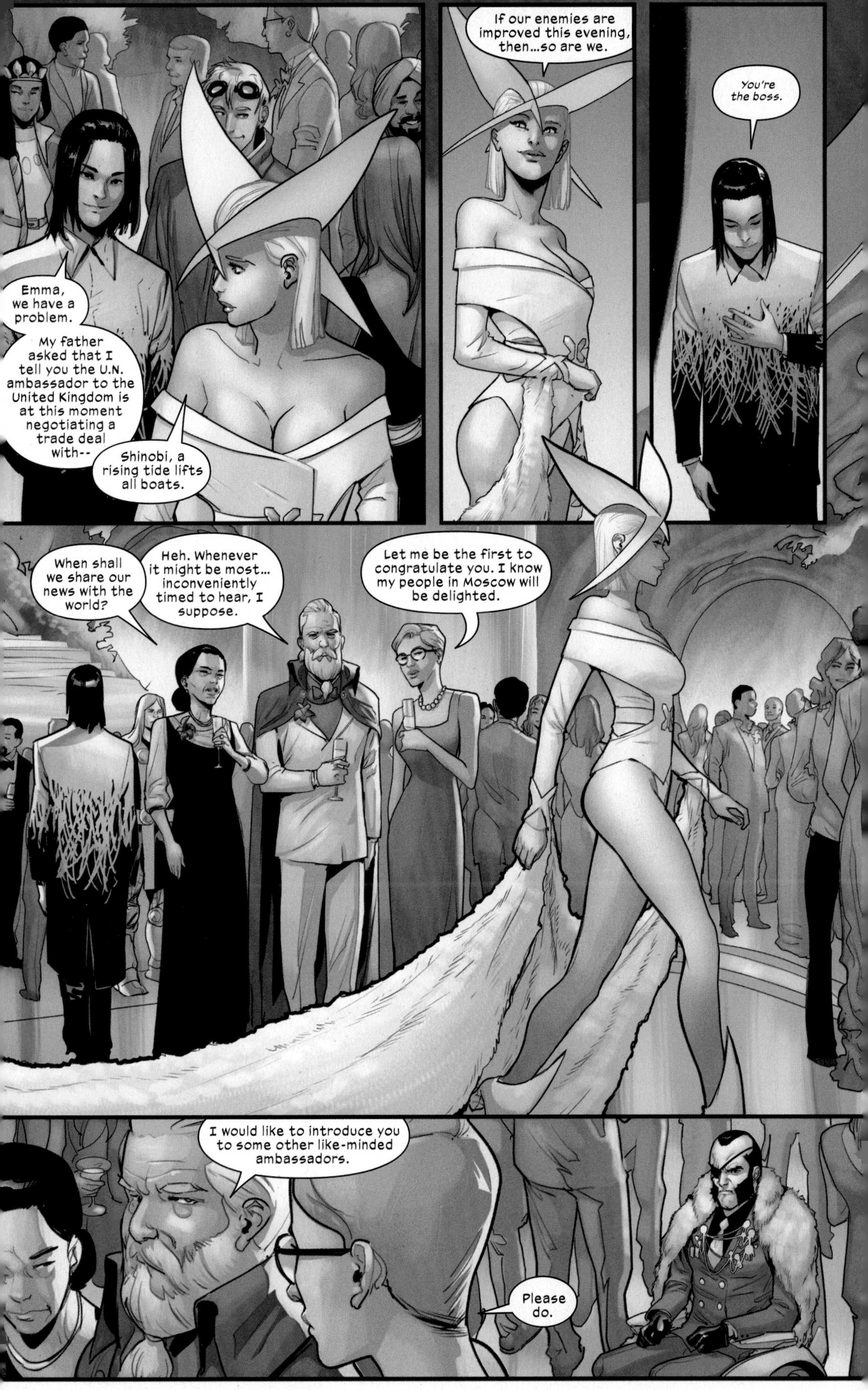

Emma, we have a problem.
My father asked that I tell you the U.N. ambassador to the United Kingdom is at this moment negotiating a trade deal with--
Shinobi, a rising tide lifts all boats.
If our enemies are improved this evening, then...so are we.
You're the boss.
When shall we share our news with the world?
Heh. Whenever it might be most... inconveniently timed to hear, I suppose.
Let me be the first to congratulate you. I know my people in Moscow will be delighted.
I would like to introduce you to some other like-minded ambassadors.
Please do.

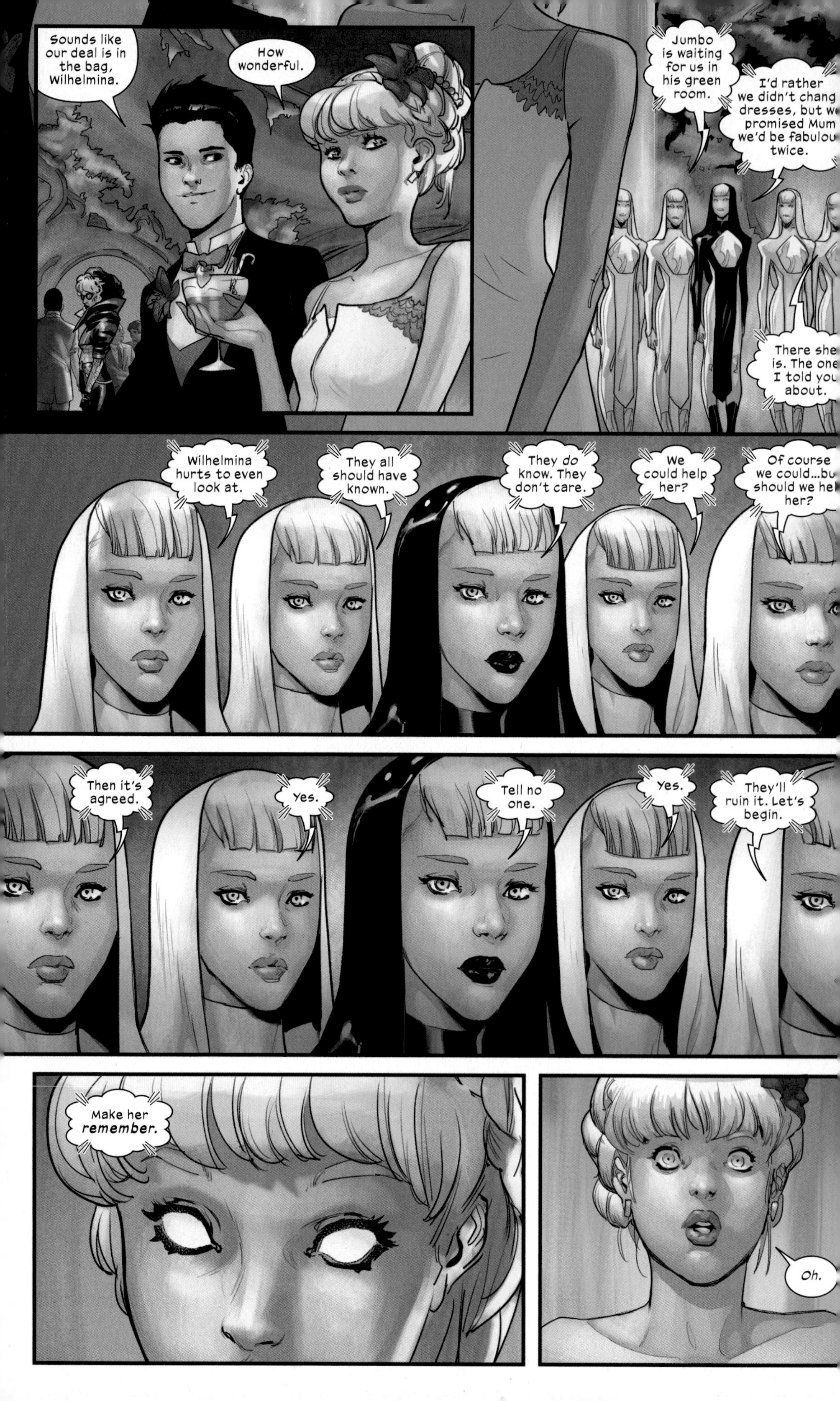
Sounds like our deal is in the bag, Wilhelmina.
How wonderful.
Jumbo is waiting for us in his green room.
I'd rather we didn't chang dresses, but w promised Mum we'd be fabulou twice.
There she is. The one I told you about.
Wilhelmina hurts to even look at.
They all should have known.
They *do* know. They don't care.
We could help her?
Of course we could...bu should we he her?
Then it's agreed.
Yes.
Tell no one.
Yes.
They'll ruin it. Let's begin.
Make her ***remember.***
Oh.

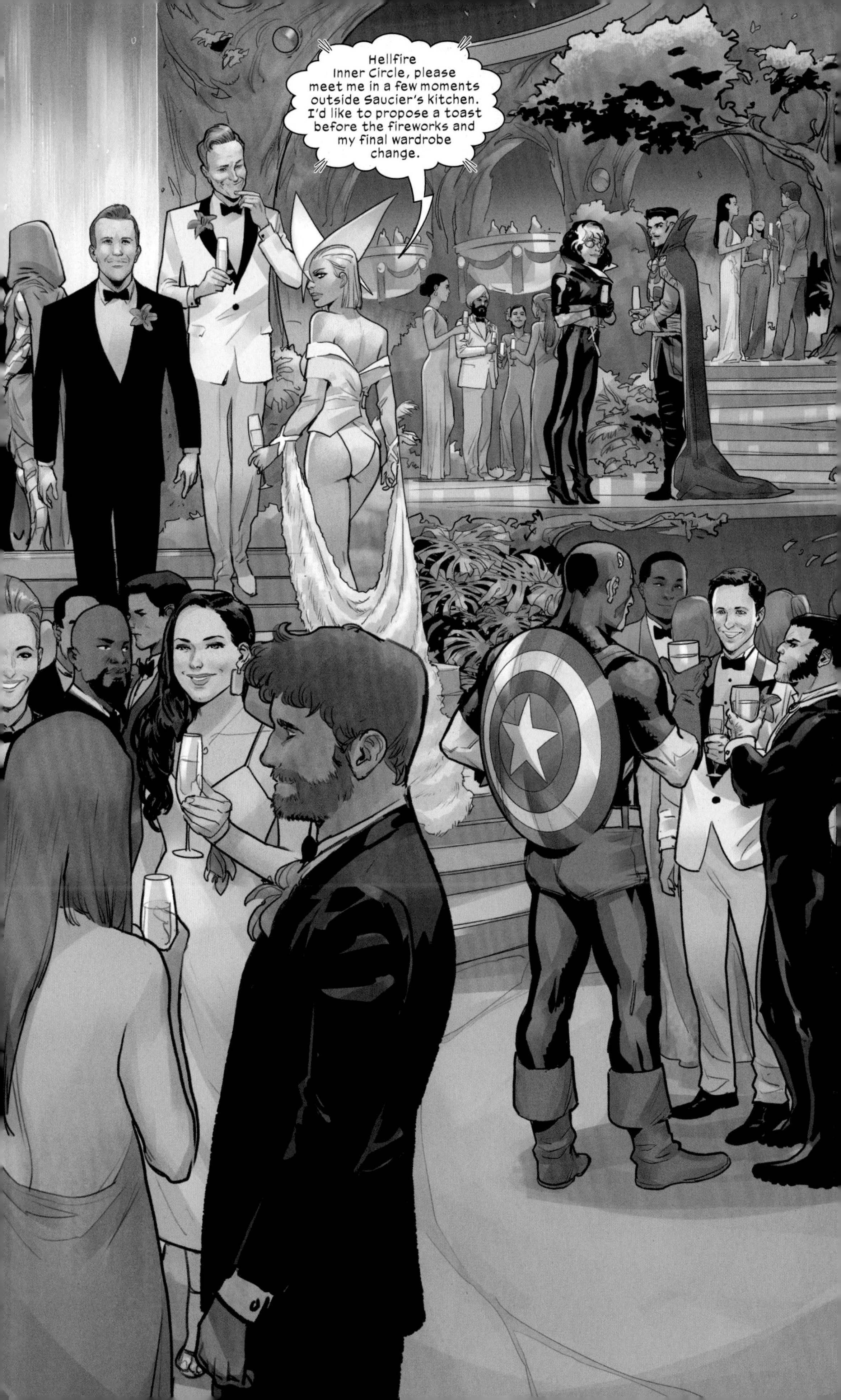
Hellfire Inner Circle, please meet me in a few moments outside Saucier's kitchen. I'd like to propose a toast before the fireworks and my final wardrobe change.

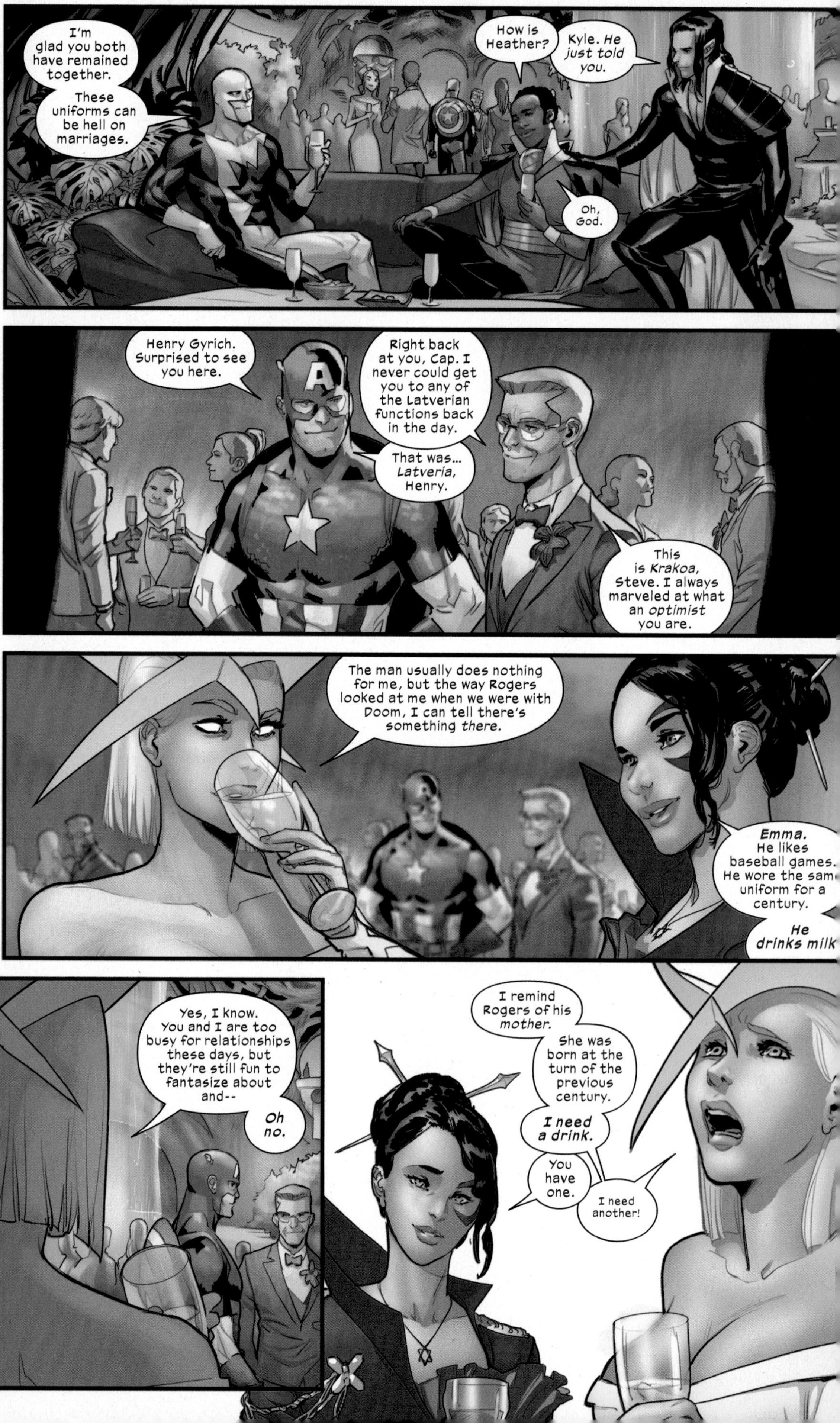
I'm glad you both have remained together.
These uniforms can be hell on marriages.
How is Heather?
Kyle. *He* just told you.
Oh, God.
Henry Gyrich. Surprised to see you here.
Right back at you, Cap. I never could get you to any of the Latverian functions back in the day.
That was... *Latveria*, Henry.
This is *Krakoa*, Steve. I always marveled at what an *optimist* you are.
The man usually does nothing for me, but the way Rogers looked at me when we were with Doom, I can tell there's something *there.*
Emma. He likes baseball games. He wore the sam uniform for a century.
He drinks milk
Yes, I know. You and I are too busy for relationships these days, but they're still fun to fantasize about and--
Oh no.
I remind Rogers of his *mother.*
She was born at the turn of the previous century.
I need a drink.
You have one.
I need another!

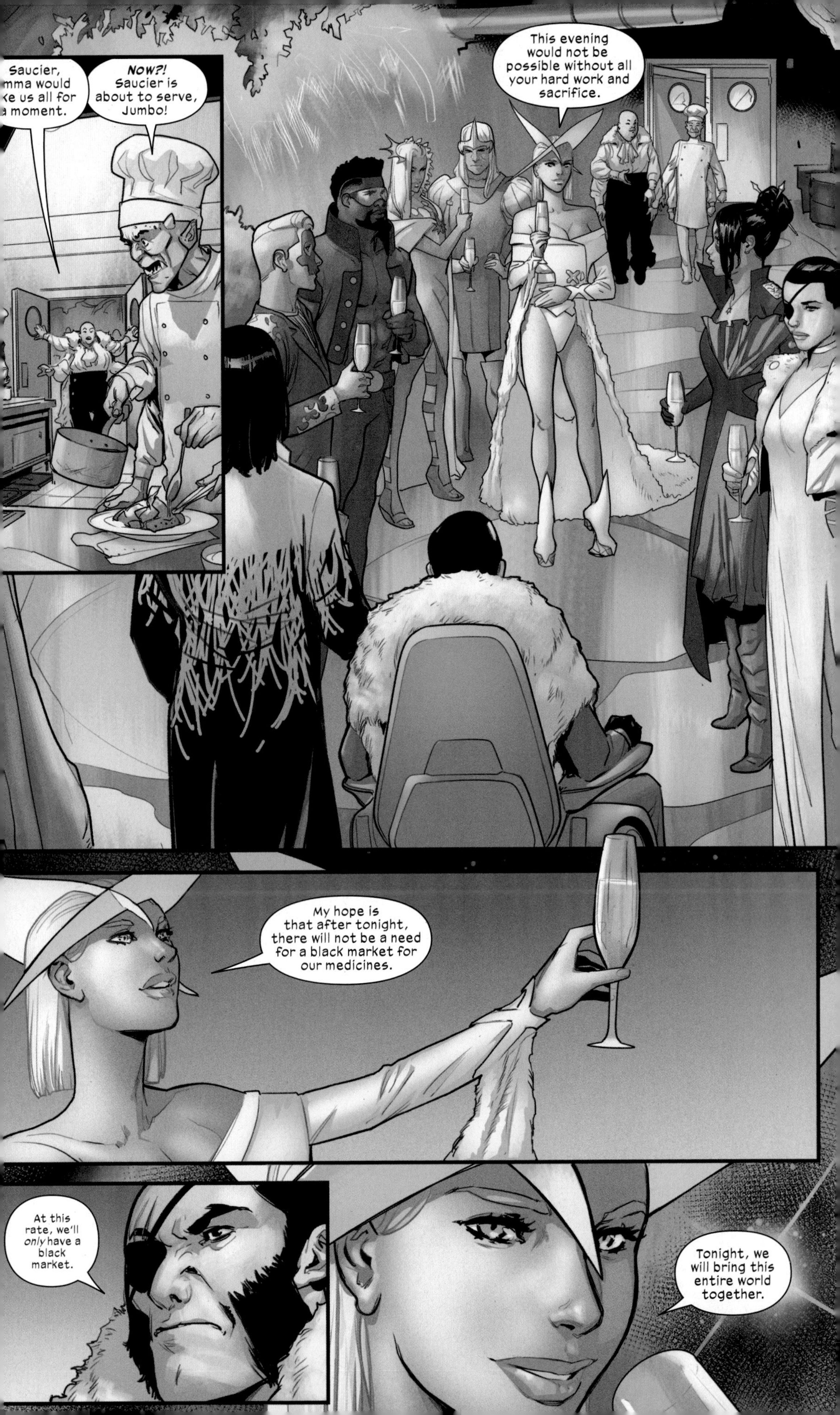
Saucier,
mma would
ke us all for
a moment.
NOW?! Saucier is about to serve, Jumbo!
This evening would not be possible without all your hard work and sacrifice.
My hope is that after tonight, there will not be a need for a black market for our medicines.
At this rate, we'll *only* have a black market.
Tonight, we will bring this entire world together.

[00_hellfire_gala_X]
[00_marauders__21]

WELCOME TO THE PARTY

The MARAUDERS have been sailing the high seas, protecting mutants and righting wrongs the world over. But Emma Frost has just thrown open the doors to the Hellfire Gala...and in one night, everything -- everything -- will change.

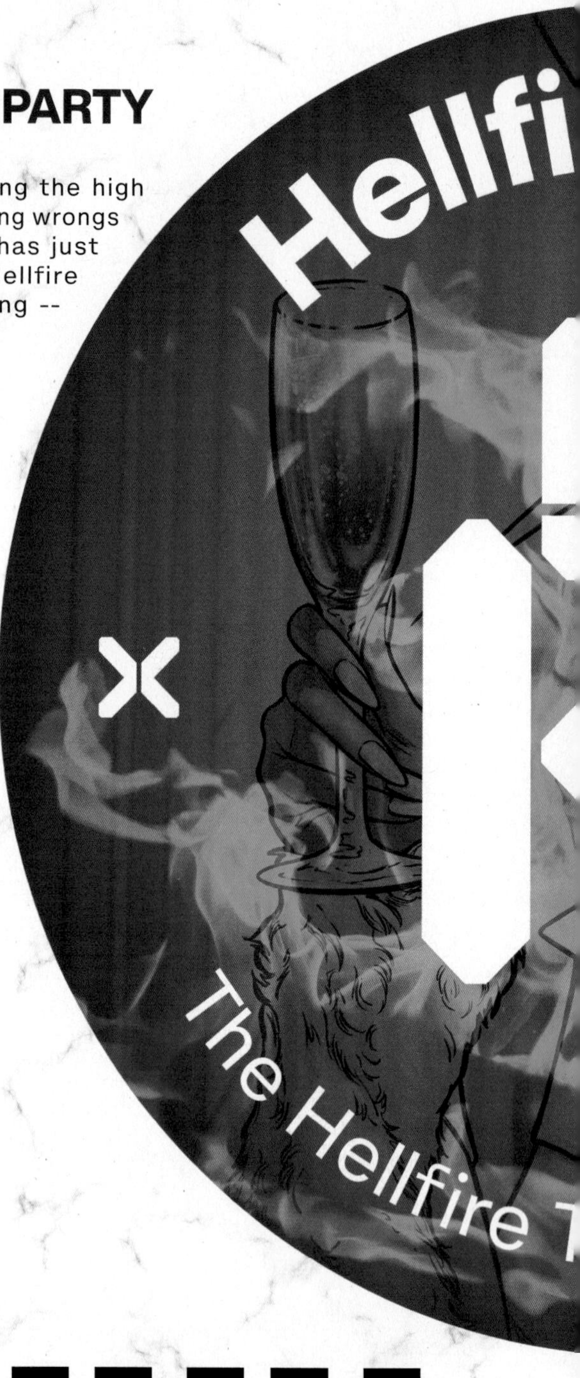

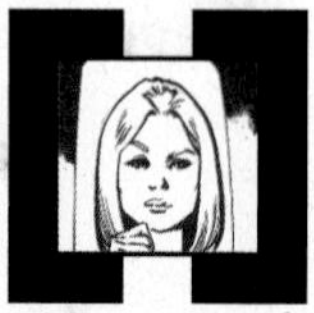
Emma Frost

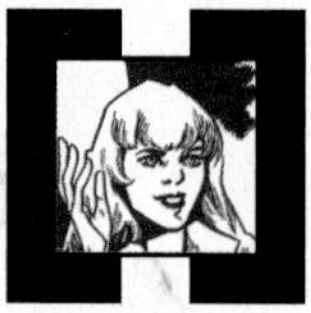
Kate Pryde

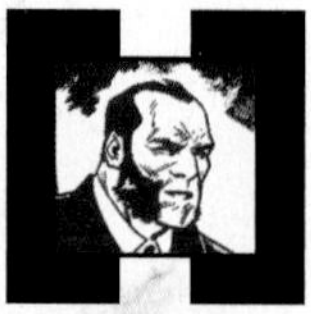
Sebastian Shaw

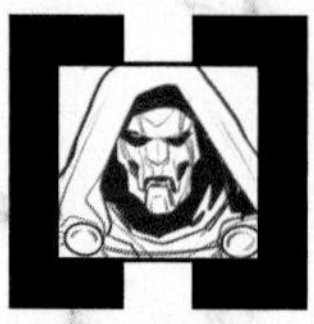
Doctor Doom

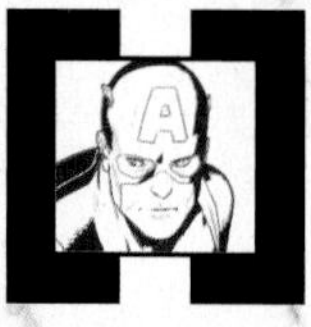
Captain America

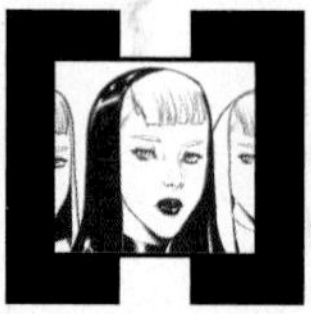
The Five-In-One

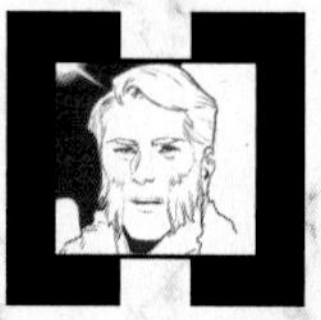
Banshee

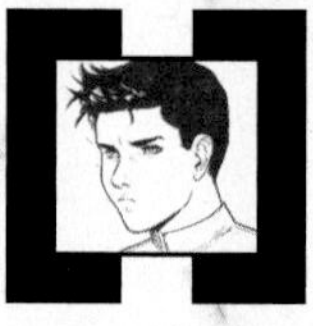
Franklin Richards

MARAUDERS

[X_21]

[ISSUE TWENTY-ONE] .... YOU ARE CORDIALLY INVITED TO THE HELLFIRE GALA ....

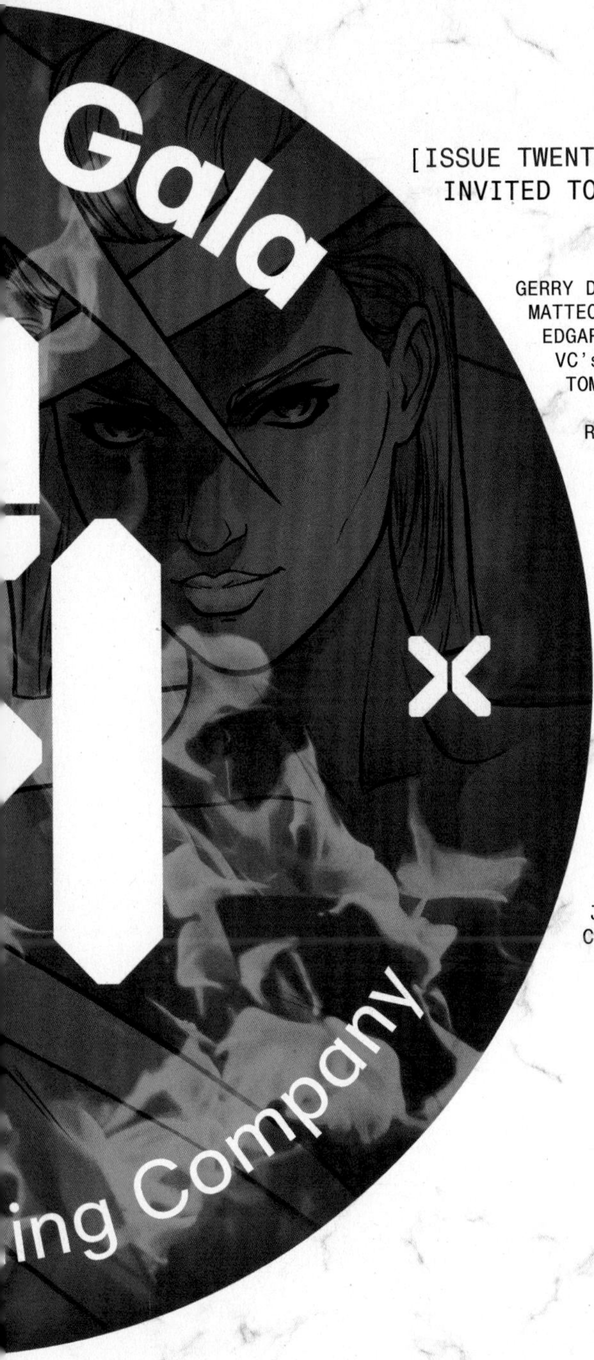
Gala
ing Company

GERRY DUGGAN ....[WRITER]
MATTEO LOLLI ....[ARTIST]
EDGAR DELGADO ....[COLOR ARTIST]
VC's CORY PETIT ....[LETTERER]
TOM MULLER ....[DESIGN]

RUSSELL DAUTERMAN & MATTHEW WILSON.... ....[COVER ARTISTS]
DAVID FINCH & FRANK D'ARMATA;
PHIL JIMENEZ & MARTE GRACIA......... ....[VARIANT COVER ARTISTS]

MATTEO LOLLI...................... ....[MARAUDERS DESIGN VARIANT COVER ARTIST]

RUSSELL DAUTERMAN ....[EMMA FROST DESIGN VARIANT COVER ARTIST]

RUSSELL DAUTERMAN & MATTHEW WILSON ....[CONNECTING COVER ARTISTS]

JONATHAN HICKMAN.........[HEAD OF X]
JAY BOWEN ....[PRODUCTION]
ANNALISE BISSA.....[ASSOCIATE EDITOR]
JORDAN D. WHITE ....[EDITOR]
C.B. CEBULSKI ....[EDITOR IN CHIEF]

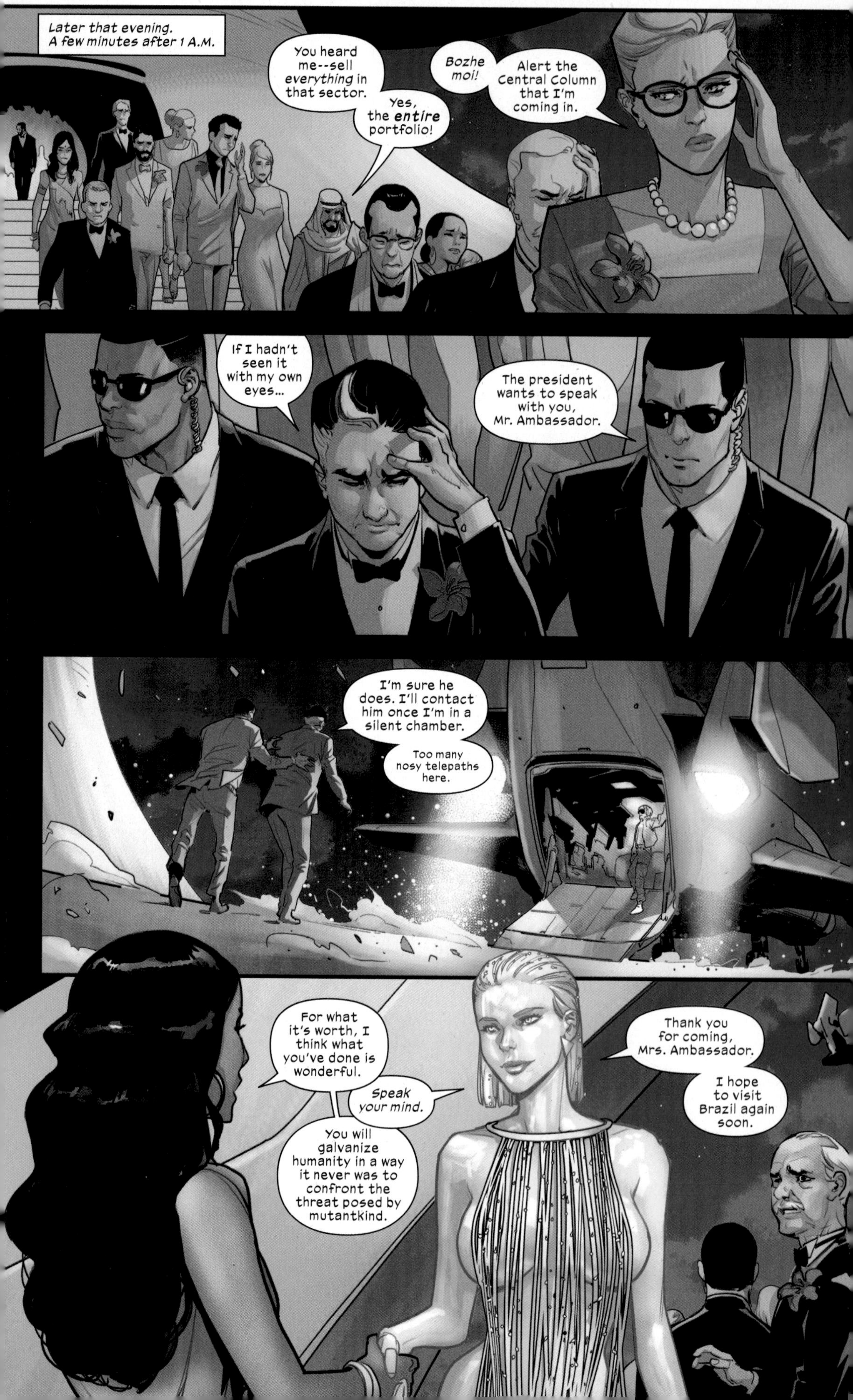
Later that evening. A few minutes after 1 A.M.
You heard me--sell *everything* in that sector.
Yes, the *entire* portfolio!
Bozhe moi!
Alert the Central Column that I'm coming in.
If I hadn't seen it with my own eyes...
The president wants to speak with you, Mr. Ambassador.
I'm sure he does. I'll contact him once I'm in a silent chamber.
Too many nosy telepaths here.
For what it's worth, I think what you've done is wonderful.
Speak your mind.
You will galvanize humanity in a way it never was to confront the threat posed by mutantkind.
Thank you for coming, Mrs. Ambassador.
I hope to visit Brazil again soon.

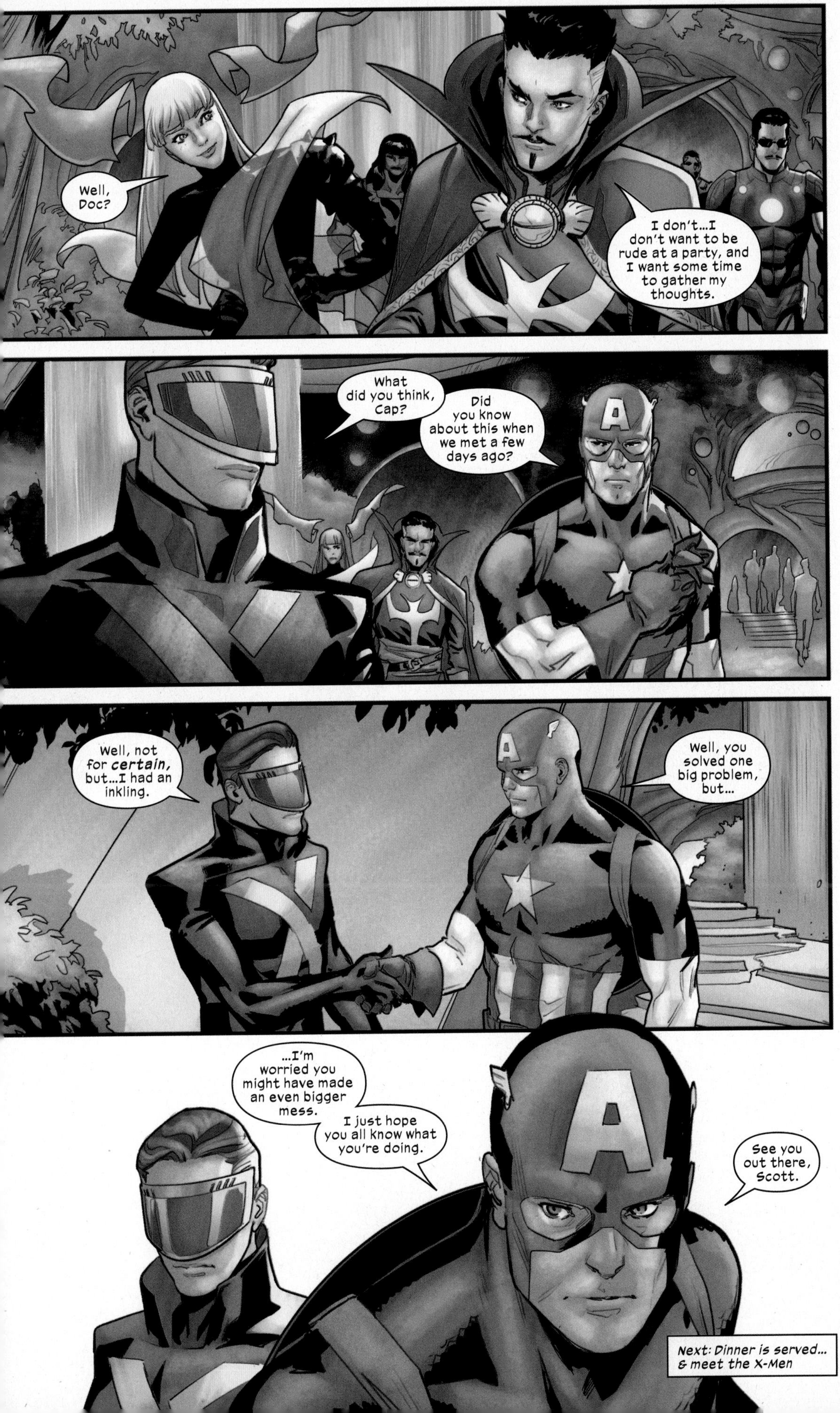
Well, Doc?
I don't...I don't want to be rude at a party, and I want some time to gather my thoughts.
What did you think, Cap?
Did you know about this when we met a few days ago?
Well, not for *certain*, but...I had an inkling.
Well, you solved one big problem, but...
...I'm worried you might have made an even bigger mess.
I just hope you all know what you're doing.
See you out there, Scott.
Next: Dinner is served... & meet the X-Men

OUT WITH THE OLD
A TALE OF HELLFIRE GALA PAST

CHRIS CLAREMONT........[WRITER]
JOHN BOLTON............[ARTIST]
GLYNIS OLIVER....[COLOR ARTIST]
TOM ORZECHOWSKI......[LETTERER]
ANN NOCENTI............[EDITOR]

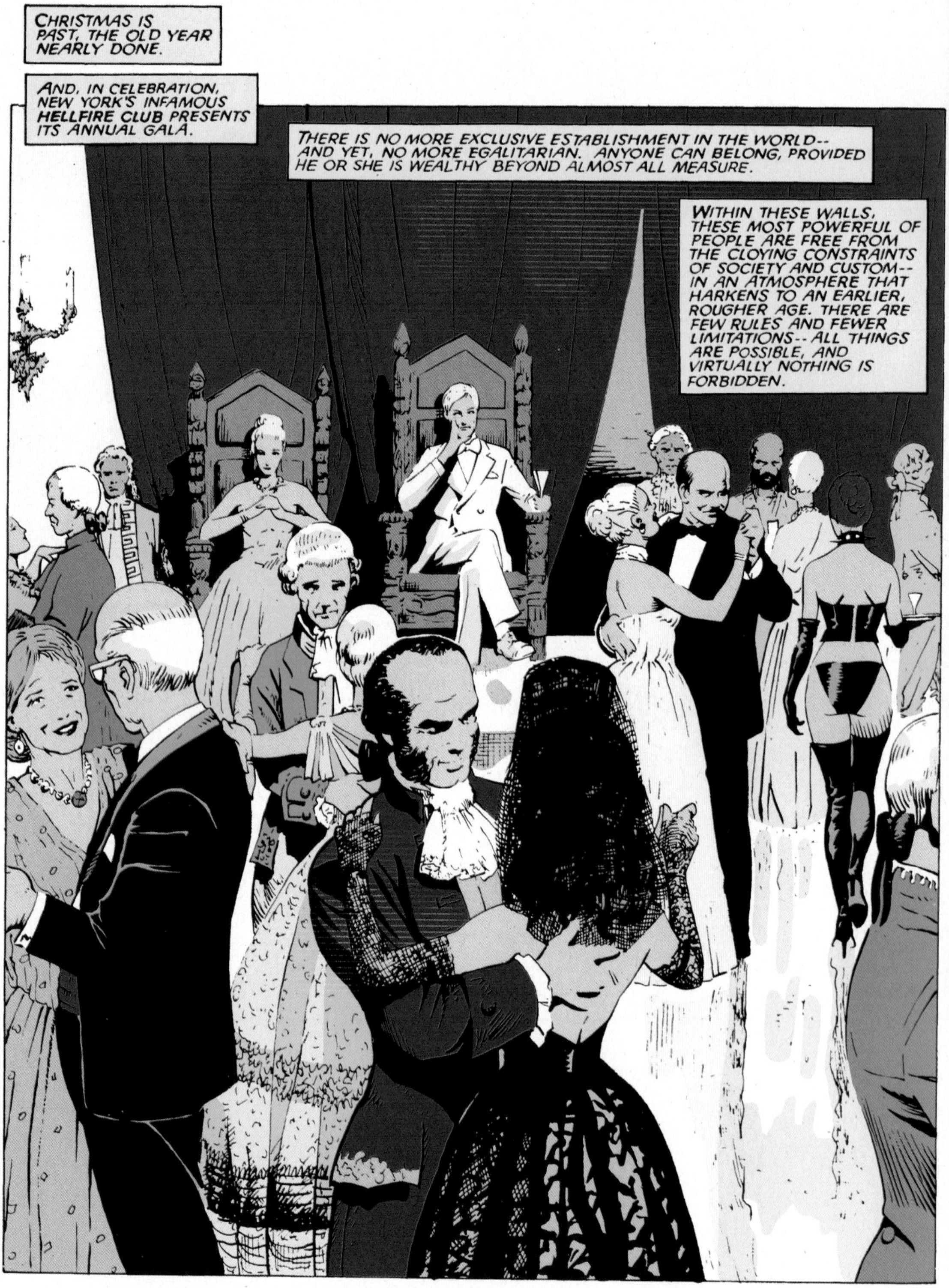
CHRISTMAS IS PAST, THE OLD YEAR NEARLY DONE.
AND, IN CELEBRATION, NEW YORK'S INFAMOUS HELLFIRE CLUB PRESENTS ITS ANNUAL GALA.
THERE IS NO MORE EXCLUSIVE ESTABLISHMENT IN THE WORLD-- AND YET, NO MORE EGALITARIAN. ANYONE CAN BELONG, PROVIDED HE OR SHE IS WEALTHY BEYOND ALMOST ALL MEASURE.
WITHIN THESE WALLS, THESE MOST POWERFUL OF PEOPLE ARE FREE FROM THE CLOYING CONSTRAINTS OF SOCIETY AND CUSTOM-- IN AN ATMOSPHERE THAT HARKENS TO AN EARLIER, ROUGHER AGE. THERE ARE FEW RULES AND FEWER LIMITATIONS-- ALL THINGS ARE POSSIBLE, AND VIRTUALLY NOTHING IS FORBIDDEN.

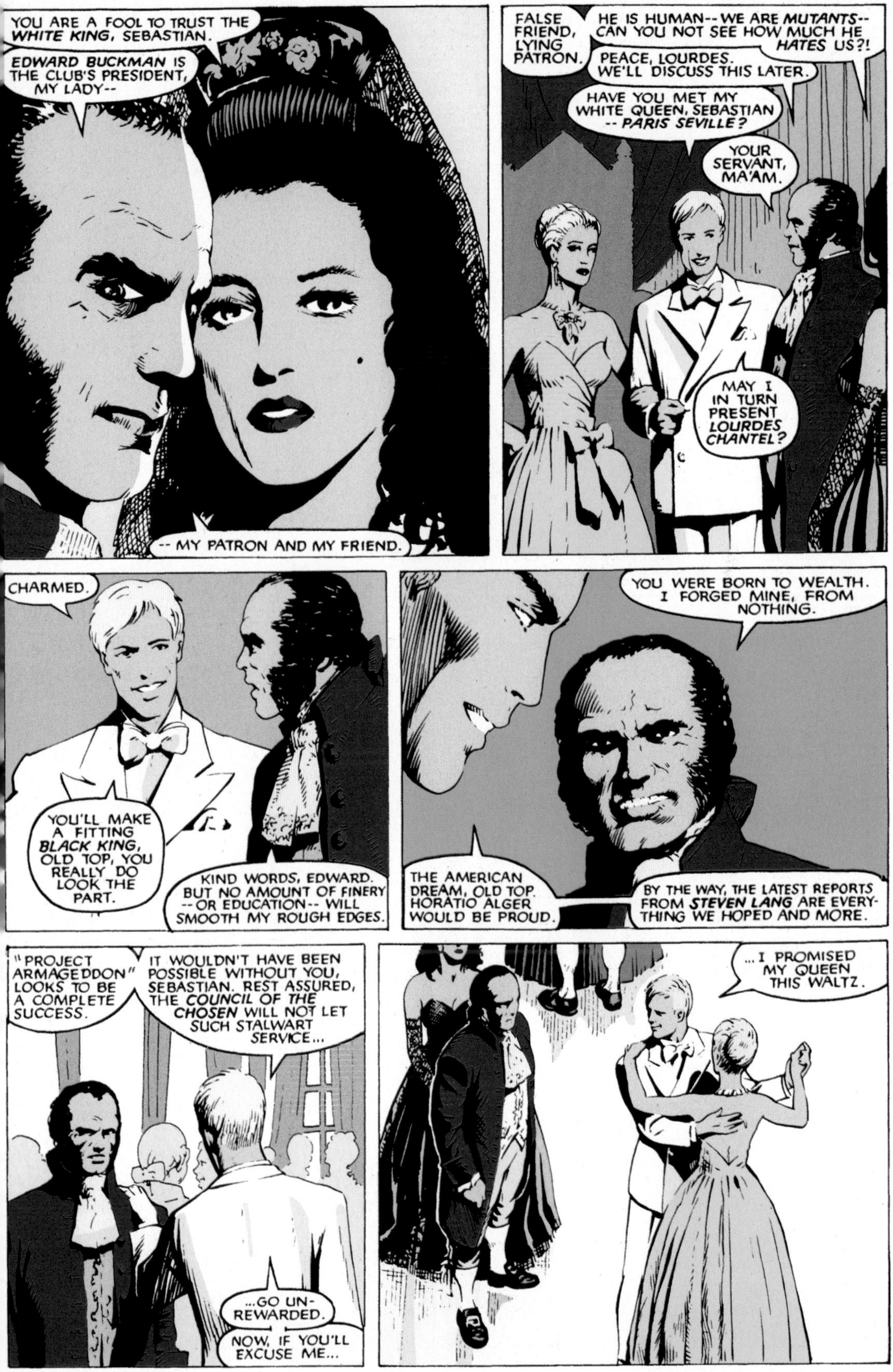

YOU ARE A FOOL TO TRUST THE WHITE KING, SEBASTIAN.
EDWARD BUCKMAN IS THE CLUB'S PRESIDENT, MY LADY--
-- MY PATRON AND MY FRIEND.
FALSE FRIEND, LYING PATRON.
HE IS HUMAN-- WE ARE MUTANTS-- CAN YOU NOT SEE HOW MUCH HE HATES US?!
PEACE, LOURDES. WE'LL DISCUSS THIS LATER.
HAVE YOU MET MY WHITE QUEEN, SEBASTIAN -- PARIS SEVILLE?
YOUR SERVANT, MA'AM.
MAY I IN TURN PRESENT LOURDES CHANTEL?
CHARMED.
YOU'LL MAKE A FITTING BLACK KING, OLD TOP, YOU REALLY DO LOOK THE PART.
KIND WORDS, EDWARD. BUT NO AMOUNT OF FINERY --OR EDUCATION-- WILL SMOOTH MY ROUGH EDGES.
YOU WERE BORN TO WEALTH. I FORGED MINE, FROM NOTHING.
THE AMERICAN DREAM, OLD TOP. HORATIO ALGER WOULD BE PROUD.
BY THE WAY, THE LATEST REPORTS FROM STEVEN LANG ARE EVERYTHING WE HOPED AND MORE.
"PROJECT ARMAGEDDON" LOOKS TO BE A COMPLETE SUCCESS.
IT WOULDN'T HAVE BEEN POSSIBLE WITHOUT YOU, SEBASTIAN. REST ASSURED, THE COUNCIL OF THE CHOSEN WILL NOT LET SUCH STALWART SERVICE...
...GO UN-REWARDED.
NOW, IF YOU'LL EXCUSE ME...
...I PROMISED MY QUEEN THIS WALTZ.

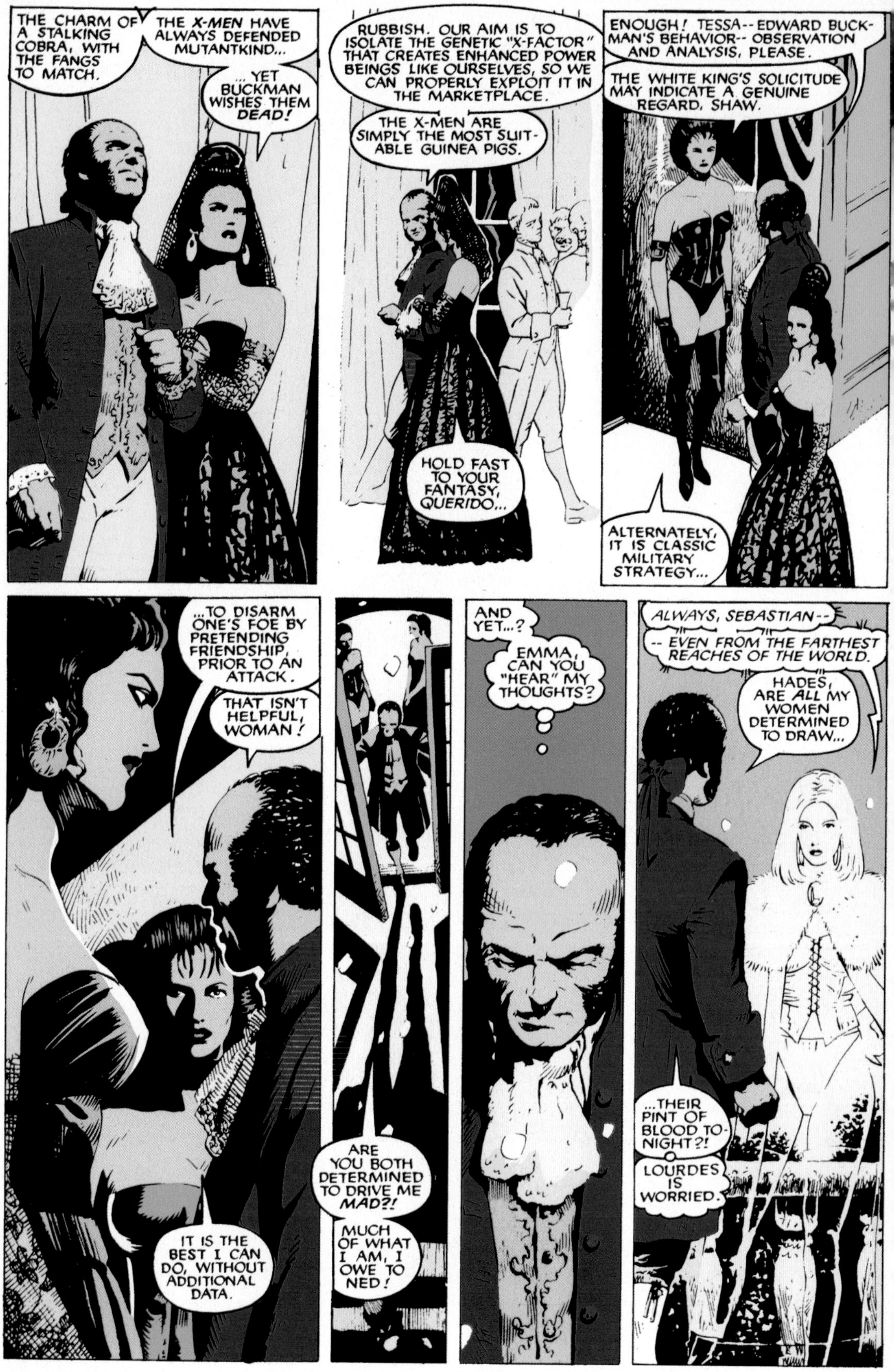
THE CHARM OF A STALKING COBRA, WITH THE FANGS TO MATCH.
THE X-MEN HAVE ALWAYS DEFENDED MUTANTKIND...
... YET BUCKMAN WISHES THEM DEAD!
RUBBISH. OUR AIM IS TO ISOLATE THE GENETIC "X-FACTOR" THAT CREATES ENHANCED POWER BEINGS LIKE OURSELVES, SO WE CAN PROPERLY EXPLOIT IT IN THE MARKETPLACE.
THE X-MEN ARE SIMPLY THE MOST SUITABLE GUINEA PIGS.
HOLD FAST TO YOUR FANTASY, QUERIDO...
ENOUGH! TESSA--EDWARD BUCKMAN'S BEHAVIOR-- OBSERVATION AND ANALYSIS, PLEASE.
THE WHITE KING'S SOLICITUDE MAY INDICATE A GENUINE REGARD, SHAW.
ALTERNATELY, IT IS CLASSIC MILITARY STRATEGY...
...TO DISARM ONE'S FOE BY PRETENDING FRIENDSHIP, PRIOR TO AN ATTACK.
THAT ISN'T HELPFUL, WOMAN!
IT IS THE BEST I CAN DO, WITHOUT ADDITIONAL DATA.
ARE YOU BOTH DETERMINED TO DRIVE ME MAD?!
MUCH OF WHAT I AM, I OWE TO NED!
AND YET...?
EMMA, CAN YOU "HEAR" MY THOUGHTS?
ALWAYS, SEBASTIAN--
-- EVEN FROM THE FARTHEST REACHES OF THE WORLD.
HADES, ARE ALL MY WOMEN DETERMINED TO DRAW...
...THEIR PINT OF BLOOD TONIGHT?!
LOURDES IS WORRIED.

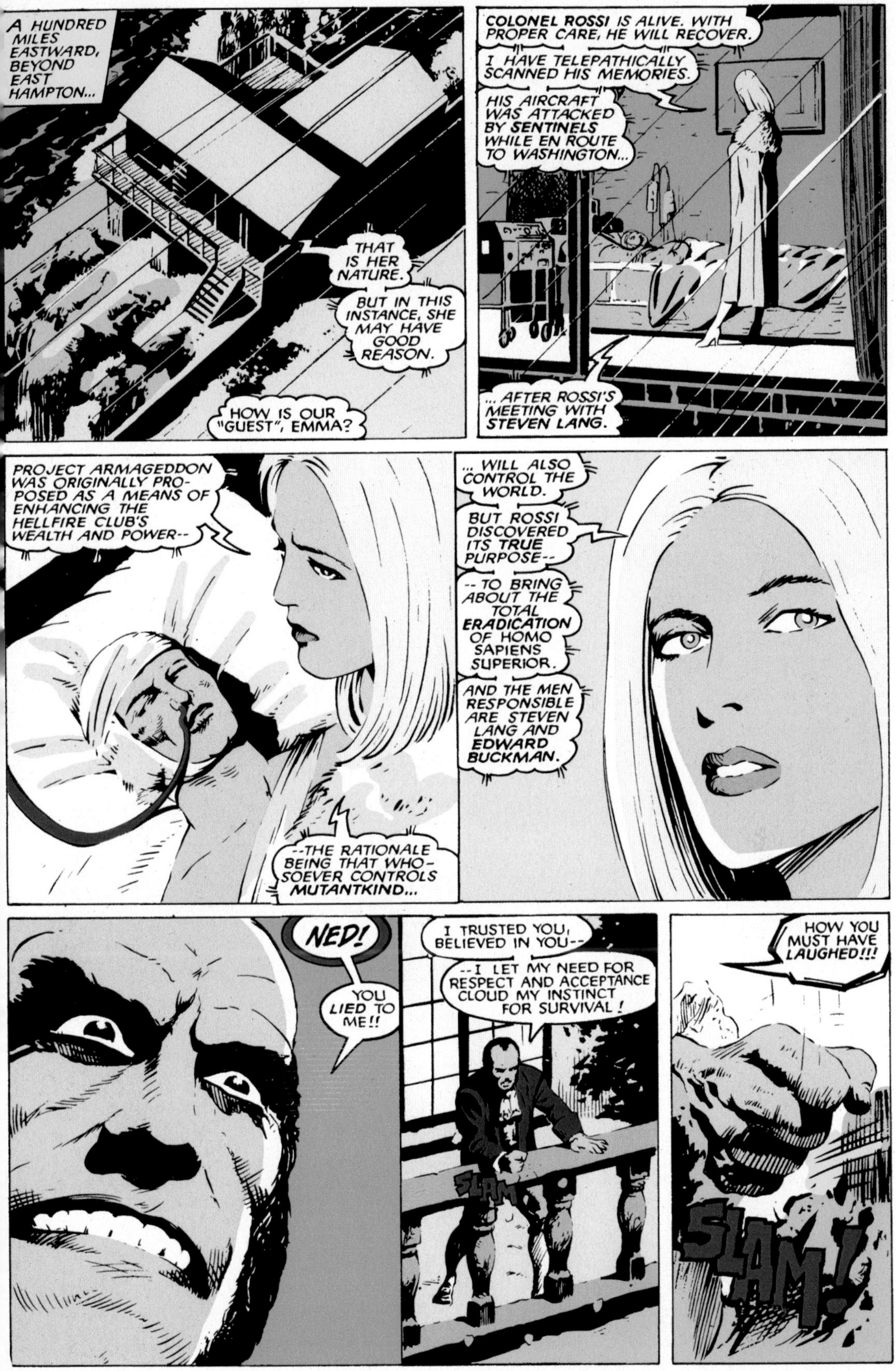
A HUNDRED MILES EASTWARD, BEYOND EAST HAMPTON...
HOW IS OUR "GUEST", EMMA?
THAT IS HER NATURE.
BUT IN THIS INSTANCE, SHE MAY HAVE GOOD REASON.
COLONEL ROSSI IS ALIVE. WITH PROPER CARE, HE WILL RECOVER.
I HAVE TELEPATHICALLY SCANNED HIS MEMORIES.
HIS AIRCRAFT WAS ATTACKED BY SENTINELS WHILE EN ROUTE TO WASHINGTON...
...AFTER ROSSI'S MEETING WITH STEVEN LANG.
PROJECT ARMAGEDDON WAS ORIGINALLY PROPOSED AS A MEANS OF ENHANCING THE HELLFIRE CLUB'S WEALTH AND POWER--
--THE RATIONALE BEING THAT WHOSOEVER CONTROLS MUTANTKIND...
...WILL ALSO CONTROL THE WORLD.
BUT ROSSI DISCOVERED ITS TRUE PURPOSE--
--TO BRING ABOUT THE TOTAL ERADICATION OF HOMO SAPIENS SUPERIOR.
AND THE MEN RESPONSIBLE ARE STEVEN LANG AND EDWARD BUCKMAN.
NED!
YOU LIED TO ME!!
I TRUSTED YOU, BELIEVED IN YOU--
--I LET MY NEED FOR RESPECT AND ACCEPTANCE CLOUD MY INSTINCT FOR SURVIVAL!
SLAM
HOW YOU MUST HAVE LAUGHED!!!
SLAM!

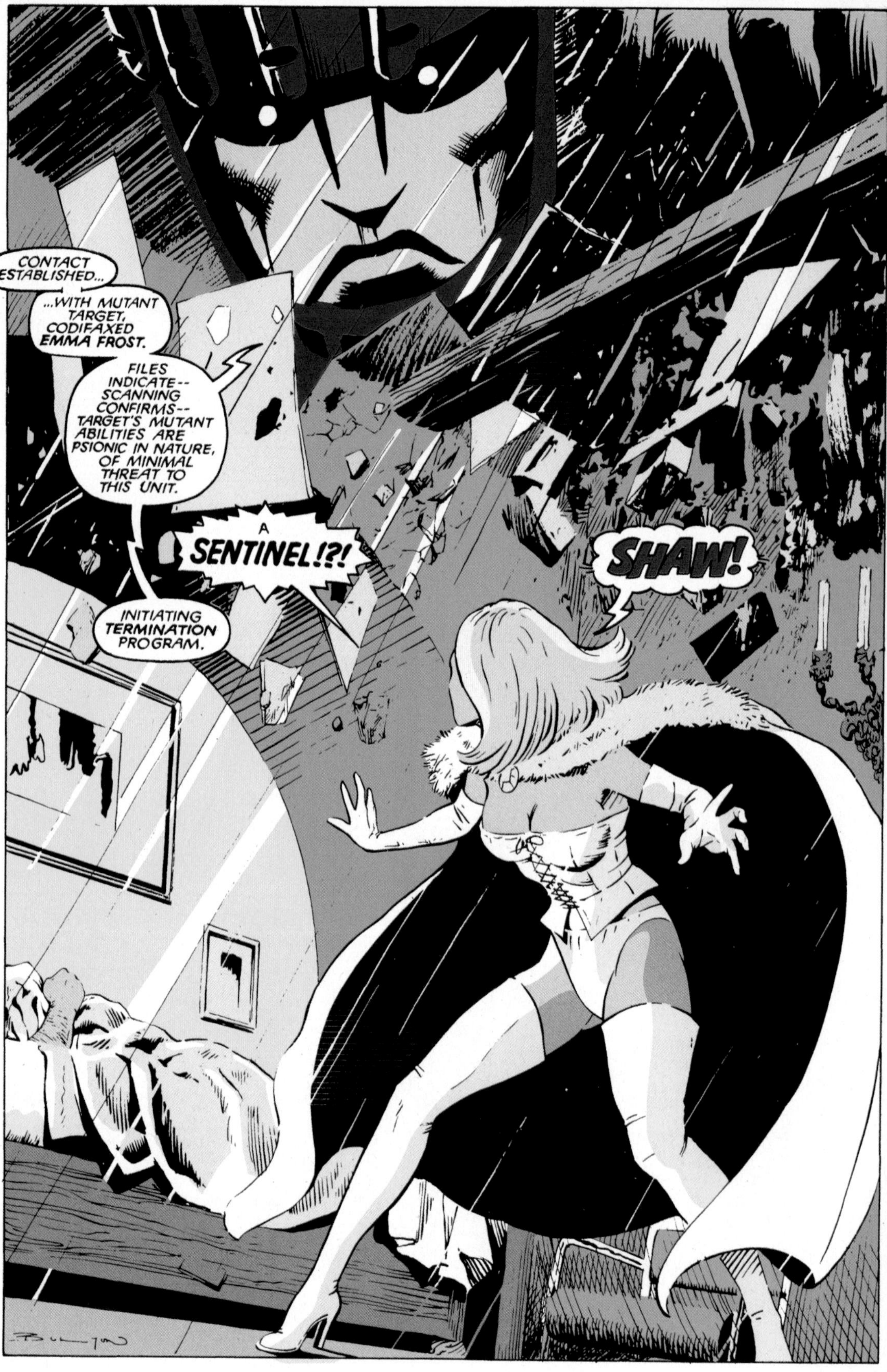

CONTACT ESTABLISHED...
...WITH MUTANT TARGET, CODIFAXED EMMA FROST.
FILES INDICATE-- SCANNING CONFIRMS-- TARGET'S MUTANT ABILITIES ARE PSIONIC IN NATURE, OF MINIMAL THREAT TO THIS UNIT.
A SENTINEL!?!
SHAW!
INITIATING TERMINATION PROGRAM.

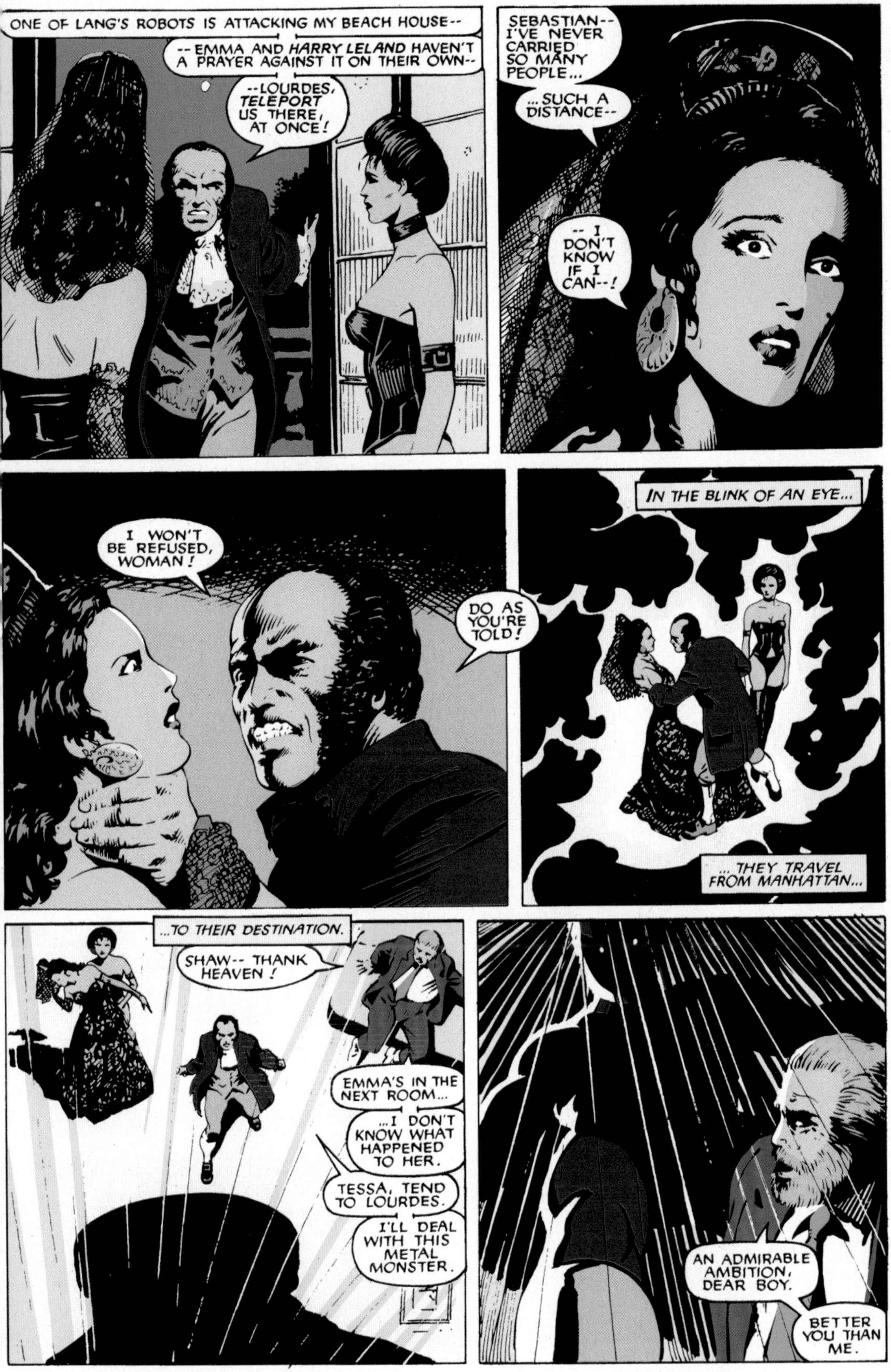

ONE OF LANG'S ROBOTS IS ATTACKING MY BEACH HOUSE--
-- EMMA AND HARRY LELAND HAVEN'T A PRAYER AGAINST IT ON THEIR OWN--
--LOURDES, TELEPORT US THERE, AT ONCE!
SEBASTIAN-- I'VE NEVER CARRIED SO MANY PEOPLE...
...SUCH A DISTANCE--
-- I DON'T KNOW IF I CAN--!
I WON'T BE REFUSED, WOMAN!
DO AS YOU'RE TOLD!
IN THE BLINK OF AN EYE...
...THEY TRAVEL FROM MANHATTAN...
...TO THEIR DESTINATION.
SHAW-- THANK HEAVEN!
EMMA'S IN THE NEXT ROOM...
...I DON'T KNOW WHAT HAPPENED TO HER.
TESSA, TEND TO LOURDES.
I'LL DEAL WITH THIS METAL MONSTER.
AN ADMIRABLE AMBITION, DEAR BOY.
BETTER YOU THAN ME.

BRILLIANT LAWYER YOU MAY BE, HARRY--

--BUT CONSIDERABLY LESS THAN A MAN.

NERVE GAS!

GOT TO FLATTEN THE REMAINING WALLS, SO THE WIND CAN BLOW THE GAS AWAY BEFORE IT CAN DO US ANY HARM!

A GOOD PUNCH--

--THE HARDER I STRIKE ANYTHING, THE STRONGER I GET--

--A FEW MORE LIKE IT AND I'LL BE UNBEATA-- WHU-AH?!!

SHAW!

LOURDES, STAY BACK! YOU'RE STILL TOO WEAK!

I DON'T CARE, TESSA!

I WON'T LET HIM BE HARMED!

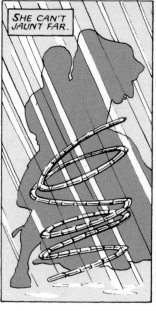

SHE CAN'T JAUNT FAR.

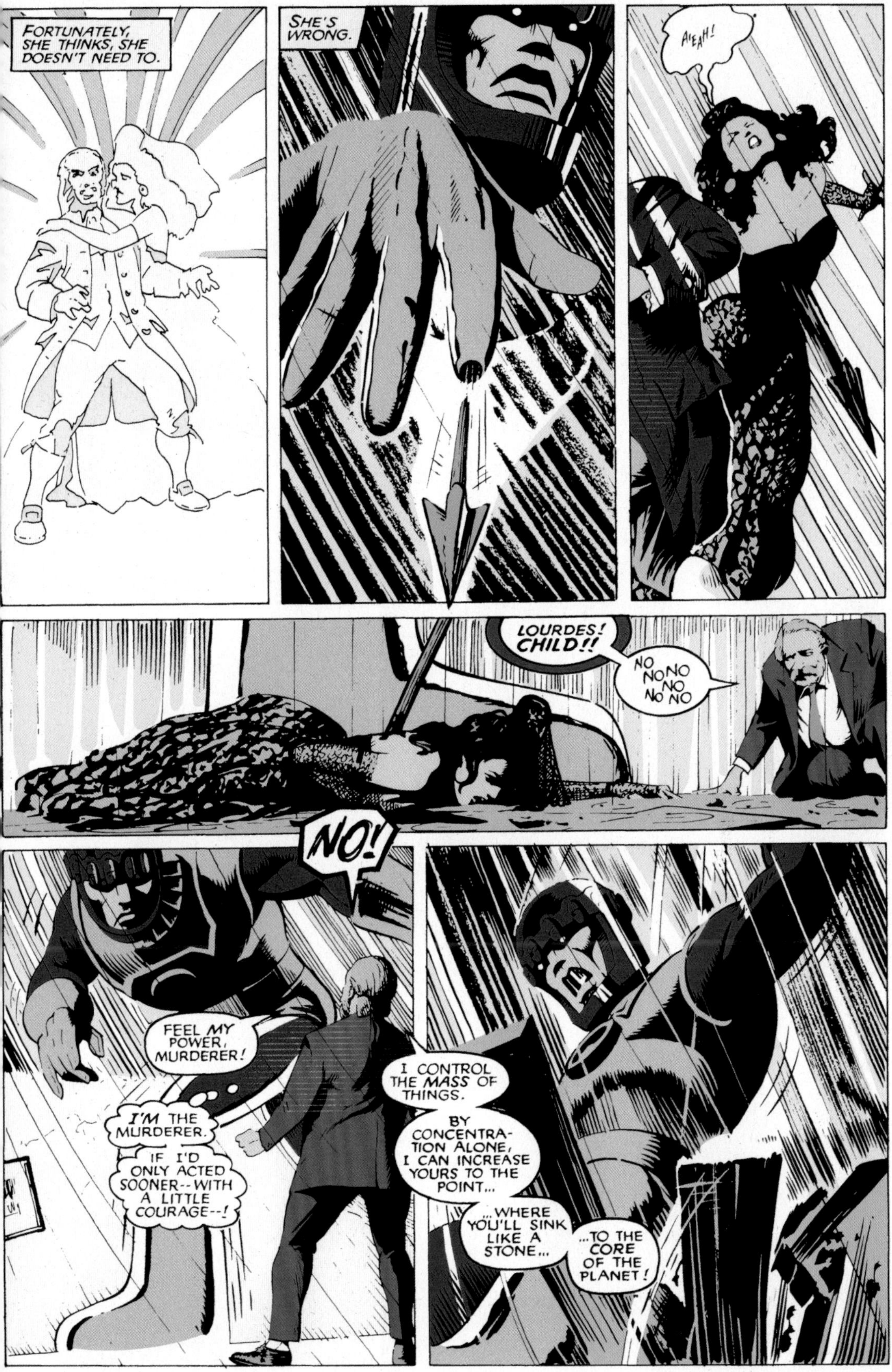
FORTUNATELY, SHE THINKS, SHE DOESN'T NEED TO.
SHE'S WRONG.
AIEEAH!
LOURDES! CHILD!!
NO NO NO NO NO NO NO
NO!
FEEL MY POWER, MURDERER!
I'M THE MURDERER.
IF I'D ONLY ACTED SOONER--WITH A LITTLE COURAGE--!
I CONTROL THE MASS OF THINGS.
BY CONCENTRATION ALONE, I CAN INCREASE YOURS TO THE POINT...
...WHERE YOU'LL SINK LIKE A STONE...
...TO THE CORE OF THE PLANET!

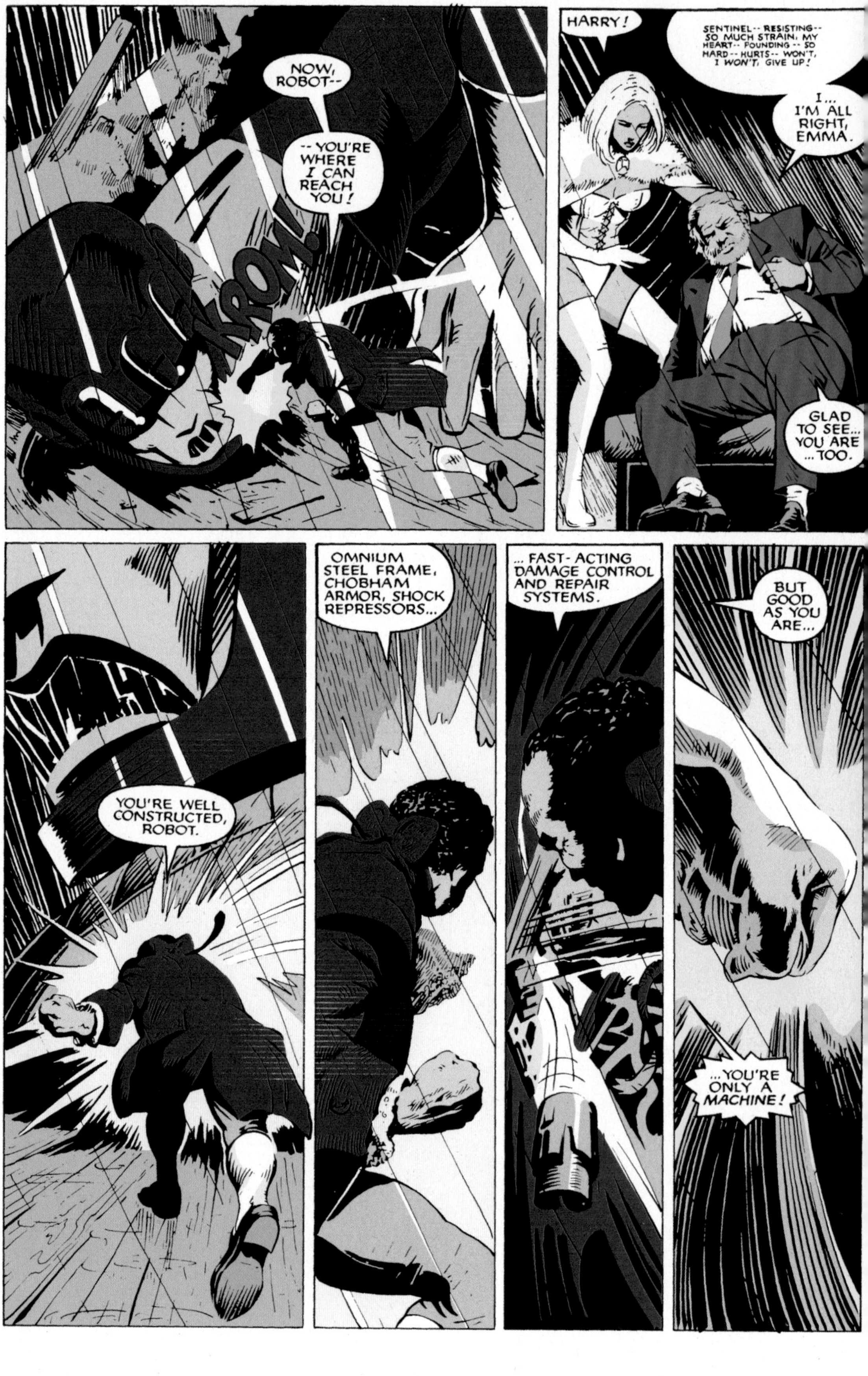

NOW, ROBOT--
-- YOU'RE WHERE I CAN REACH YOU!
KROM!
HARRY!
SENTINEL-- RESISTING-- SO MUCH STRAIN. MY HEART-- POUNDING -- SO HARD-- HURTS-- WON'T, I WON'T, GIVE UP!
I... I'M ALL RIGHT, EMMA.
GLAD TO SEE... YOU ARE ...TOO.
YOU'RE WELL CONSTRUCTED, ROBOT.
OMNIUM STEEL FRAME, CHOBHAM ARMOR, SHOCK REPRESSORS...
... FAST-ACTING DAMAGE CONTROL AND REPAIR SYSTEMS.
BUT GOOD AS YOU ARE...
...YOU'RE ONLY A MACHINE!

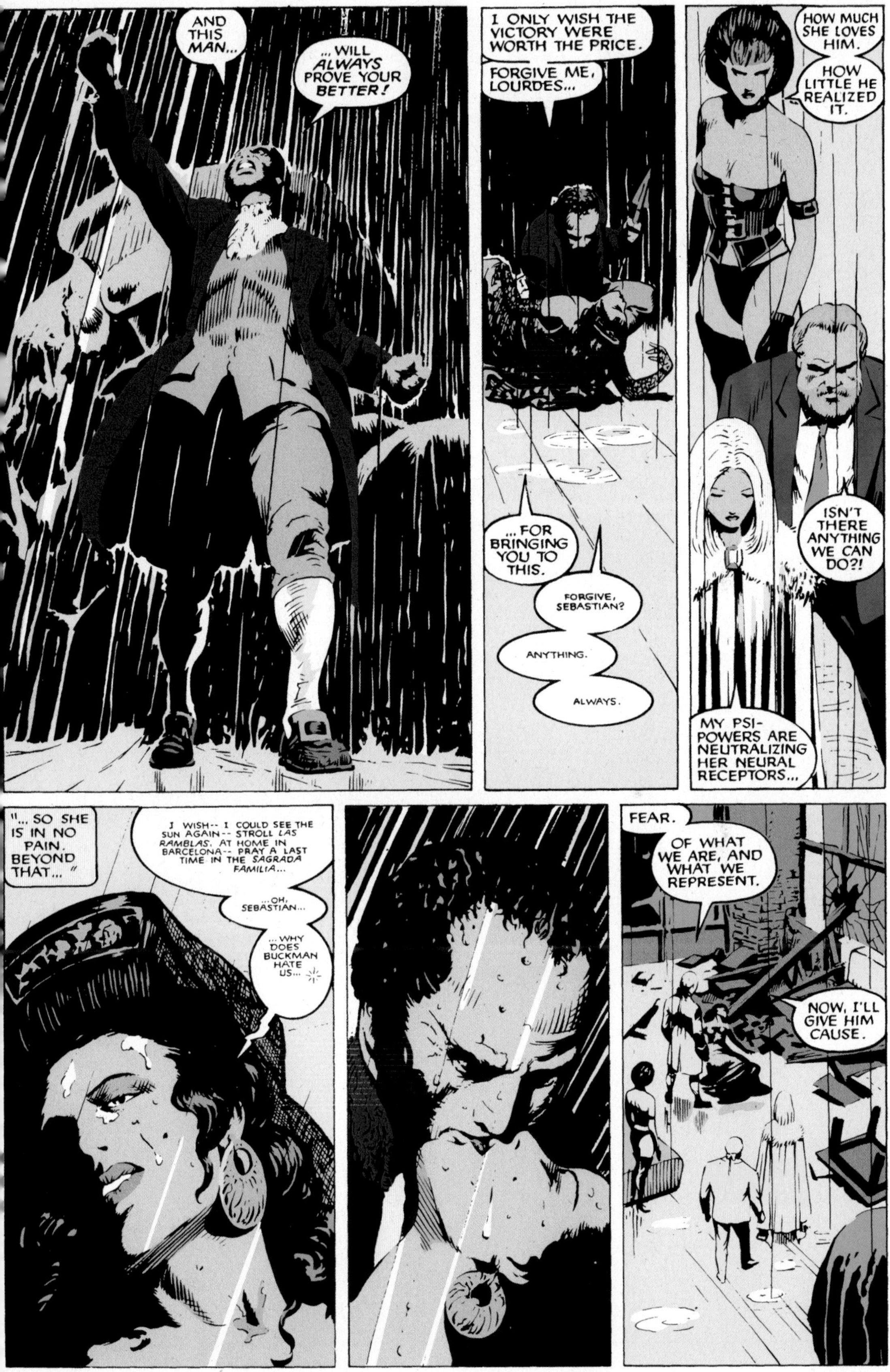
AND THIS MAN...
...WILL ALWAYS PROVE YOUR BETTER!
I ONLY WISH THE VICTORY WERE WORTH THE PRICE.
FORGIVE ME, LOURDES...
...FOR BRINGING YOU TO THIS.
FORGIVE, SEBASTIAN?
ANYTHING.
ALWAYS.
HOW MUCH SHE LOVES HIM.
HOW LITTLE HE REALIZED IT.
ISN'T THERE ANYTHING WE CAN DO?!
MY PSI-POWERS ARE NEUTRALIZING HER NEURAL RECEPTORS...
"...SO SHE IS IN NO PAIN. BEYOND THAT..."
I WISH-- I COULD SEE THE SUN AGAIN-- STROLL LAS RAMBLAS, AT HOME IN BARCELONA-- PRAY A LAST TIME IN THE SAGRADA FAMILIA...
...OH, SEBASTIAN...
...WHY DOES BUCKMAN HATE US...
FEAR.
OF WHAT WE ARE, AND WHAT WE REPRESENT.
NOW, I'LL GIVE HIM CAUSE.

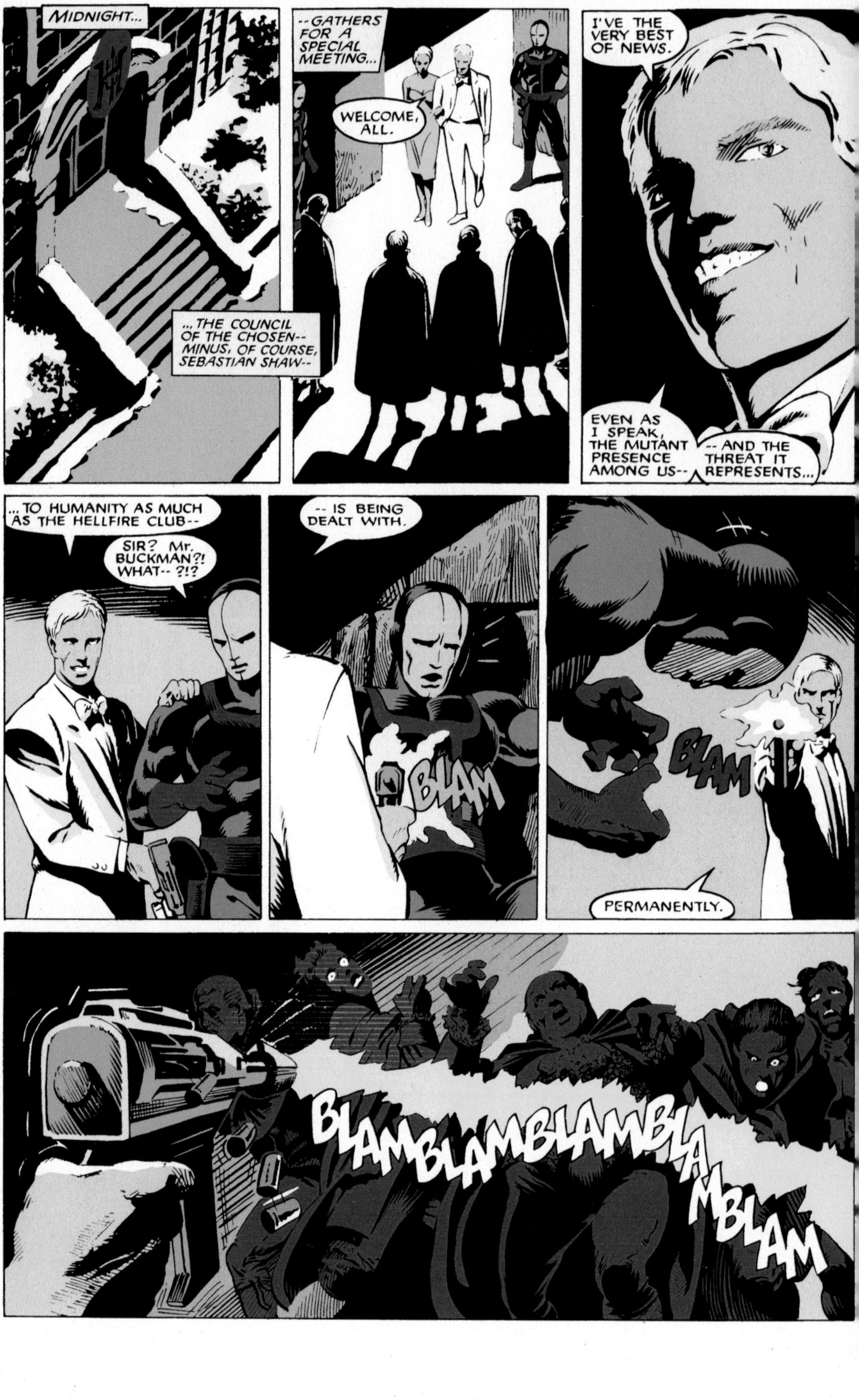
MIDNIGHT...
...THE COUNCIL OF THE CHOSEN-- MINUS, OF COURSE, SEBASTIAN SHAW--
--GATHERS FOR A SPECIAL MEETING...
WELCOME, ALL.
I'VE THE VERY BEST OF NEWS.
EVEN AS I SPEAK, THE MUTANT PRESENCE AMONG US--
--AND THE THREAT IT REPRESENTS...
...TO HUMANITY AS MUCH AS THE HELLFIRE CLUB--
SIR? Mr. BUCKMAN?! WHAT-- ?!?
-- IS BEING DEALT WITH.
BLAM
BLAM
PERMANENTLY.
BLAMBLAMBLAMBLAMBLAM

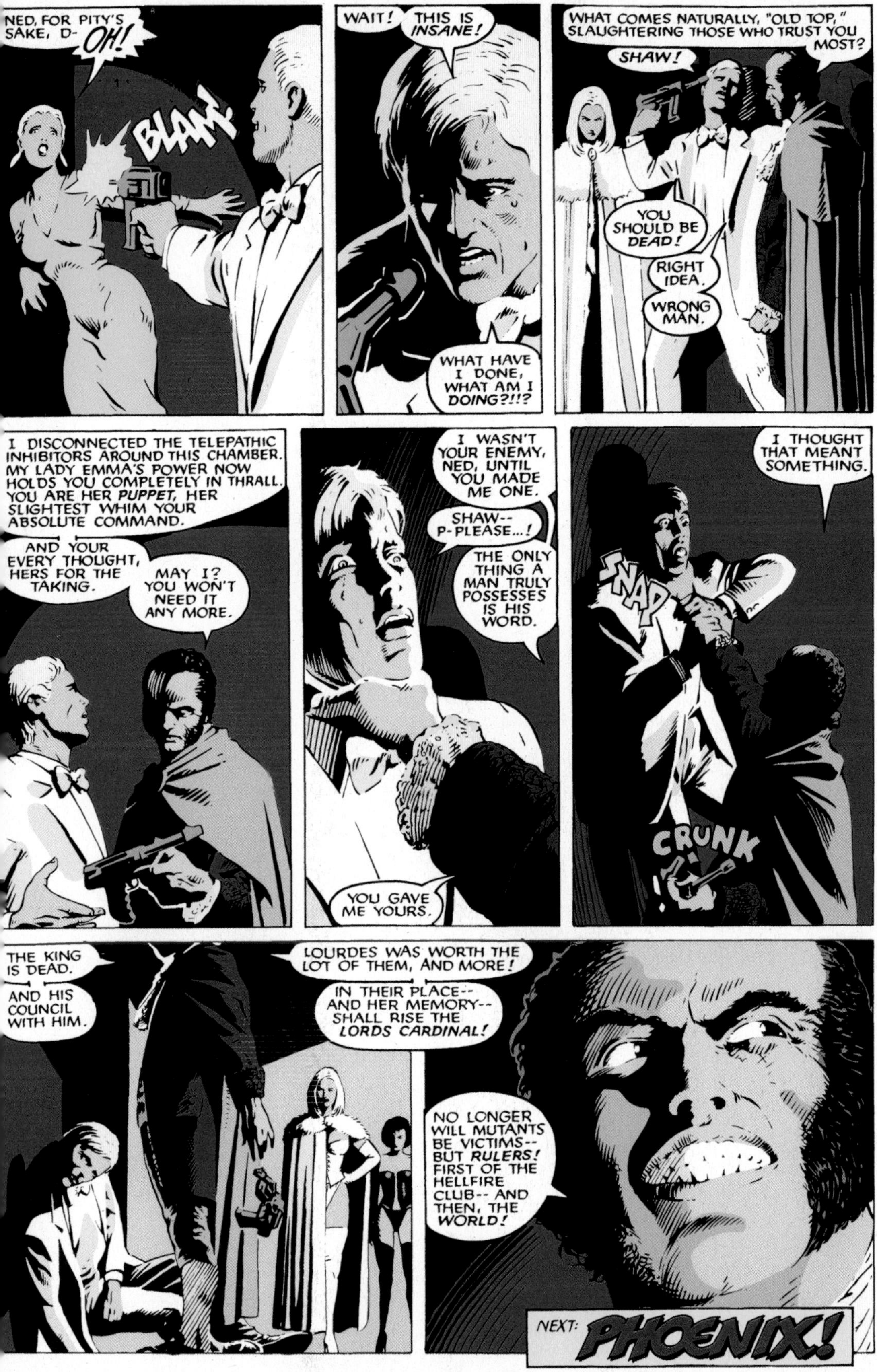

NED, FOR PITY'S SAKE, D- OH!
BLAM
WAIT!
THIS IS INSANE!
WHAT HAVE I DONE, WHAT AM I DOING?!!?
WHAT COMES NATURALLY, "OLD TOP," SLAUGHTERING THOSE WHO TRUST YOU MOST?
SHAW!
YOU SHOULD BE DEAD!
RIGHT IDEA.
WRONG MAN.
I DISCONNECTED THE TELEPATHIC INHIBITORS AROUND THIS CHAMBER. MY LADY EMMA'S POWER NOW HOLDS YOU COMPLETELY IN THRALL. YOU ARE HER PUPPET, HER SLIGHTEST WHIM YOUR ABSOLUTE COMMAND.
AND YOUR EVERY THOUGHT, HERS FOR THE TAKING.
MAY I? YOU WON'T NEED IT ANY MORE.
I WASN'T YOUR ENEMY, NED, UNTIL YOU MADE ME ONE.
SHAW-- P-PLEASE...!
THE ONLY THING A MAN TRULY POSSESSES IS HIS WORD.
YOU GAVE ME YOURS.
I THOUGHT THAT MEANT SOMETHING.
SNAP
CRUNK
THE KING IS DEAD.
AND HIS COUNCIL WITH HIM.
LOURDES WAS WORTH THE LOT OF THEM, AND MORE!
IN THEIR PLACE-- AND HER MEMORY-- SHALL RISE THE LORDS CARDINAL!
NO LONGER WILL MUTANTS BE VICTIMS-- BUT RULERS! FIRST OF THE HELLFIRE CLUB-- AND THEN, THE WORLD!
NEXT: PHOENIX!

[CXM].....007]
[HFG]....1987]

[reign_of_x]

[kra_]
[koa_]

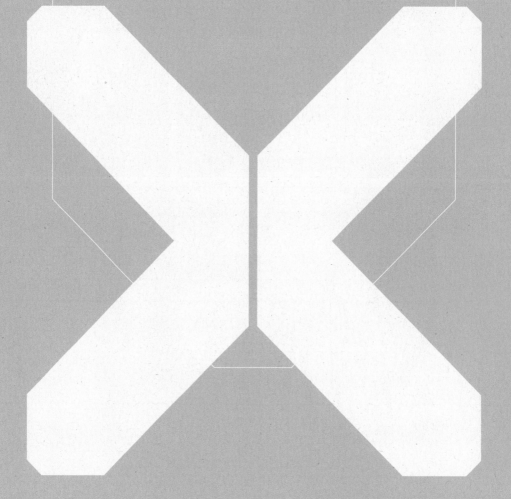

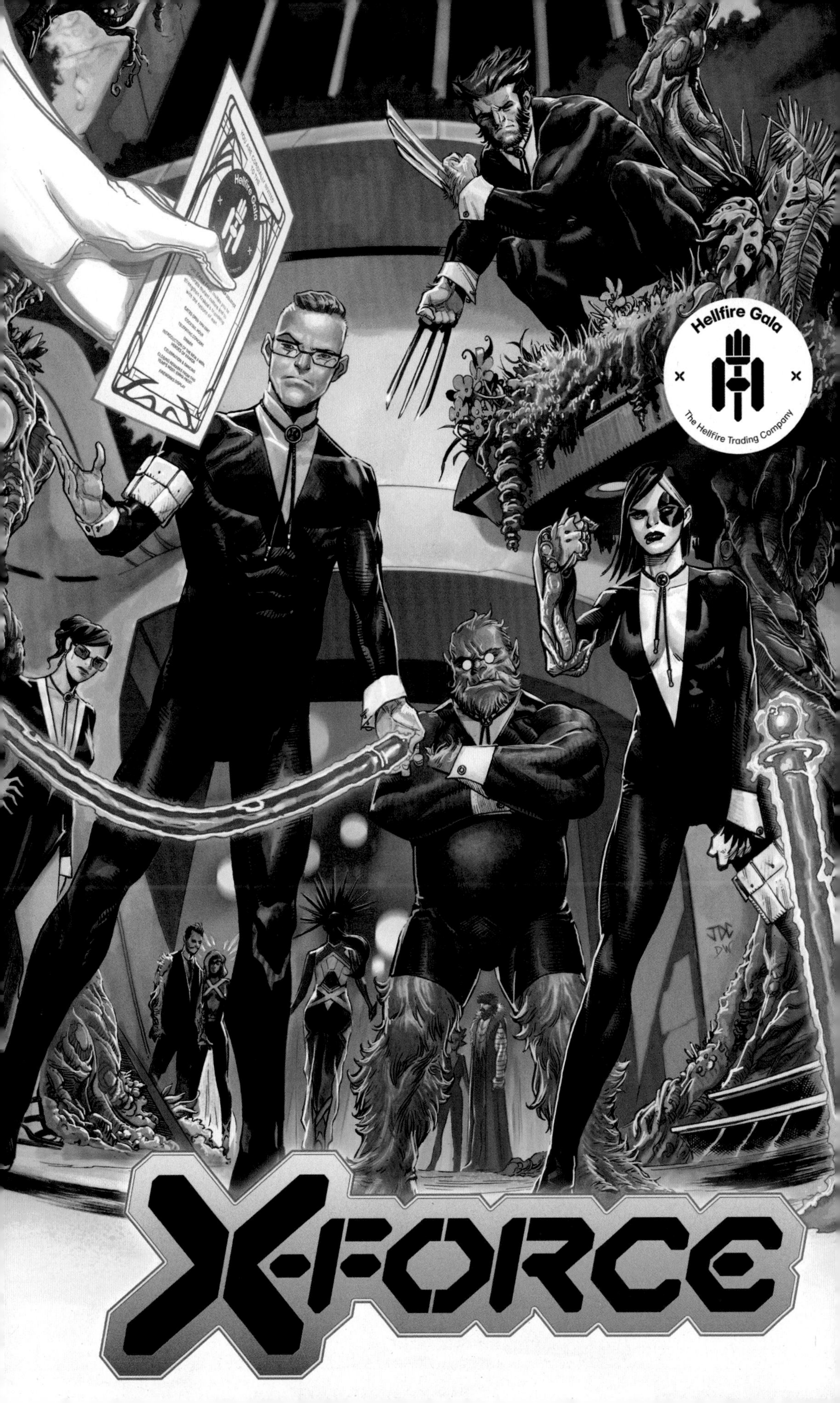
Hellfire Gala
The Hellfire Trading Company
X-FORCE

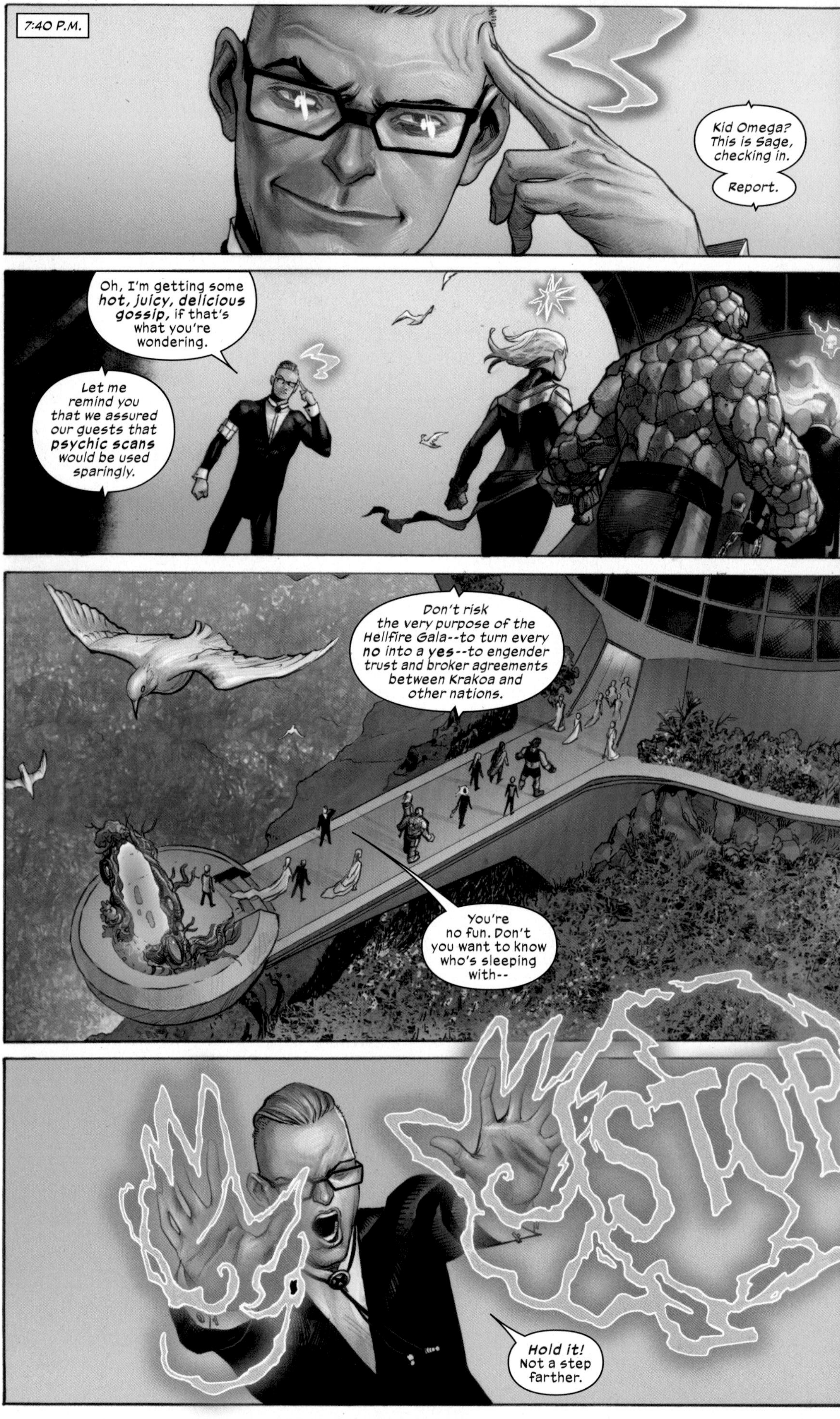
7:40 P.M.
Kid Omega? This is Sage, checking in.
Report.
Oh, I'm getting some hot, juicy, delicious gossip, if that's what you're wondering.
Let me remind you that we assured our guests that psychic scans would be used sparingly.
Don't risk the very purpose of the Hellfire Gala--to turn every no into a yes--to engender trust and broker agreements between Krakoa and other nations.
You're no fun. Don't you want to know who's sleeping with--
STOP
Hold it! Not a step farther.

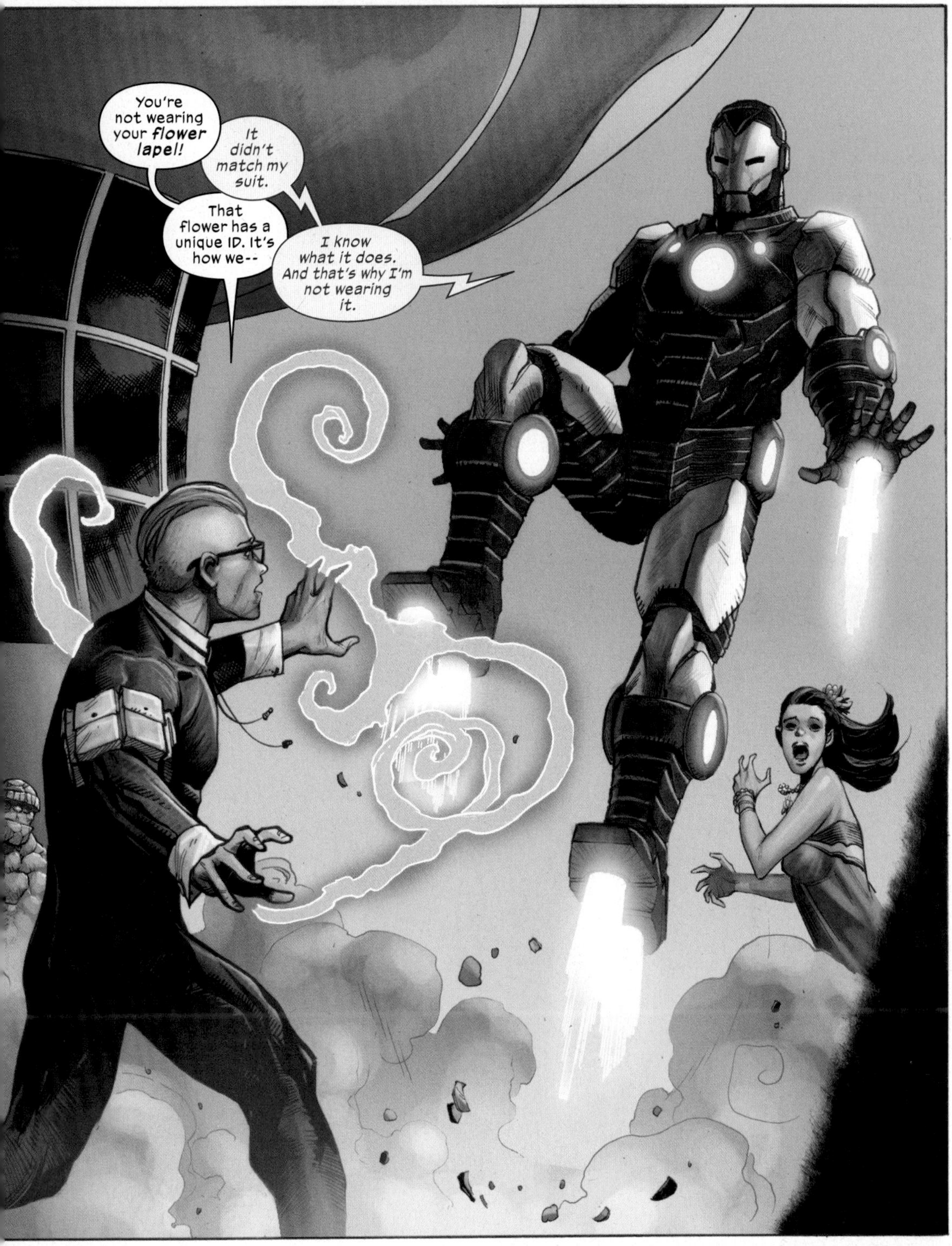

You're not wearing your *flower lapel!*
It didn't match my suit.
That flower has a unique ID. It's how we--
I know what it does. And that's why I'm not wearing it.

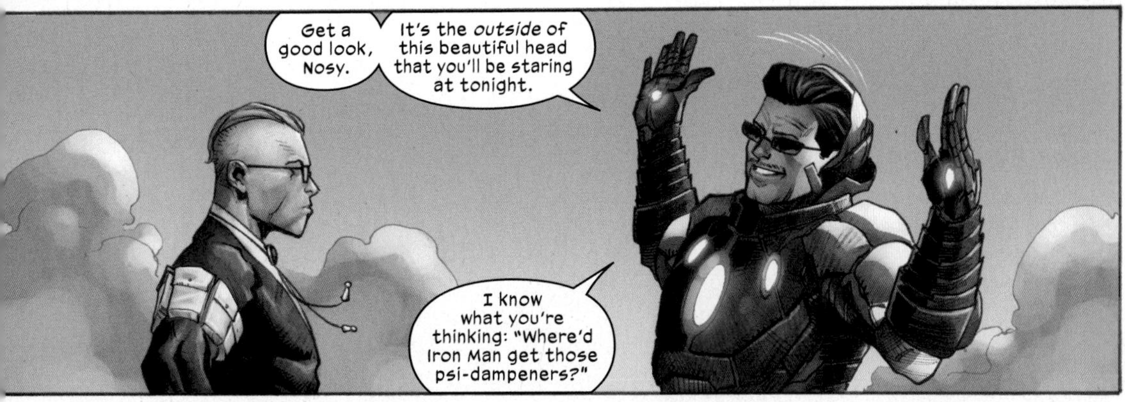

Get a good look, Nosy.
It's the *outside* of this beautiful head that you'll be staring at tonight.
I know what you're thinking: "Where'd Iron Man get those psi-dampeners?"

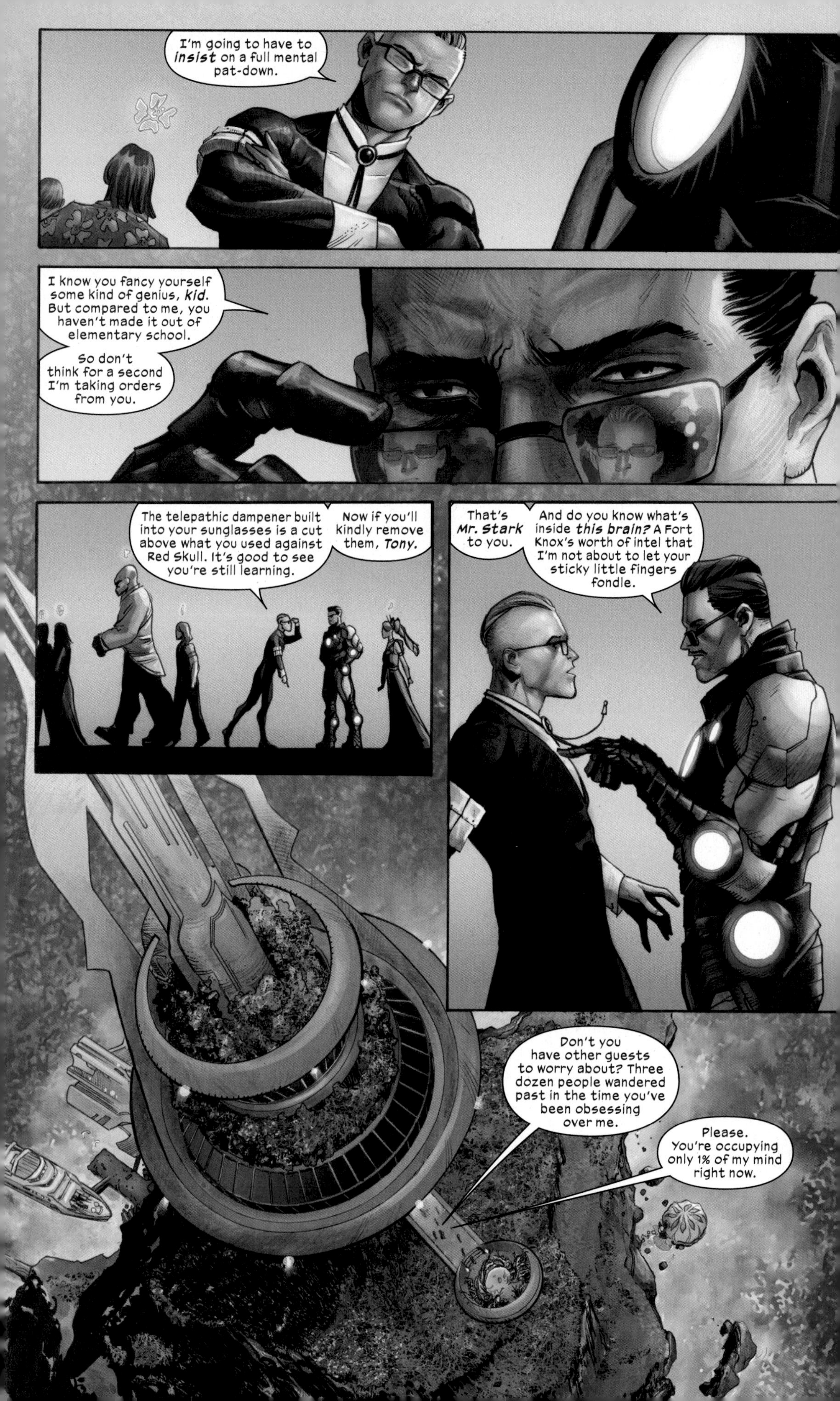
I'm going to have to *insist* on a full mental pat-down.
I know you fancy yourself some kind of genius, *kid.* But compared to me, you haven't made it out of elementary school.
So don't think for a second I'm taking orders from you.
The telepathic dampener built into your sunglasses is a cut above what you used against Red Skull. It's good to see you're still learning.
Now if you'll kindly remove them, *Tony.*
That's *Mr. Stark* to you.
And do you know what's inside *this brain?* A Fort Knox's worth of intel that I'm not about to let your sticky little fingers fondle.
Don't you have other guests to worry about? Three dozen people wandered past in the time you've been obsessing over me.
Please. You're occupying only 1% of my mind right now.

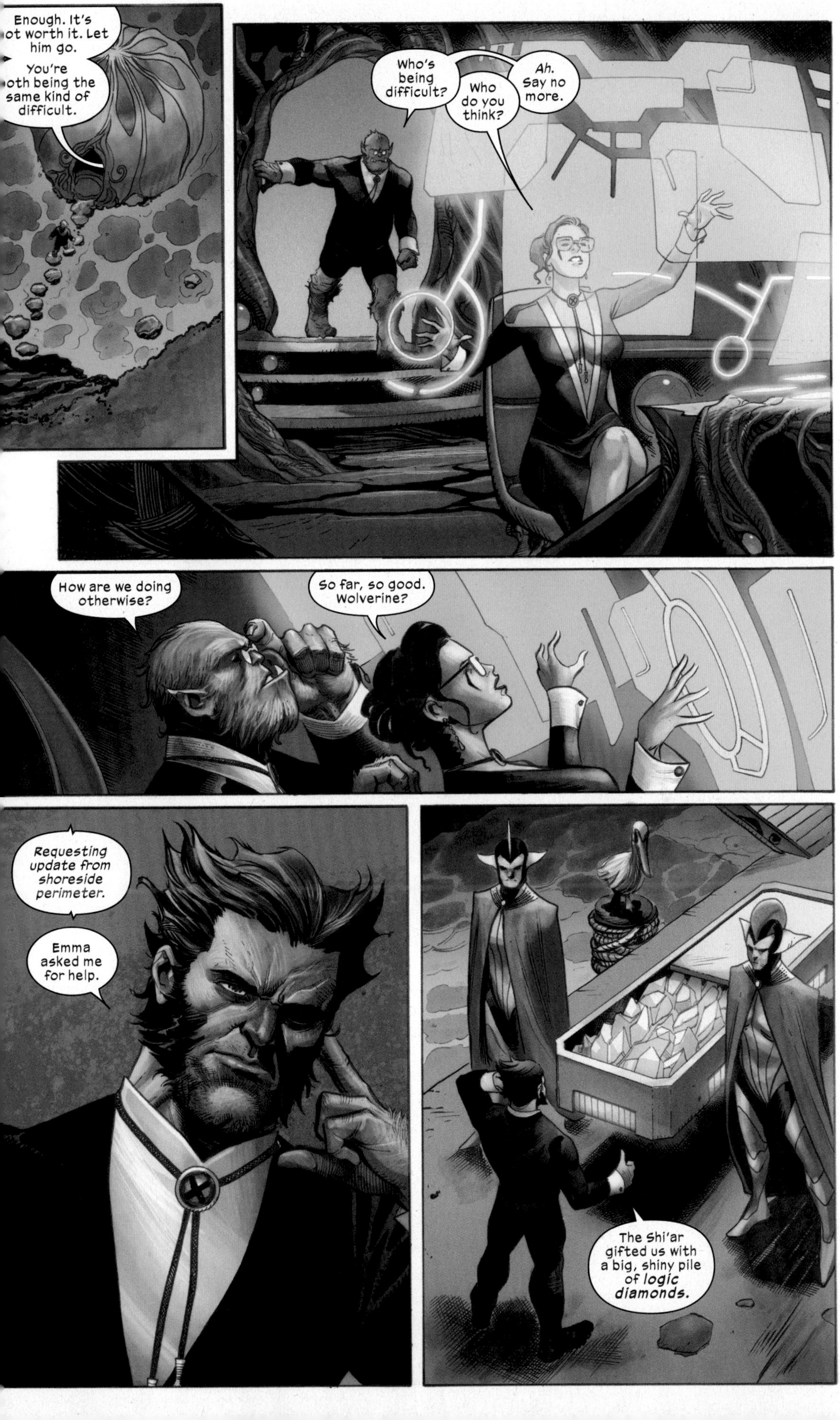

Enough. It's
ot worth it. Let
him go.
You're
oth being the
same kind of
difficult.
Who's
being
difficult?
Who
do you
think?
Ah.
Say no
more.
How are we doing
otherwise?
So far, so good.
Wolverine?
Requesting
update from
shoreside
perimeter.
Emma
asked me
for help.
The Shi'ar
gifted us with
a big, shiny pile
of logic
diamonds.

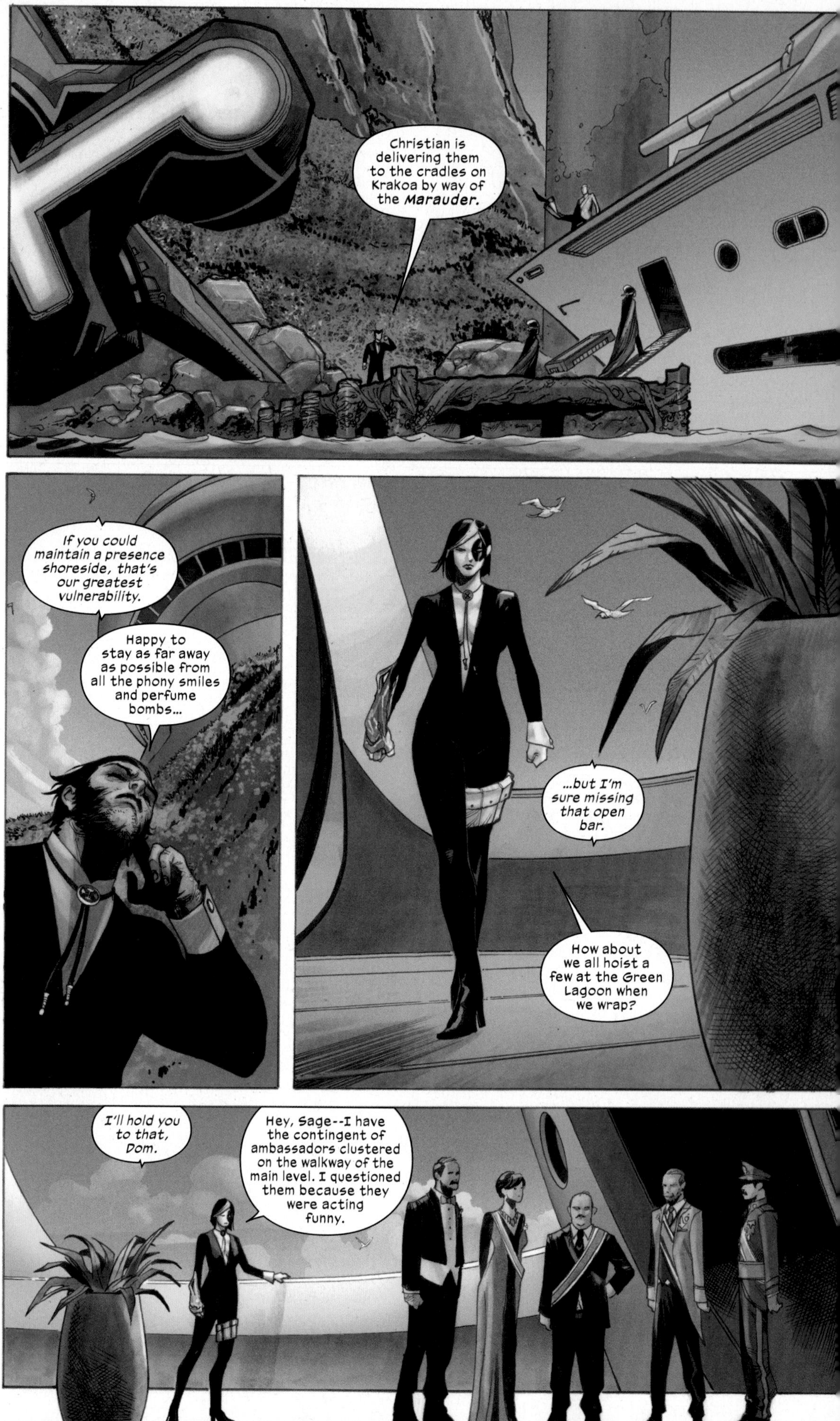

Christian is delivering them to the cradles on Krakoa by way of the *Marauder.*
If you could maintain a presence shoreside, that's our greatest vulnerability.
Happy to stay as far away as possible from all the phony smiles and perfume bombs...
...but I'm sure missing that open bar.
How about we all hoist a few at the Green Lagoon when we wrap?
I'll hold you to that, Dom.
Hey, Sage--I have the contingent of ambassadors clustered on the walkway of the main level. I questioned them because they were acting funny.

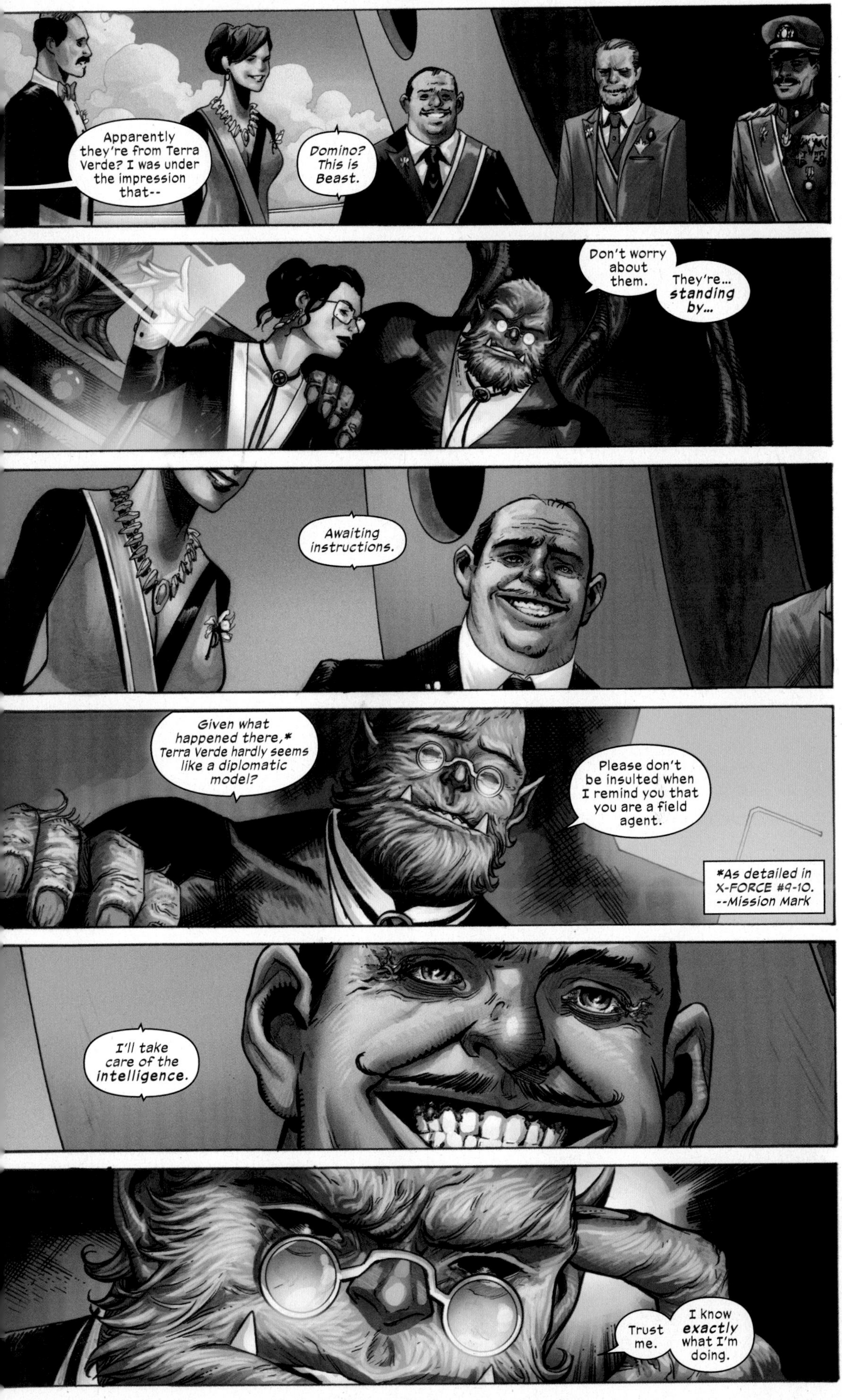

Apparently they're from Terra Verde? I was under the impression that--
Domino? This is Beast.
Don't worry about them.
They're... *standing* by...
Awaiting instructions.
Given what happened there,* Terra Verde hardly seems like a diplomatic model?
Please don't be insulted when I remind you that you are a field agent.
*As detailed in X-FORCE #9-10. --Mission Mark
I'll take care of the **intelligence**.
Trust me.
I know *exactly* what I'm doing.

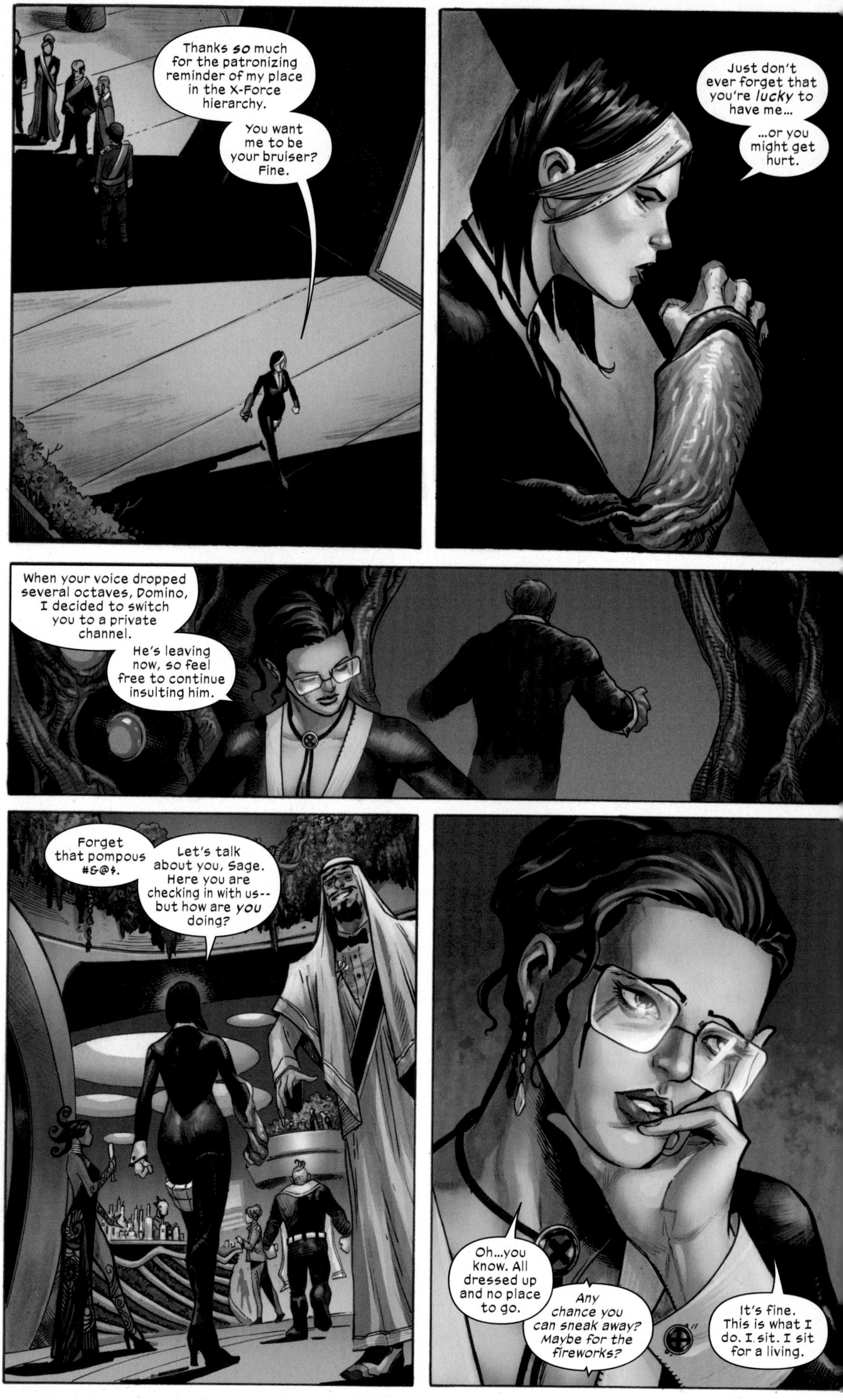

Thanks *so* much for the patronizing reminder of my place in the X-Force hierarchy.
You want me to be your bruiser? Fine.
Just don't ever forget that you're *lucky* to have me...
...or you might get hurt.
When your voice dropped several octaves, Domino, I decided to switch you to a private channel.
He's leaving now, so feel free to continue insulting him.
Forget that pompous #&@$.
Let's talk about you, Sage. Here you are checking in with us-- but how are *you* doing?
Oh...you know. All dressed up and no place to go.
Any chance you can sneak away? Maybe for the fireworks?
It's fine. This is what I do. I sit. I sit for a living.

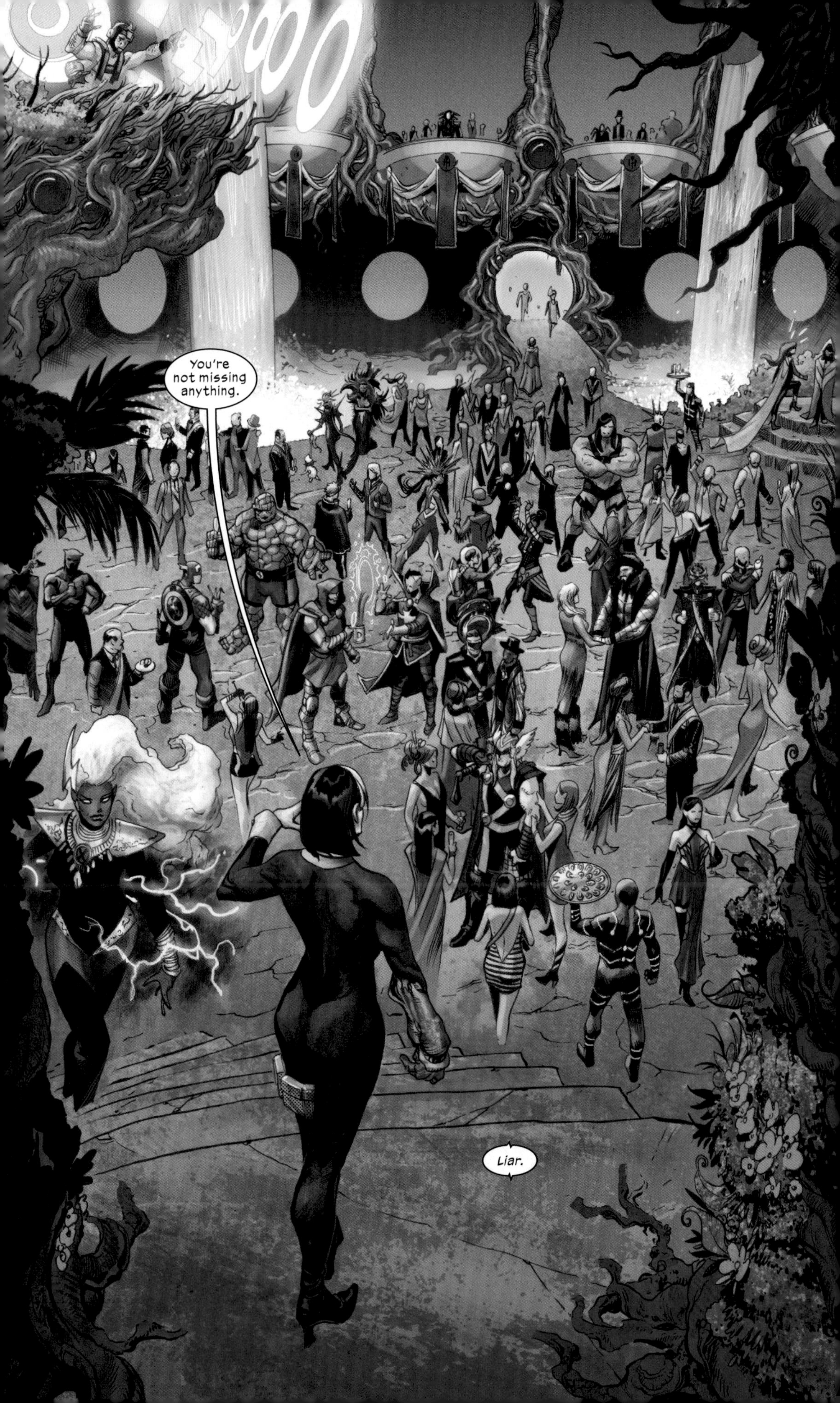
You're not missing anything.
Liar.

INVITE-ONLY

The Hellfire Gala, the most anticipated party of the year where mutant and humans alike gather in celebration. But not everyone is raising their glasses in merriment. Away from the protection of Krakoa and mingling with guests and diplomats from all ends of the earth -- each with their own history and aspirations toward the mutant community -- X-Force has their hands full keeping the party safe.

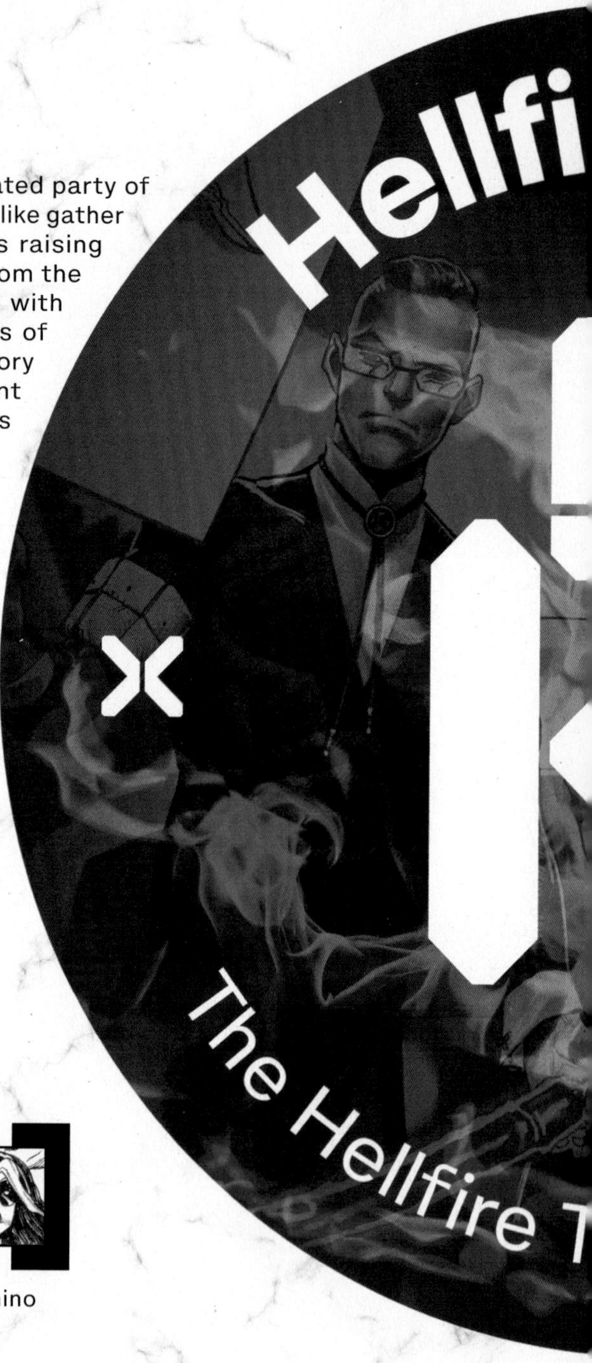
Hellfi
The Hellfire T

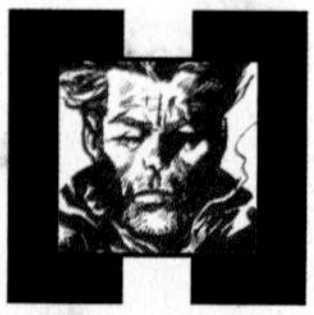
Wolverine

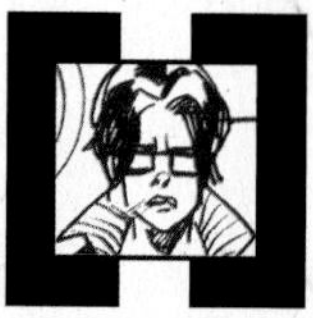
Sage

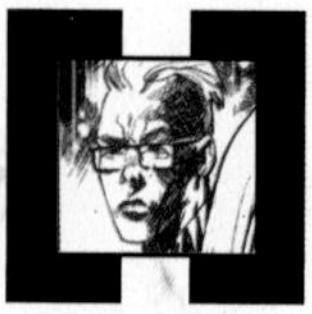
Kid Omega

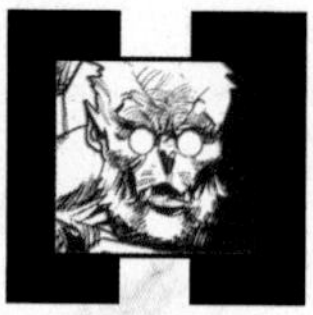
Beast

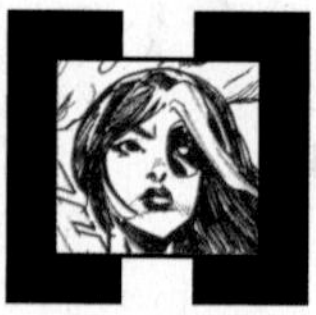
Domino

X-FORCE

[X_20]

[ISSUE TWENTY] ....
.... THE SECRET GARDEN

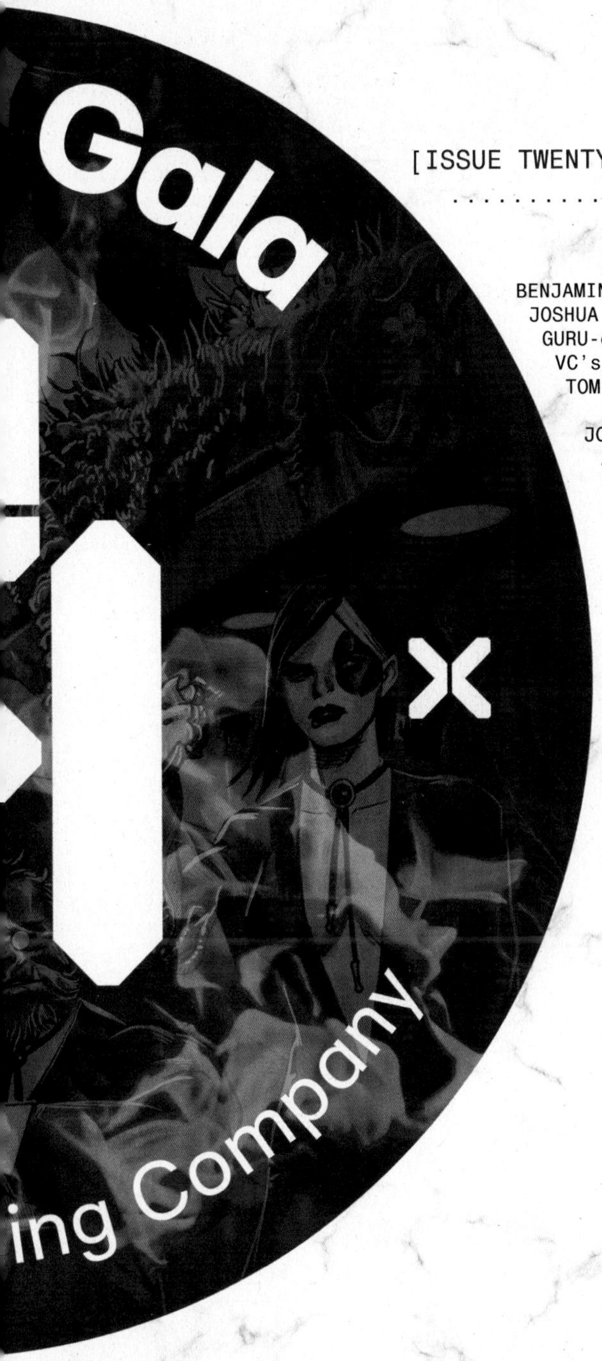
Gala
ing Company

BENJAMIN PERCY .... [WRITER]
JOSHUA CASSARA .... [ARTIST]
GURU-eFX .... [COLOR ARTIST]
VC's JOE CARAMAGNA .... [LETTERER]
TOM MULLER .... [DESIGN]

JOSHUA CASSARA & DEAN WHITE...........
.... [COVER ARTISTS]

JOSHUA CASSARA ....
[X-FORCE DESIGN VARIANT COVER ARTIST]

RUSSELL DAUTERMAN ....
[EMMA DESIGN VARIANT COVER ARTIST]

RUSSELL DAUTERMAN & MATTHEW WILSON
.... [CONNECTING COVER ARTISTS]

JONATHAN HICKMAN .... [HEAD OF X]
JAY BOWEN.............. [PRODUCTION]
LAUREN AMARO ..... [ASSISTANT EDITOR]
MARK BASSO .... [EDITOR]
JORDAN D. WHITE ..... [SENIOR EDITOR]
C.B. CEBULSKI...... [EDITOR IN CHIEF]

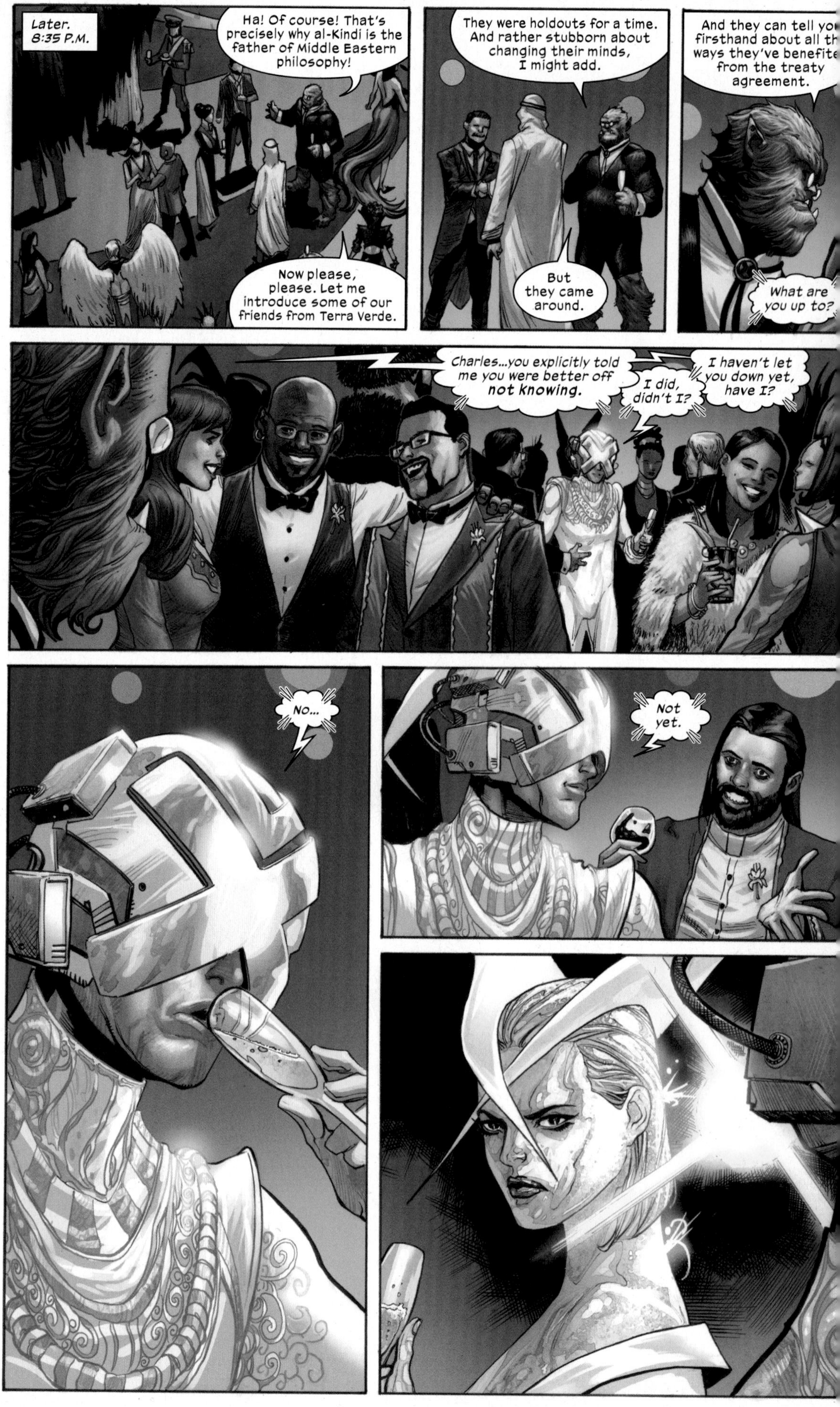
Later.
8:35 P.M.
Ha! Of course! That's precisely why al-Kindi is the father of Middle Eastern philosophy!
Now please, please. Let me introduce some of our friends from Terra Verde.
They were holdouts for a time. And rather stubborn about changing their minds, I might add.
But they came around.
And they can tell yo firsthand about all th ways they've benefite from the treaty agreement.
What are you up to?
Charles...you explicitly told me you were better off not knowing.
I did, didn't I?
I haven't let you down yet, have I?
No...
Not yet.

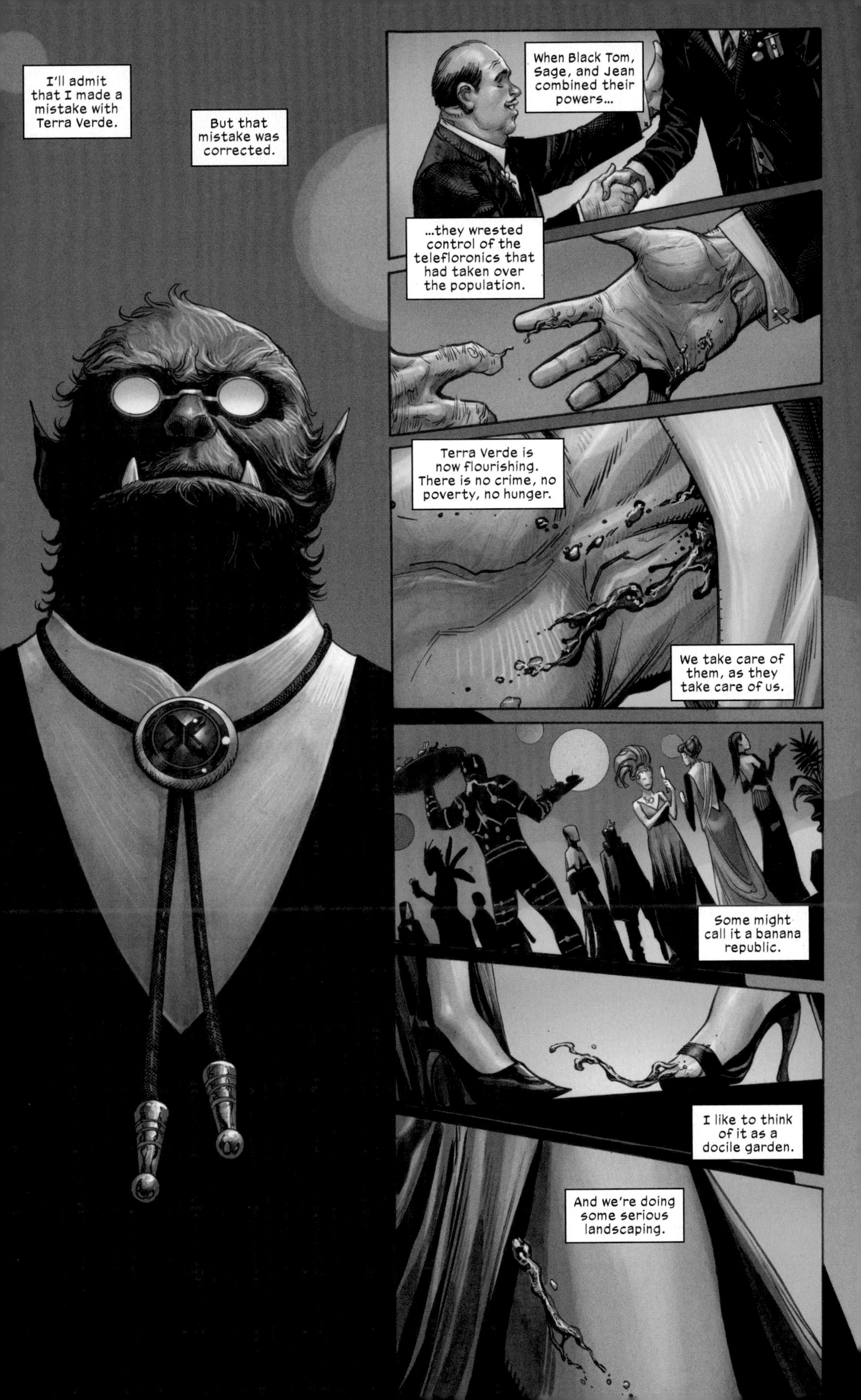
I'll admit that I made a mistake with Terra Verde.
But that mistake was corrected.
When Black Tom, Sage, and Jean combined their powers...
...they wrested control of the telefloronics that had taken over the population.
Terra Verde is now flourishing. There is no crime, no poverty, no hunger.
We take care of them, as they take care of us.
Some might call it a banana republic.
I like to think of it as a docile garden.
And we're doing some serious landscaping.

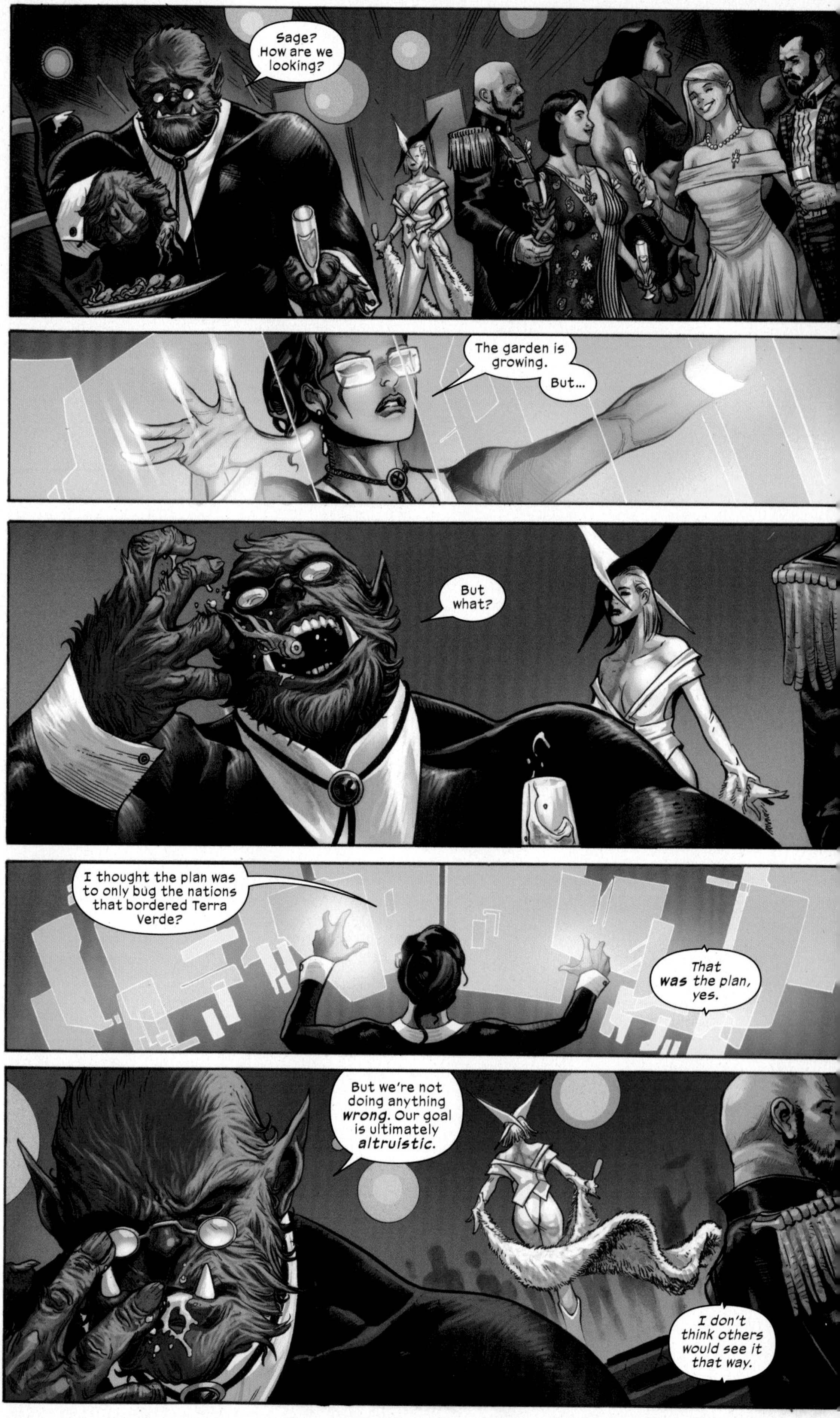
Sage? How are we looking?
The garden is growing.
But...
But what?
I thought the plan was to only bug the nations that bordered Terra Verde?
That *was* the plan, yes.
But we're not doing anything *wrong*. Our goal is ultimately *altruistic*.
I don't think others would see it that way.

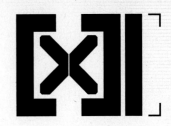

BEAST'S ARGUMENT

Imagine the following scenario. The clouds part and a god descends. His mighty voice booms like thunder as He offers to the world a gift: the gift of His watchful gaze. He would keep an eye out for all of His children and warn and protect them from harm. He wanted evildoers struck down. He wanted the good to prosper. His all-knowing wisdom would allow that.

Most people would fall to their knees and bring their hands together in a prayer of gratitude. "Thank you!" they would say. "We are loved!" they would say.

But if you change this scenario even slightly -- and say, swap out the celestial figure with a certain blue-furred mutant -- then suddenly everyone is opposed.

Because most people are stupid and illogical.

So what if I have ears in every embassy? Or in Avengers Mountain? So what if you lose the privacy you never had? My aim is to keep the world safe.

—

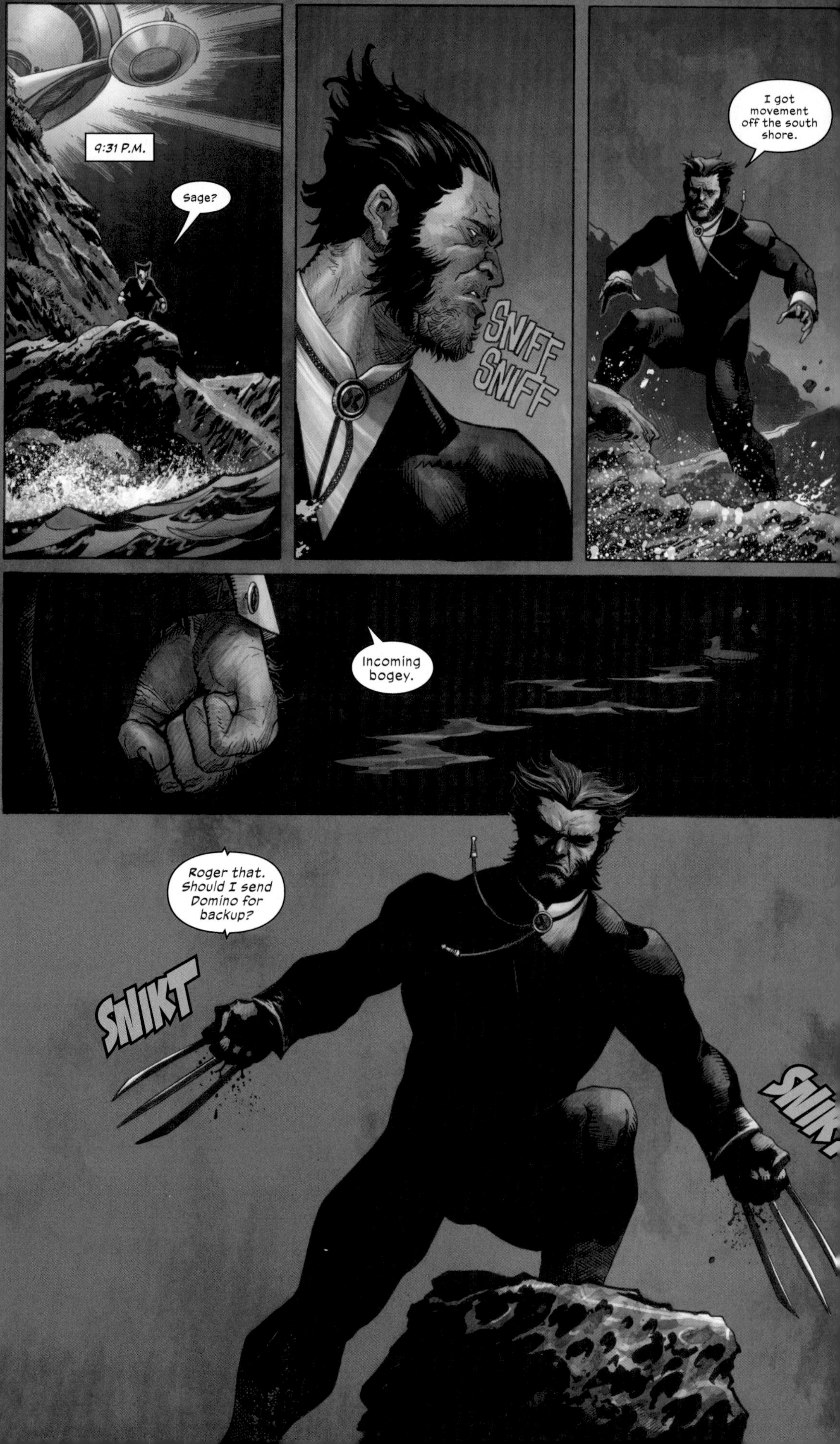
9:31 P.M.
Sage?
SNIFF SNIFF
I got movement off the south shore.
Incoming bogey.
Roger that. Should I send Domino for backup?
SNIKT
SNIKT

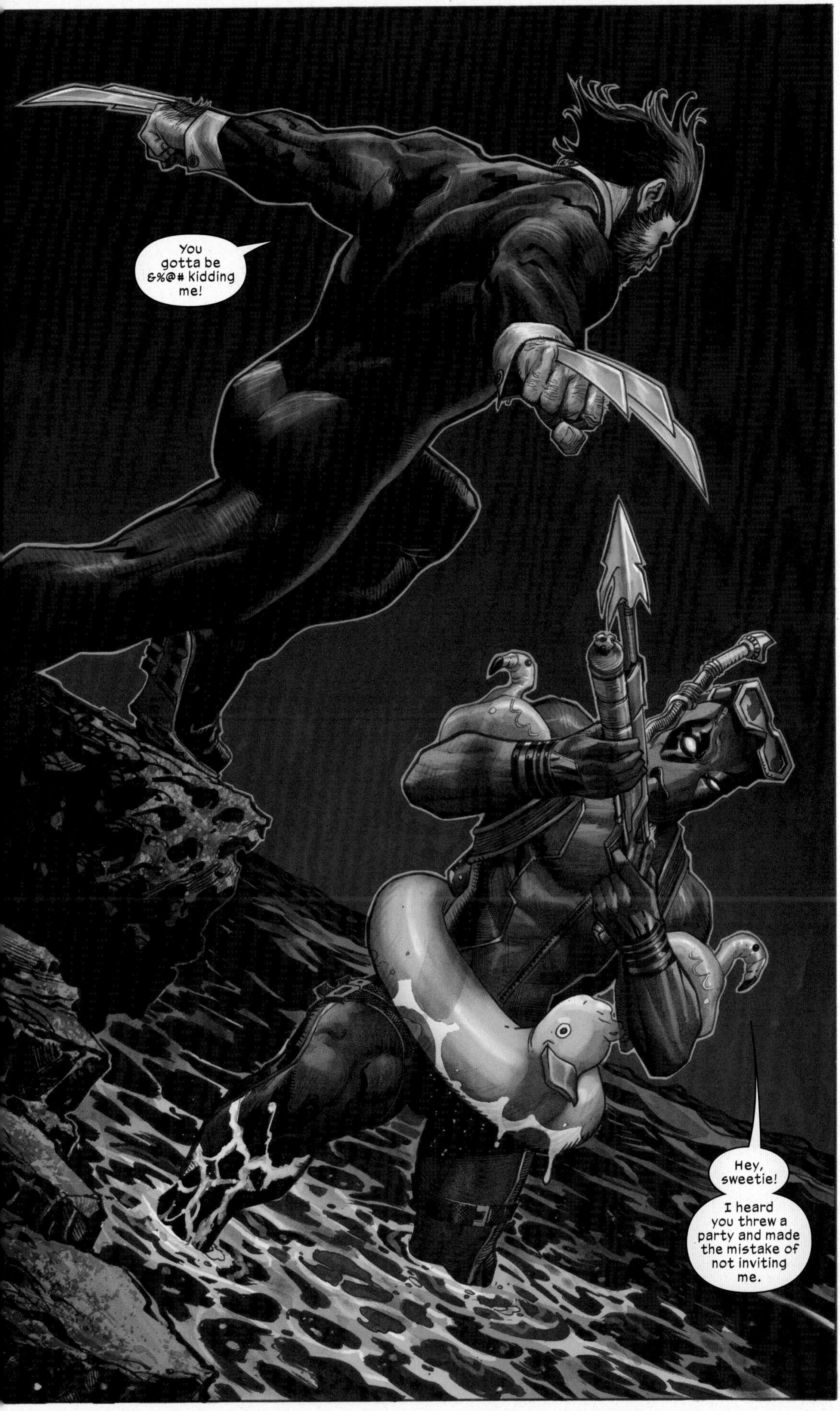
You gotta be &%@# kidding me!
Hey, sweetie!
I heard you threw a party and made the mistake of not inviting me.

You can't be here, Wade.

That hurts my feelings!

FWAP

Are you really this stupid?

I'm a mutant!

You're no mutant!

I'm an honorary mutant, then! Which means I'm allowed to get #!%&@faced at mutant parties!

This is a diplomatic summit.

Not a kegger party.

You're so rough and hairy and smelly and gross. I love it.

How about you and me work up a data page about how we fit together?

Can I be the little spoon and you be the big spoon?

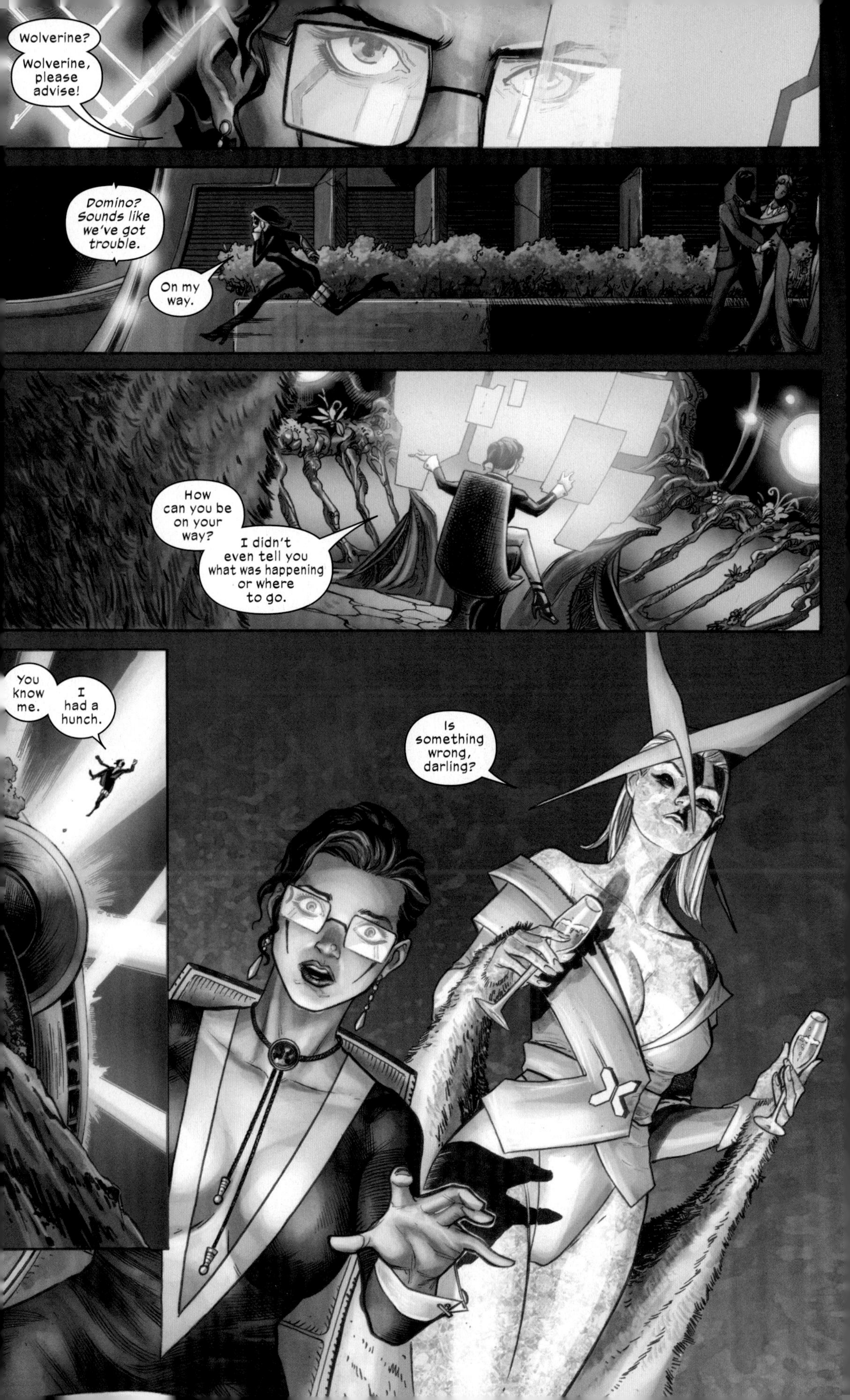
Wolverine?
Wolverine, please advise!
Domino? Sounds like we've got trouble.
On my way.
How can you be on your way?
I didn't even tell you what was happening or where to go.
You know me.
I had a hunch.
Is something wrong, darling?

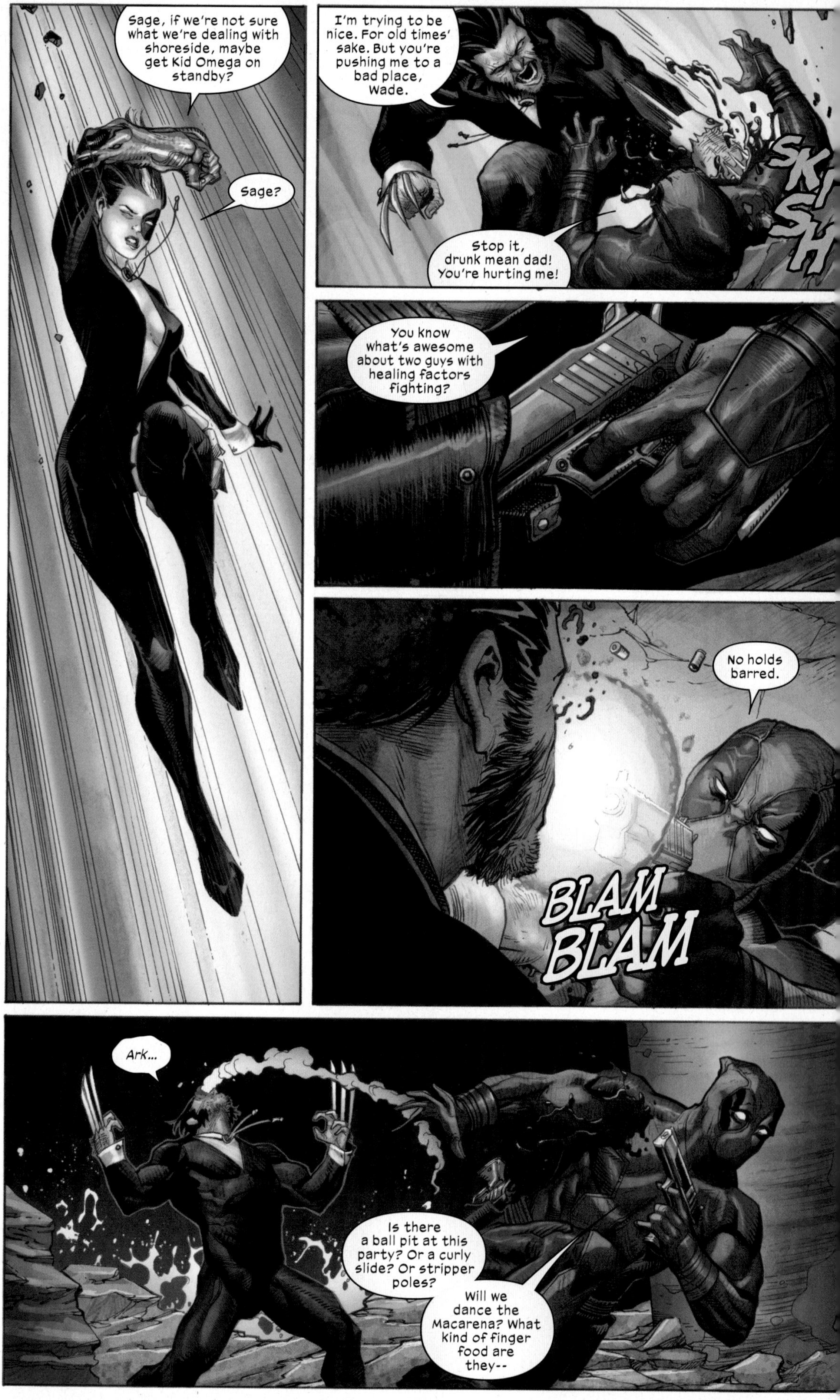

Sage, if we're not sure what we're dealing with shoreside, maybe get Kid Omega on standby?
Sage?
I'm trying to be nice. For old times' sake. But you're pushing me to a bad place, Wade.
SKISH
Stop it, drunk mean dad! You're hurting me!
You know what's awesome about two guys with healing factors fighting?
No holds barred.
BLAM BLAM
Ark...
Is there a ball pit at this party? Or a curly slide? Or stripper poles?
Will we dance the Macarena? What kind of finger food are they--

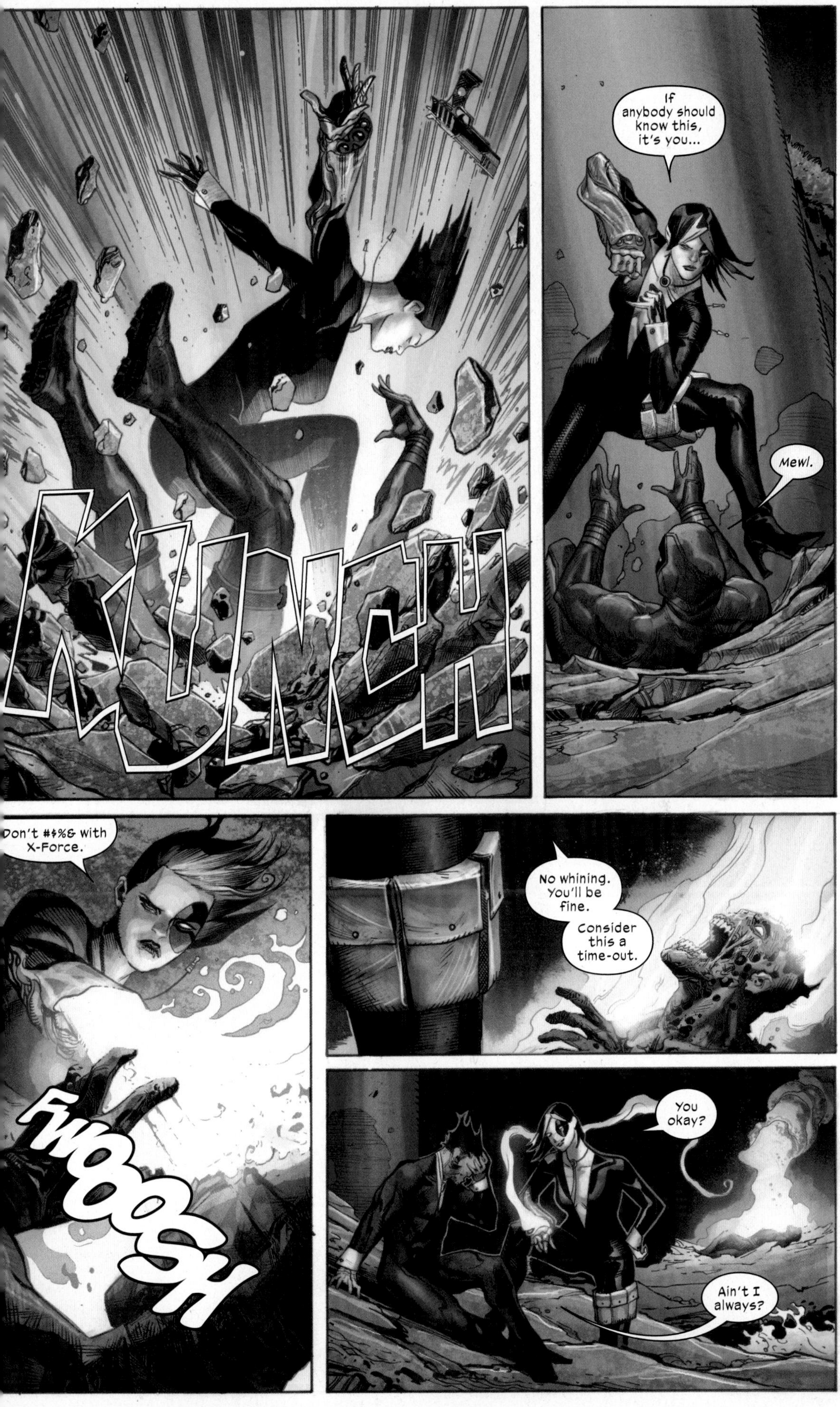
KUNCH
If anybody should know this, it's you...
Mewl.
Don't #$%& with X-Force.
FWOOSH
No whining. You'll be fine.
Consider this a time-out.
You okay?
Ain't I always?

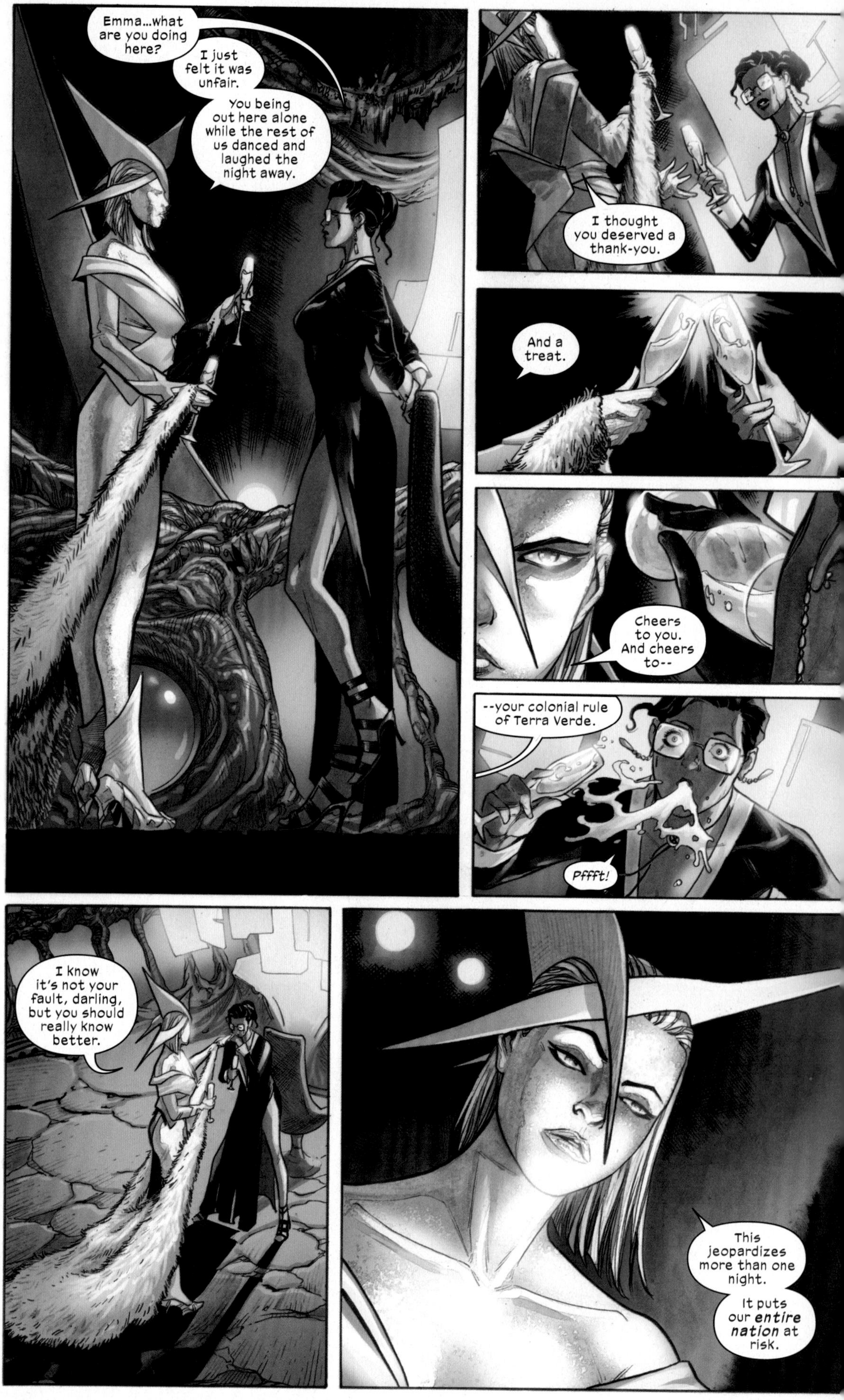
Emma...what are you doing here?
I just felt it was unfair.
You being out here alone while the rest of us danced and laughed the night away.
I thought you deserved a thank-you.
And a treat.
Cheers to you. And cheers to--
--your colonial rule of Terra Verde.
Pffft!
I know it's not your fault, darling, but you should really know better.
This jeopardizes more than one night.
It puts our *entire nation* at risk.

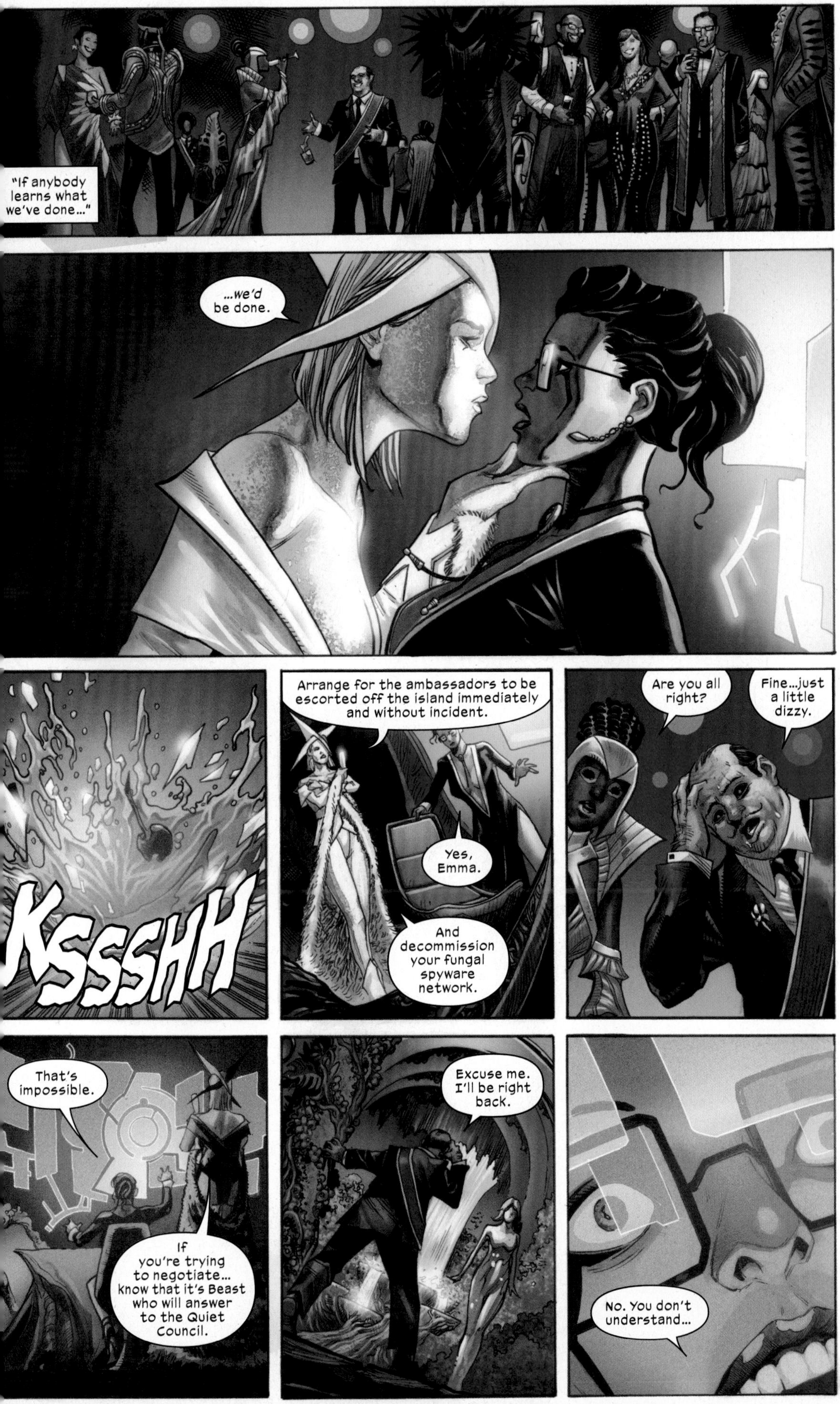
"If anybody learns what we've done..."
...we'd be done.
KSSSHH
Arrange for the ambassadors to be escorted off the island immediately and without incident.
Yes, Emma.
And decommission your fungal spyware network.
Are you all right?
Fine...just a little dizzy.
That's impossible.
If you're trying to negotiate... know that it's Beast who will answer to the Quiet Council.
Excuse me. I'll be right back.
No. You don't understand...

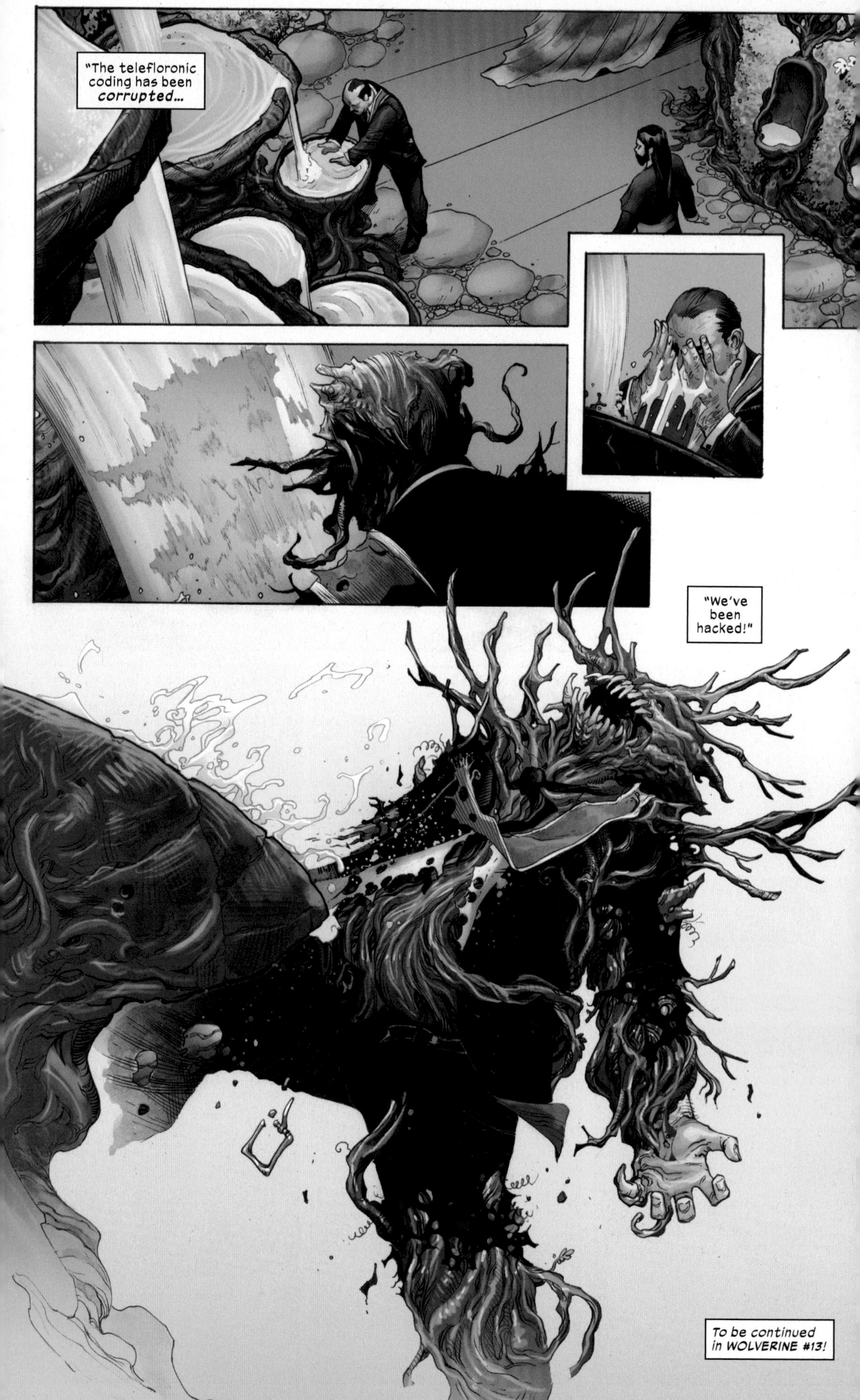
"The telefloronic coding has been *corrupted*...
"We've been hacked!"
To be continued in WOLVERINE #13!

[x-force_[0.20]
[x-force_[0.20]

You know you want it. You know you
want me in you, X-Force.

-- DEADPOOL

[x-force_[0.XX]
[x-force_[0.XX]

[x-force_[0.20].]
[x-force_[0.20].]

[x-force_alpha.]

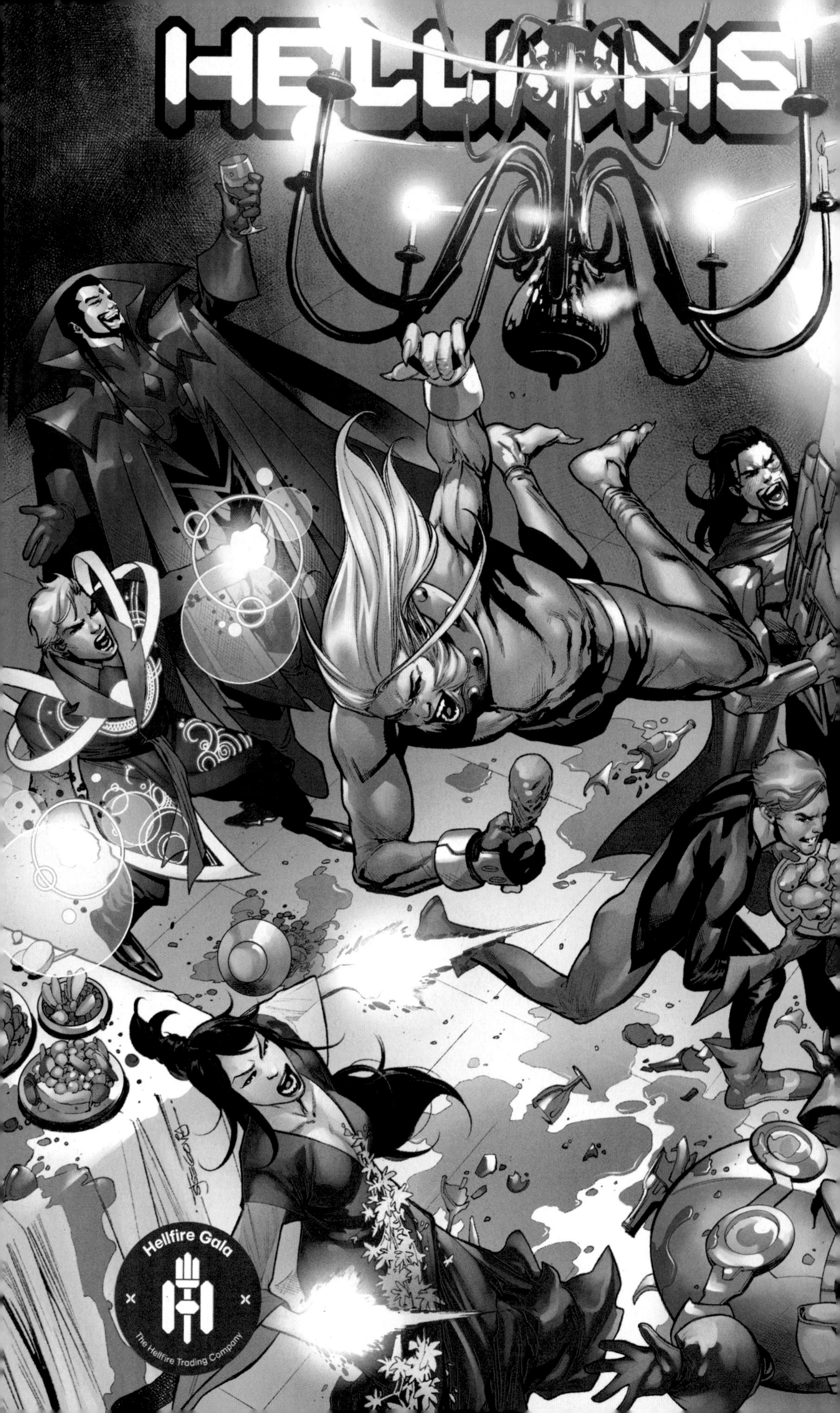
HELLIONS
Hellfire Gala
The Hellfire Trading Company

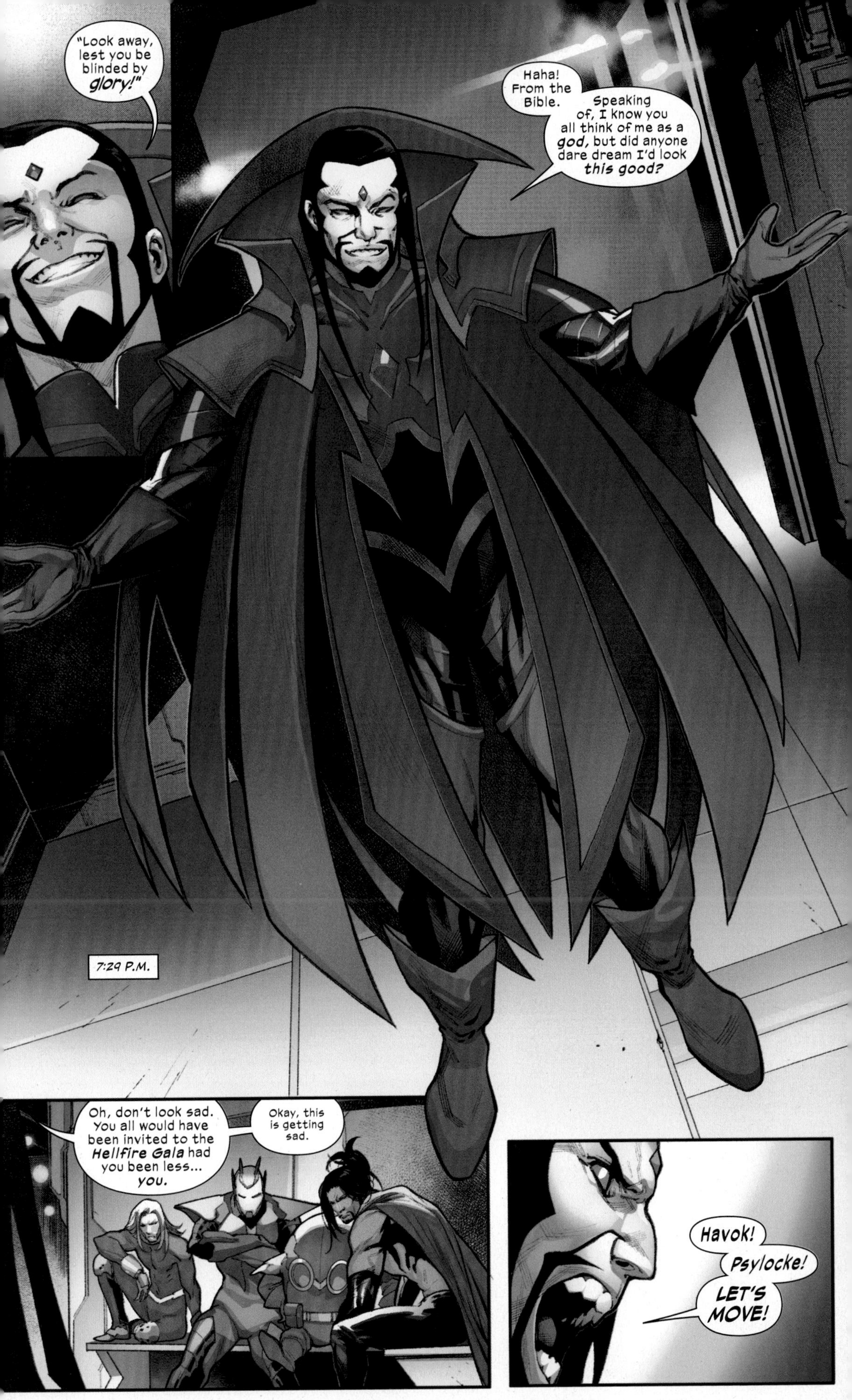
"Look away, lest you be blinded by glory!"
Haha! From the Bible.
Speaking of, I know you all think of me as a god, but did anyone dare dream I'd look this good?
7:29 P.M.
Oh, don't look sad. You all would have been invited to the Hellfire Gala had you been less... you.
Okay, this is getting sad.
Havok!
Psylocke!
LET'S MOVE!

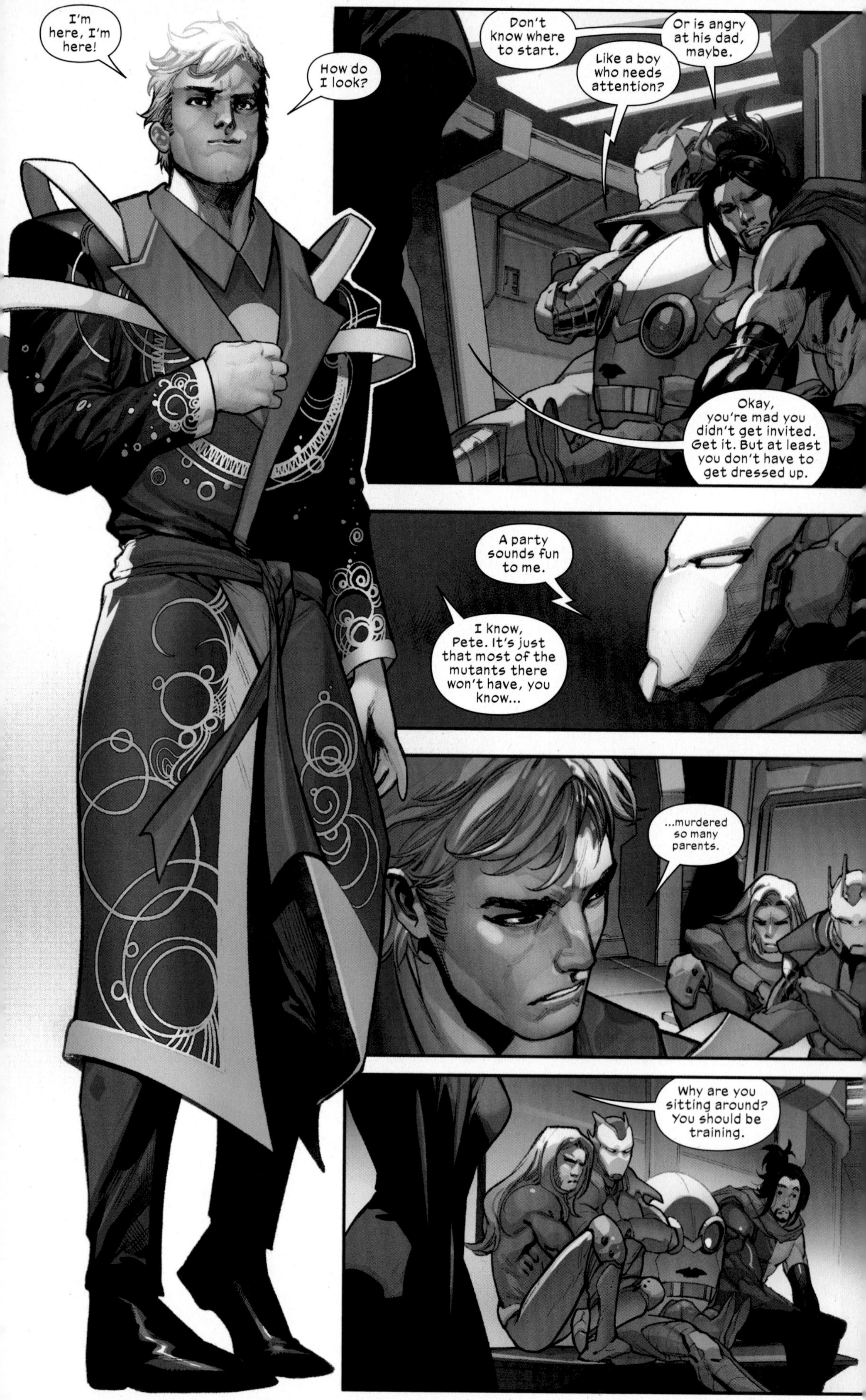
I'm here, I'm here!
How do I look?
Don't know where to start.
Or is angry at his dad, maybe.
Like a boy who needs attention?
Okay, you're mad you didn't get invited. Get it. But at least you don't have to get dressed up.
A party sounds fun to me.
I know, Pete. It's just that most of the mutants there won't have, you know...
...murdered so many parents.
Why are you sitting around? You should be training.

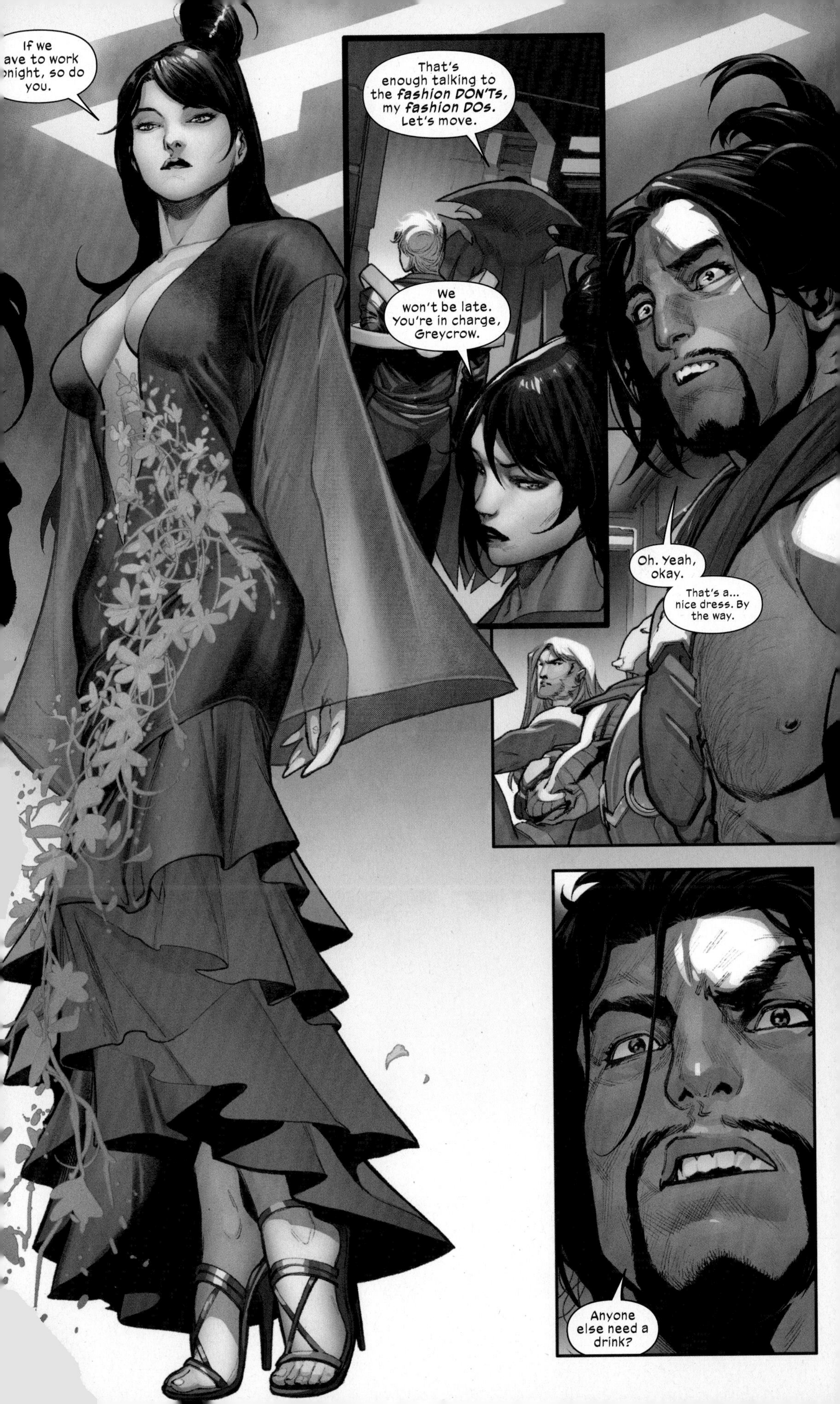
If we
ave to work
onight, so do
you.
That's enough talking to the *fashion DON'Ts*, my *fashion DOs.* Let's move.
We won't be late. You're in charge, Greycrow.
Oh. Yeah, okay.
That's a... nice dress. By the way.
Anyone else need a drink?

V.I.P.S ONLY, LOSERS

You didn't get an invite to the Hellfire Gala? That makes sense -- this is the most prestigious geopolitical event of the year, they can't let just anyone in. In fact, that's why half the Hellions weren't invited -- who would trust those delinquents around the crème de la crème of mutant and human society? Sure, that might put an even bigger strain on already fraught team dynamics (what with Mister Sinister having left his team to die in Arakko to further his own genetic research and having just manipulated Psylocke into lying to her teammates and covering for his new developing clone farm by holding her daughter's consciousness hostage), but that's the price of prestige.

Get used to it, there's no way you or the rest of the Hellions are getting into this event -- wait, don't turn the page! DON'T -- !

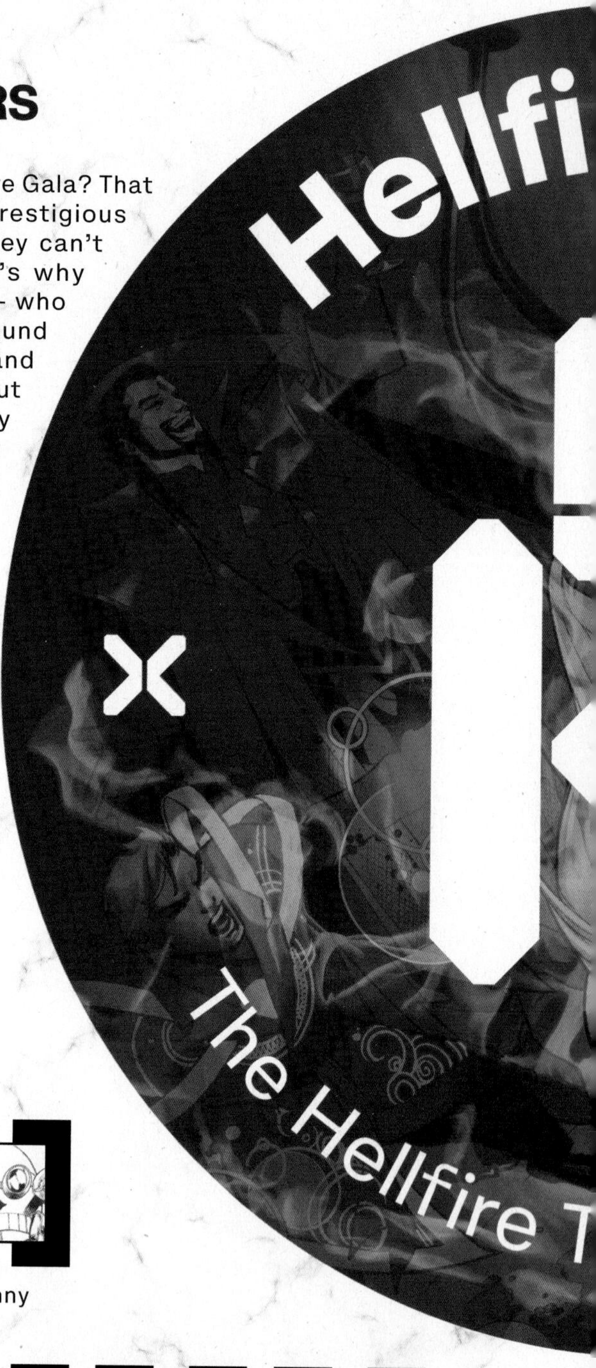
Hellfi
The Hellfire T

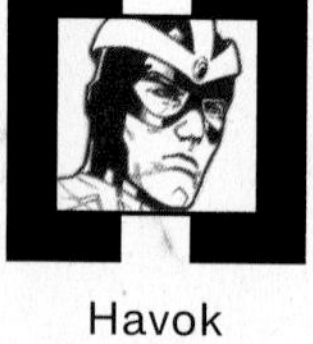
Havok

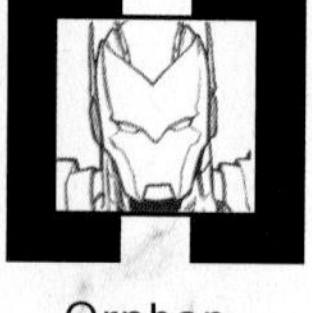
Orphan-Maker

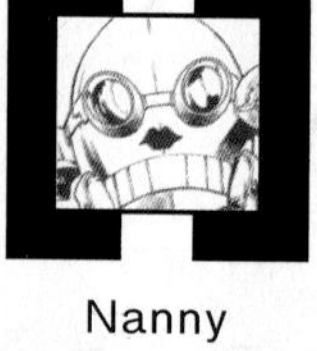
Nanny

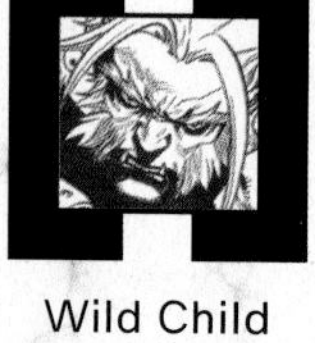
Wild Child

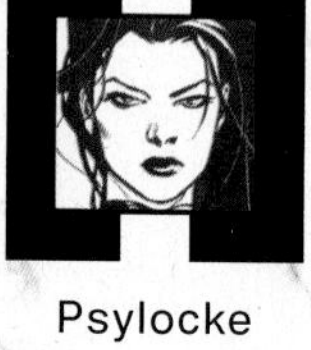
Psylocke

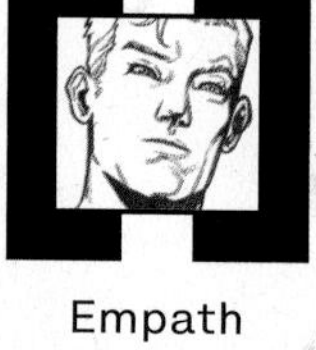
Empath

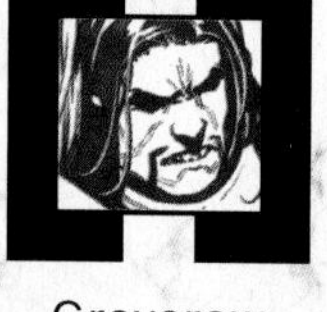
Greycrow

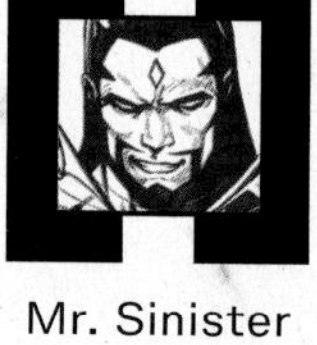
Mr. Sinister

[00_hellfire_gala_X]
[00_hellions__12]

HELLIONS

[X_12]

[ISSUE TWELVE] ....
............................GATECRASHING

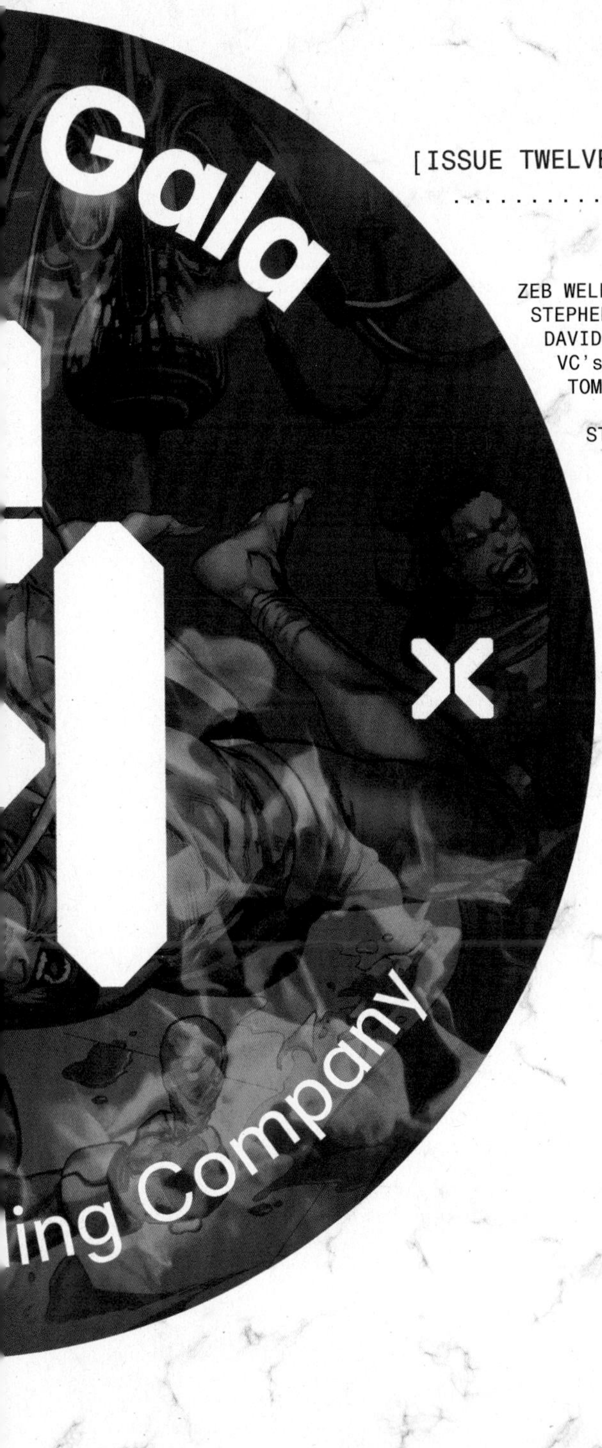

Gala
ing Company

ZEB WELLS ....[WRITER]
STEPHEN SEGOVIA ....[ARTIST]
DAVID CURIEL ....[COLOR ARTIST]
VC's ARIANA MAHER ....[LETTERER]
TOM MULLER ....[DESIGN]

STEPHEN SEGOVIA & RAIN BEREDO
.......................[COVER ARTISTS]

STEPHEN SEGOVIA.....................
[HELLIONS DESIGN VARIANT COVER ARTIST]

RUSSELL DAUTERMAN..................
[ANGEL DESIGN VARIANT COVER ARTIST]

RUSSELL DAUTERMAN & MATTHEW WILSON
........[CONNECTING COVER ARTISTS]

JONATHAN HICKMAN ....[HEAD OF X]
JAY BOWEN..............[PRODUCTION]
LAUREN AMARO.....[ASSISTANT EDITOR]
MARK BASSO ....[EDITOR]
JORDAN D. WHITE .....[SENIOR EDITOR]
C.B. CEBULSKI ......[EDITOR IN CHIEF]

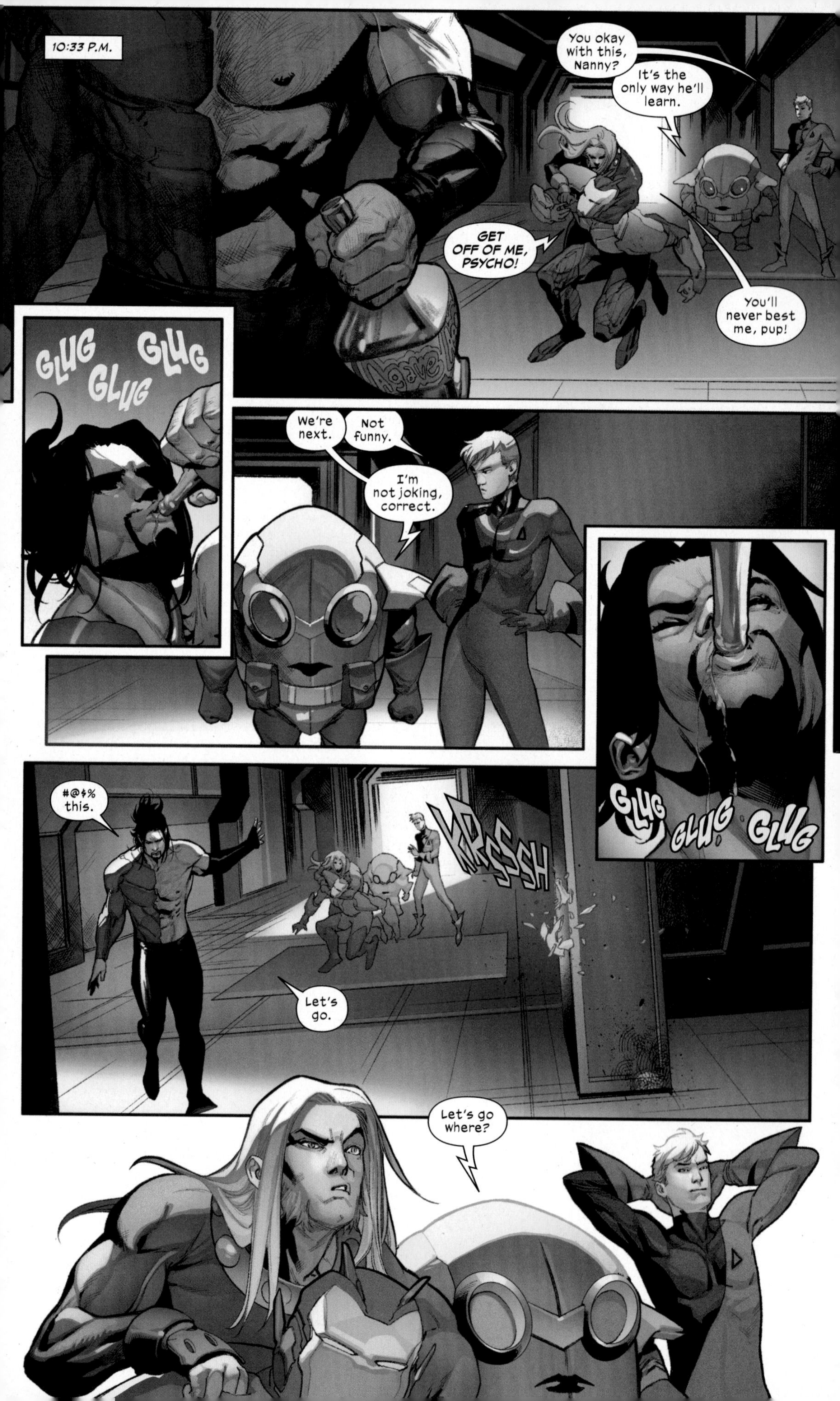

10:33 P.M.
You okay with this, Nanny?
It's the only way he'll learn.
GET OFF OF ME, PSYCHO!
You'll never best me, pup!
GLUG GLUG GLUG
We're next.
Not funny.
I'm not joking, correct.
GLUG GLUG GLUG
#@$% this.
KRSSSH
Let's go.
Let's go where?

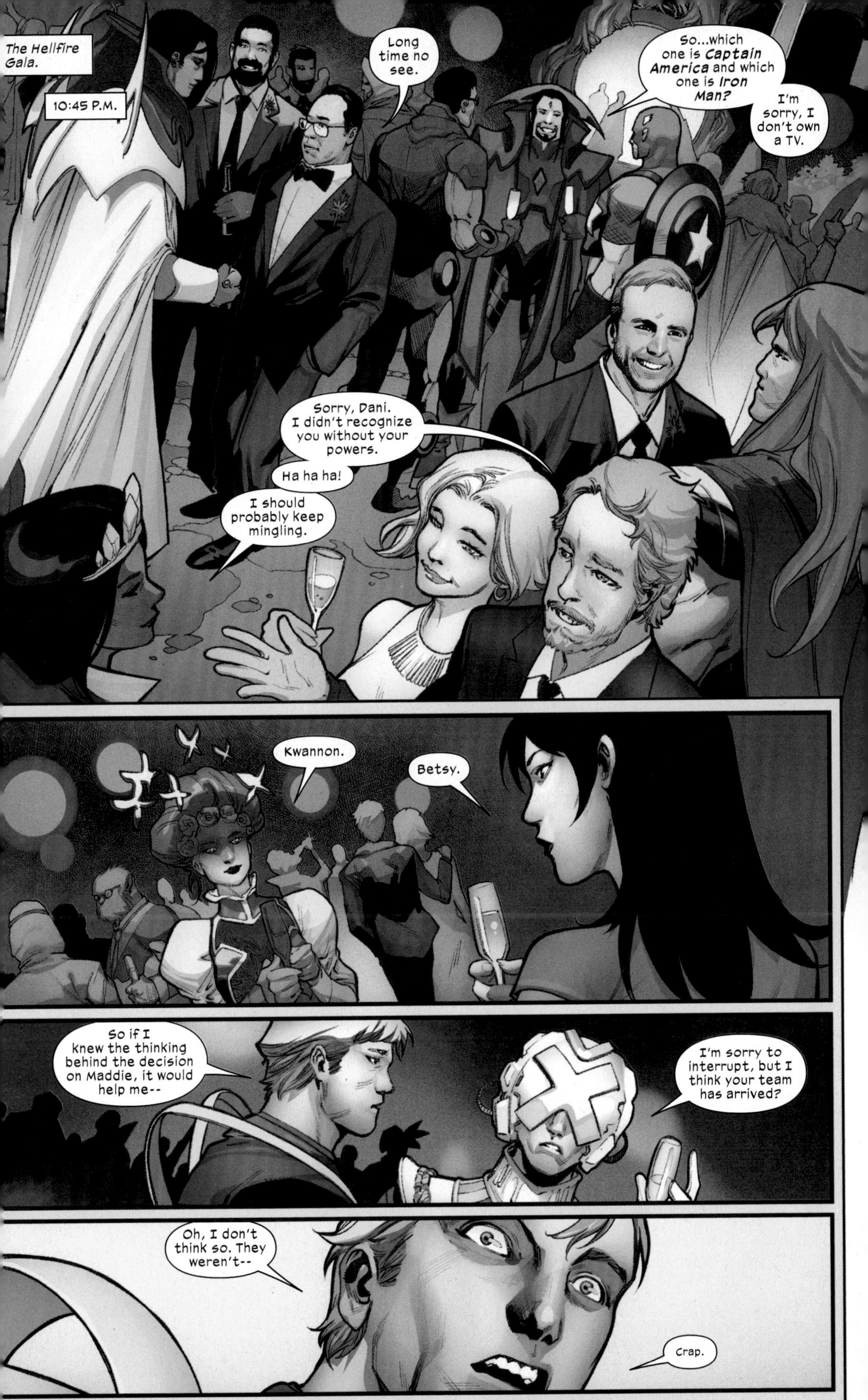

The Hellfire Gala.
10:45 P.M.
Long time no see.
So...which one is *Captain America* and which one is *Iron Man?*
I'm sorry, I don't own a TV.
Sorry, Dani. I didn't recognize you without your powers.
Ha ha ha!
I should probably keep mingling.
Kwannon.
Betsy.
So if I knew the thinking behind the decision on Maddie, it would help me--
I'm sorry to interrupt, but I think your team has arrived?
Oh, I don't think so. They weren't--
Crap.

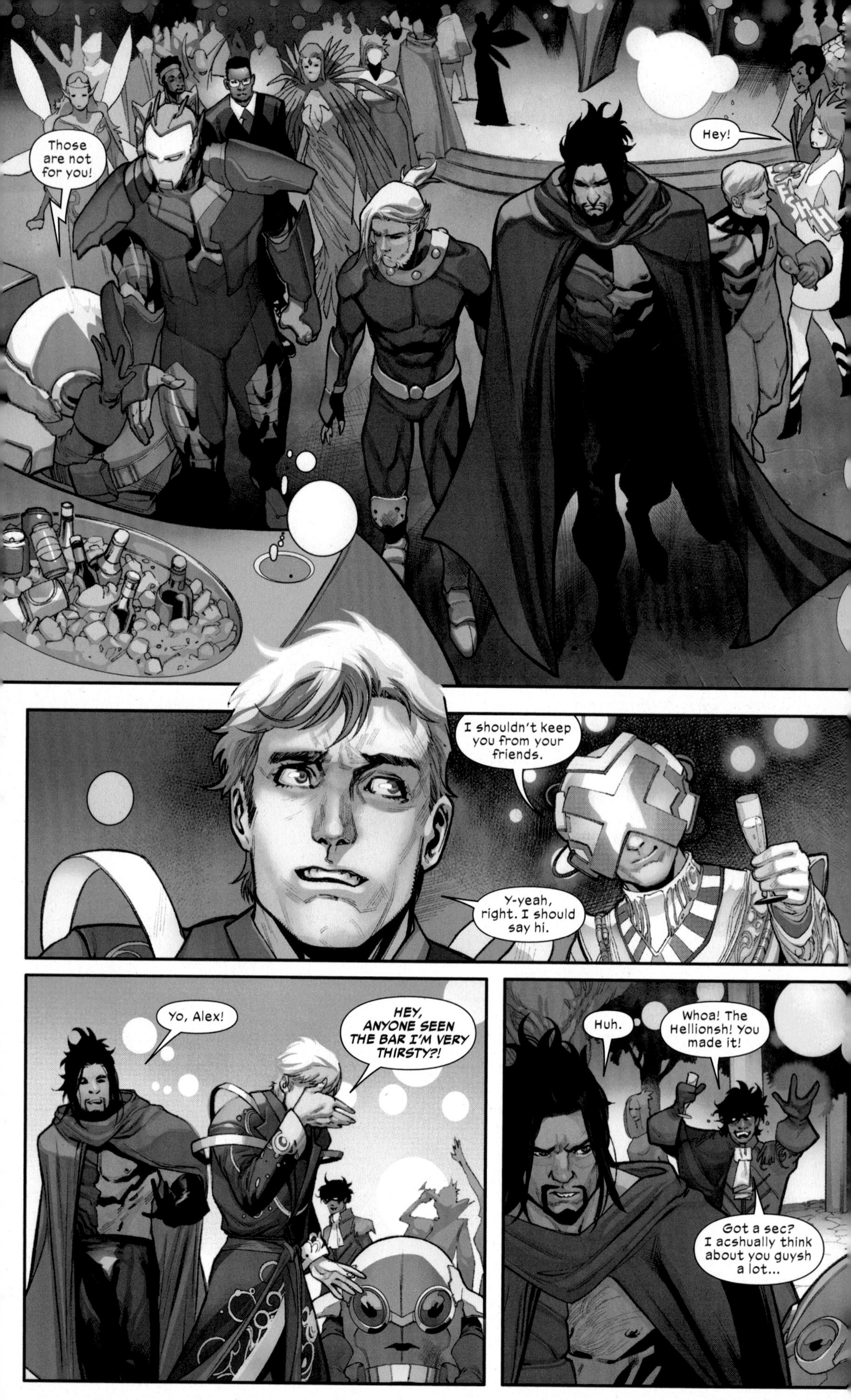

Those are not for you!
Hey!
I shouldn't keep you from your friends.
Y-yeah, right. I should say hi.
Yo, Alex!
HEY, ANYONE SEEN THE BAR I'M VERY THIRSTY?!
Huh.
Whoa! The Hellionsh! You made it!
Got a sec? I acshually think about you guysh a lot...

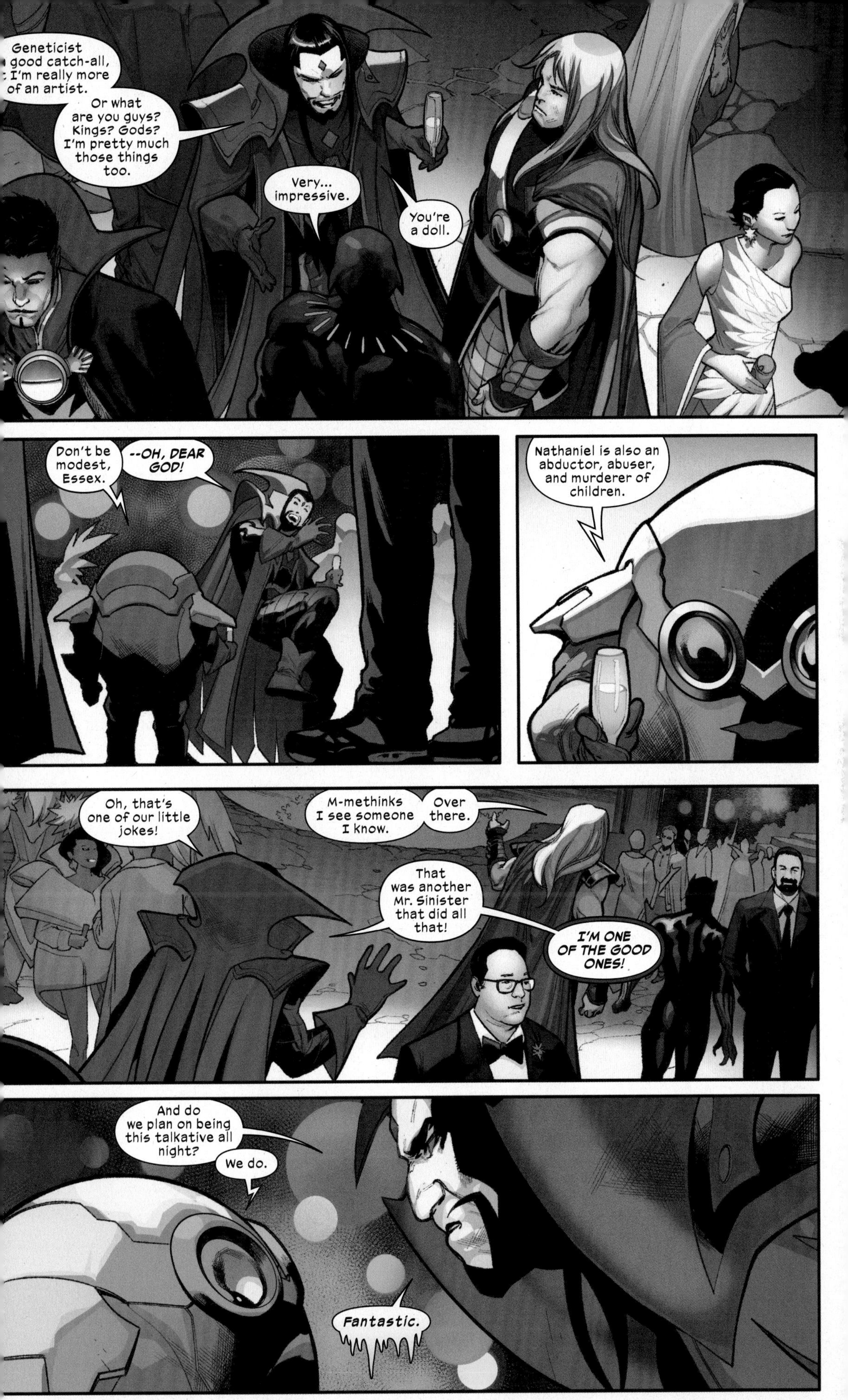

Geneticist good catch-all, I'm really more of an artist.
Or what are you guys? Kings? Gods? I'm pretty much those things too.
Very... impressive.
You're a doll.
Don't be modest, Essex.
--OH, DEAR GOD!
Nathaniel is also an abductor, abuser, and murderer of children.
Oh, that's one of our little jokes!
M-methinks I see someone I know.
Over there.
That was another Mr. Sinister that did all that!
I'M ONE OF THE GOOD ONES!
And do we plan on being this talkative all night?
We do.
Fantastic.

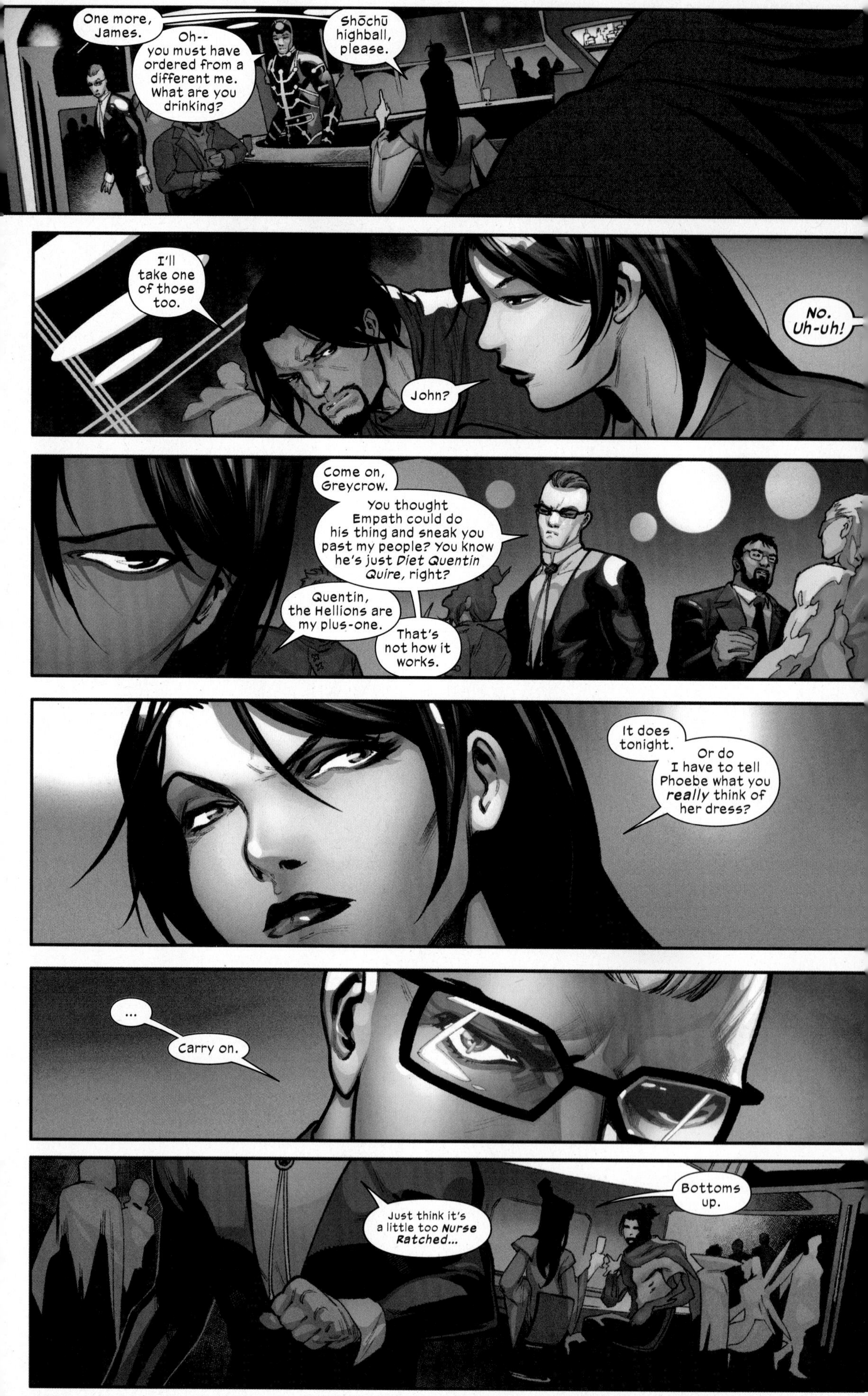

One more, James.
Oh-- you must have ordered from a different me. What are you drinking?
Shōchū highball, please.
I'll take one of those too.
John?
No. Uh-uh!
Come on, Greycrow.
You thought Empath could do his thing and sneak you past my people? You know he's just *Diet Quentin Quire,* right?
Quentin, the Hellions are my plus-one.
That's not how it works.
It does tonight.
Or do I have to tell Phoebe what you *really* think of her dress?
...
Carry on.
Just think it's a little too *Nurse Ratched...*
Bottoms up.

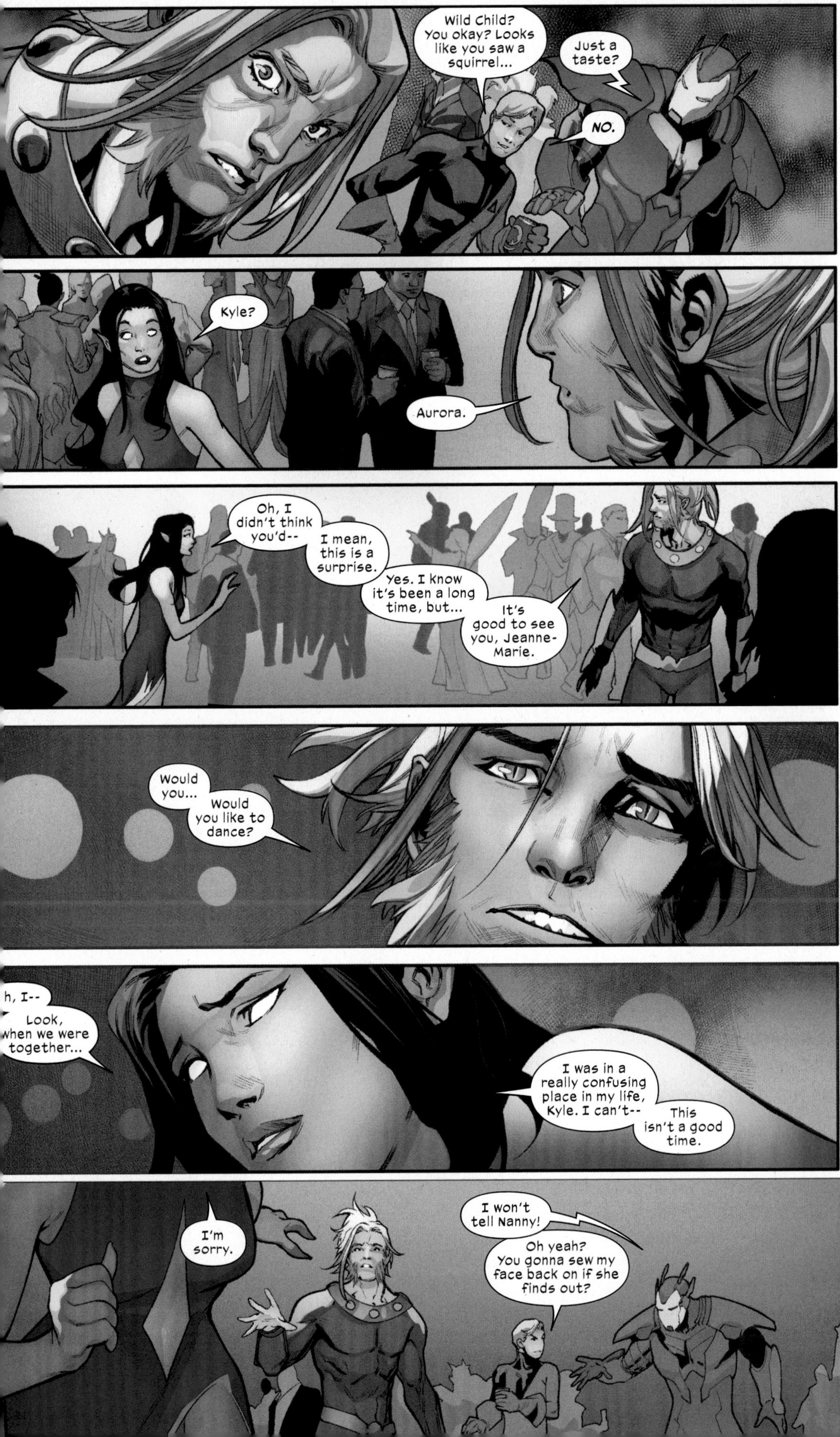

Wild Child? You okay? Looks like you saw a squirrel...
Just a taste?
NO.
Kyle?
Aurora.
Oh, I didn't think you'd--
I mean, this is a surprise.
Yes. I know it's been a long time, but...
It's good to see you, Jeanne-Marie.
Would you...
Would you like to dance?
h, I--
Look, when we were together...
I was in a really confusing place in my life, Kyle. I can't--
This isn't a good time.
I'm sorry.
I won't tell Nanny!
Oh yeah? You gonna sew my face back on if she finds out?

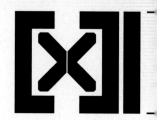

HELLFIRE GALA SECURITY & SAFETY BEST PRACTICES

THE CUCKOO AGREEMENT

Wherein the Cuckoos consent to psi-transcription so as to gather pre-evidence should an incident occur.

"IF YOU SEE SOMETHING, THINK SOMETHING."

Esme: Ouch. Gibney just got DESTROYED.

Sophie: Gibney?

Esme: Kyle. WILD CHILD. Ran into Aurora. His ex. A lot of complicated feelings. Shame, regret --

Mindee: Yeah, "ran into his ex." Got it. What's the story?

Esme: Feels like they got together when he was a lot better and she was a lot worse. She's ashamed of the whole thing. Not by him, but by who she was.

Sophie: That's hard to parse.

Esme: Yeah. Oh, and she's got someone new. Wants to feel new too.

Celeste: Don't know if this is the point of keeping an eye on things, guys.

Sophie: Cripes, Celeste. Have one of those mini-hot dogs and CHILL OUT.

Esme: Kyle was waaaaay underdressed. Is he supposed to be here?

Mindee: Phoebe, can you ask Quentin?

Phoebe: I can't hear his mind.

Esme: Maybe he's hiding from you.

Phoebe: Shut up, Esme.

Mindee: Wait, I hear him. What's a hearse ratchet?

Phoebe: ???

Esme: ???

—

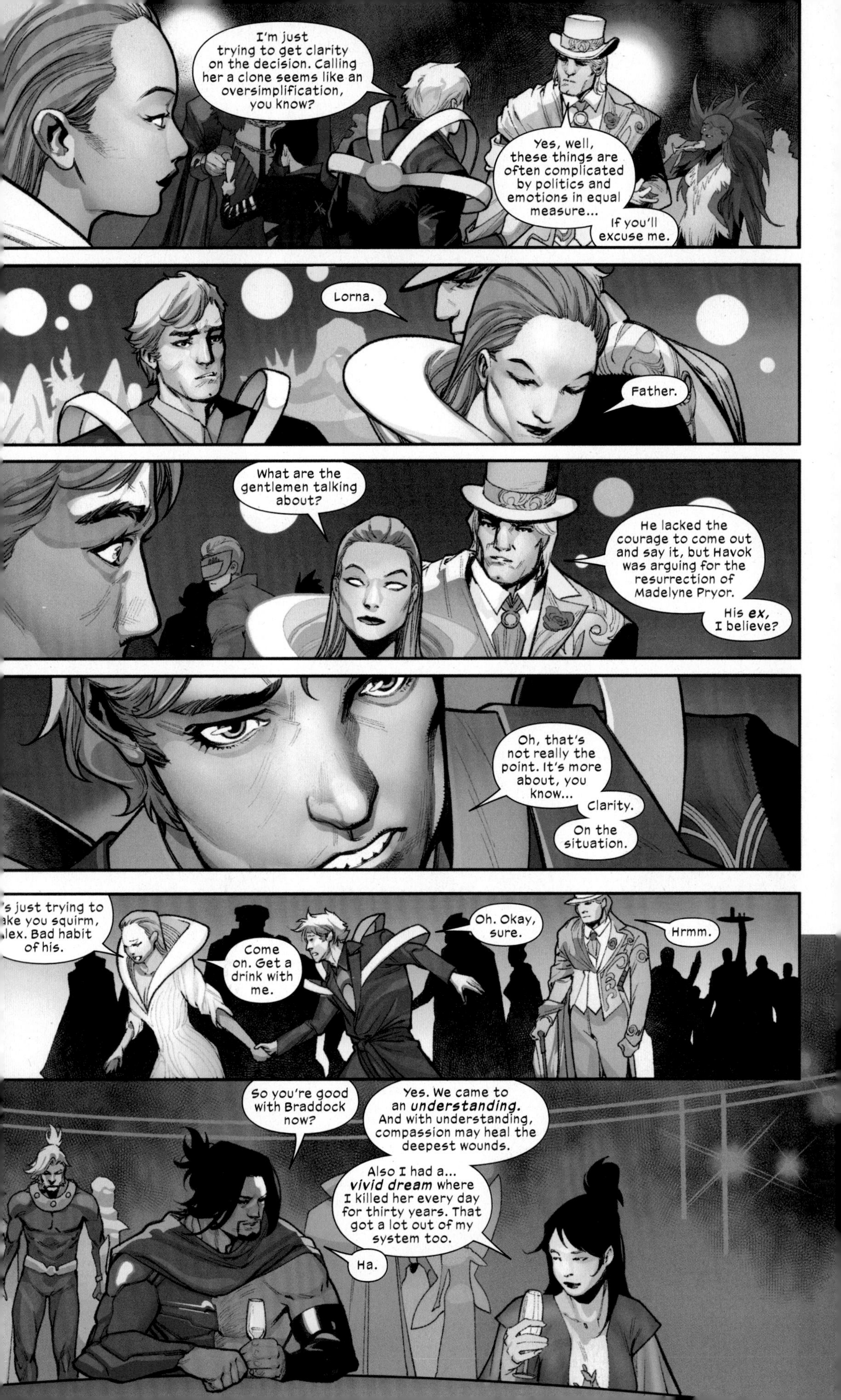

I'm just trying to get clarity on the decision. Calling her a clone seems like an oversimplification, you know?
Yes, well, these things are often complicated by politics and emotions in equal measure...
If you'll excuse me.
Lorna.
Father.
What are the gentlemen talking about?
He lacked the courage to come out and say it, but Havok was arguing for the resurrection of Madelyne Pryor.
His ex, I believe?
Oh, that's not really the point. It's more about, you know...
Clarity.
On the situation.
's just trying to ake you squirm, lex. Bad habit of his.
Come on. Get a drink with me.
Oh. Okay, sure.
Hrmm.
So you're good with Braddock now?
Yes. We came to an understanding. And with understanding, compassion may heal the deepest wounds.
Also I had a... vivid dream where I killed her every day for thirty years. That got a lot out of my system too.
Ha.

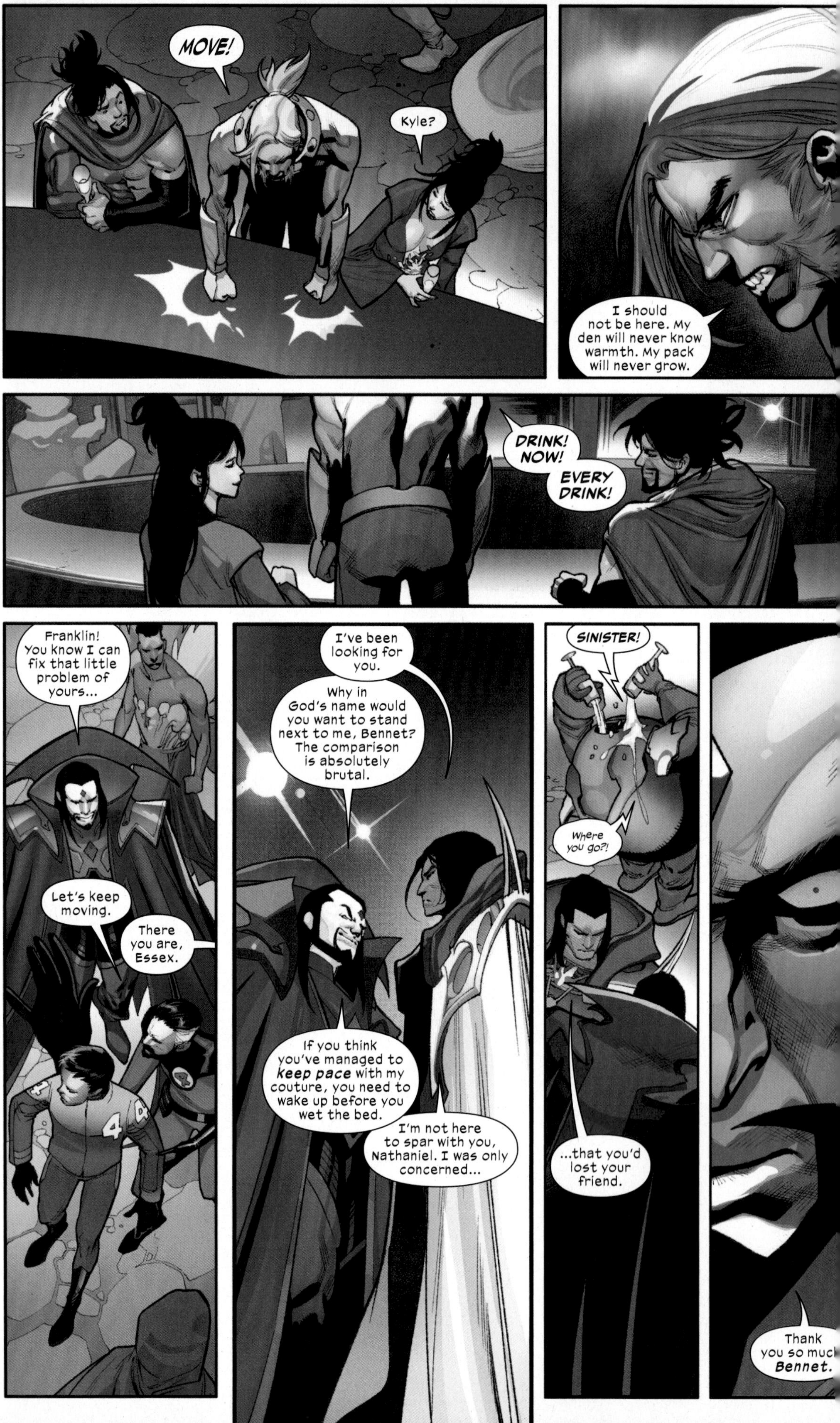
MOVE!
Kyle?
I should not be here. My den will never know warmth. My pack will never grow.
DRINK! NOW!
EVERY DRINK!
Franklin! You know I can fix that little problem of yours...
Let's keep moving.
There you are, Essex.
I've been looking for you.
Why in God's name would you want to stand next to me, Bennet? The comparison is absolutely brutal.
If you think you've managed to *keep pace* with my couture, you need to wake up before you wet the bed.
I'm not here to spar with you, Nathaniel. I was only concerned...
SINISTER!
Where you go?!
...that you'd lost your friend.
Thank you so muc
Bennet.

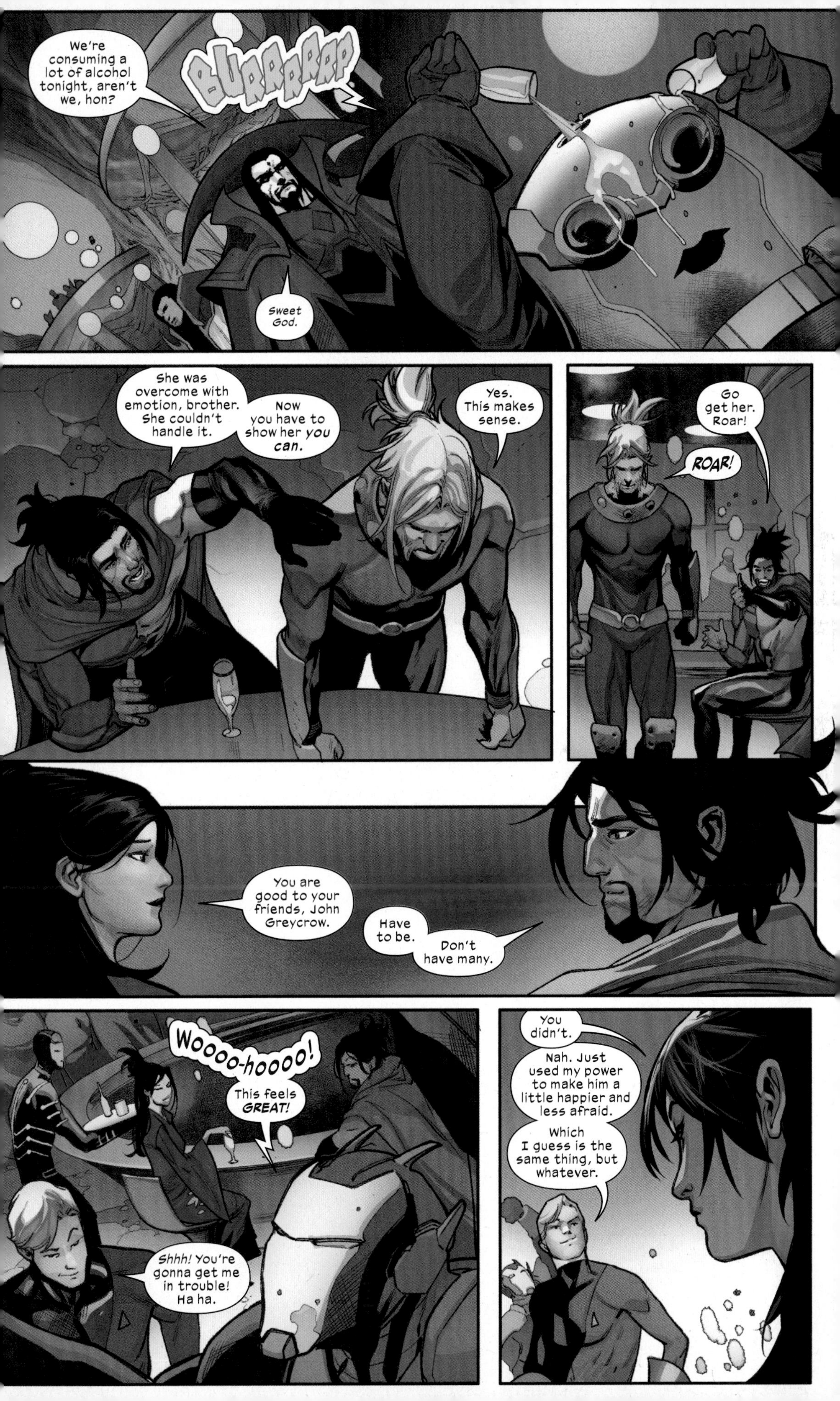
We're consuming a lot of alcohol tonight, aren't we, hon?
BURRRRRP
Sweet God.
She was overcome with emotion, brother. She couldn't handle it.
Now you have to show her *you can.*
Yes. This makes sense.
Go get her. Roar!
ROAR!
You are good to your friends, John Greycrow.
Have to be.
Don't have many.
Woooo-hoooo!
This feels GREAT!
Shhh! You're gonna get me in trouble! Ha ha.
You didn't.
Nah. Just used my power to make him a little happier and less afraid.
Which I guess is the same thing, but whatever.

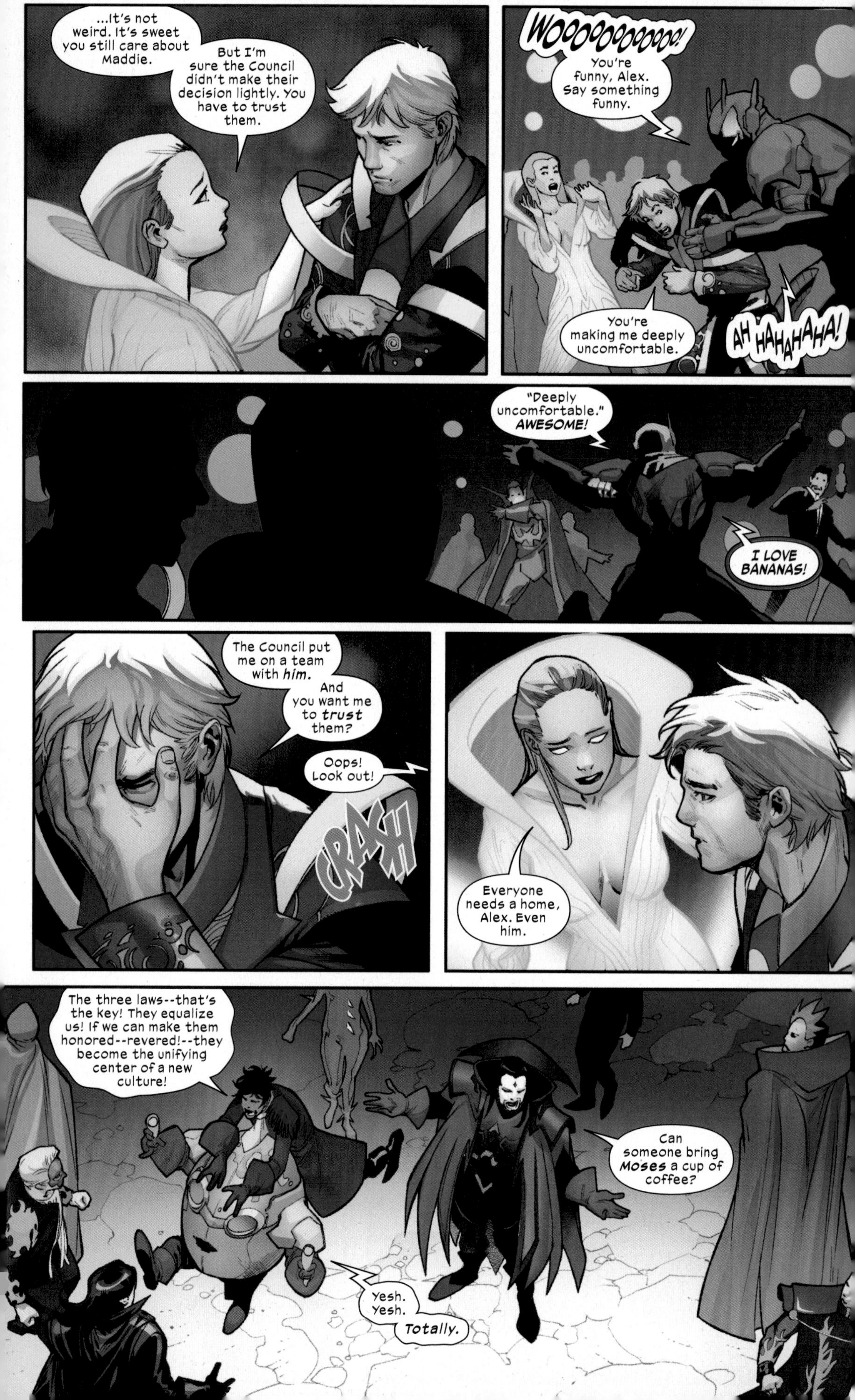
...It's not weird. It's sweet you still care about Maddie.
But I'm sure the Council didn't make their decision lightly. You have to trust them.
WOOOOOOOOOOOO!
You're funny, Alex. Say something funny.
You're making me deeply uncomfortable.
AH HAHAHAHA!
"Deeply uncomfortable." AWESOME!
I LOVE BANANAS!
The Council put me on a team with him.
And you want me to trust them?
Oops! Look out!
CRASH
Everyone needs a home, Alex. Even him.
The three laws--that's the key! They equalize us! If we can make them honored--revered!--they become the unifying center of a new culture!
Can someone bring Moses a cup of coffee?
Yesh. Yesh.
Totally.

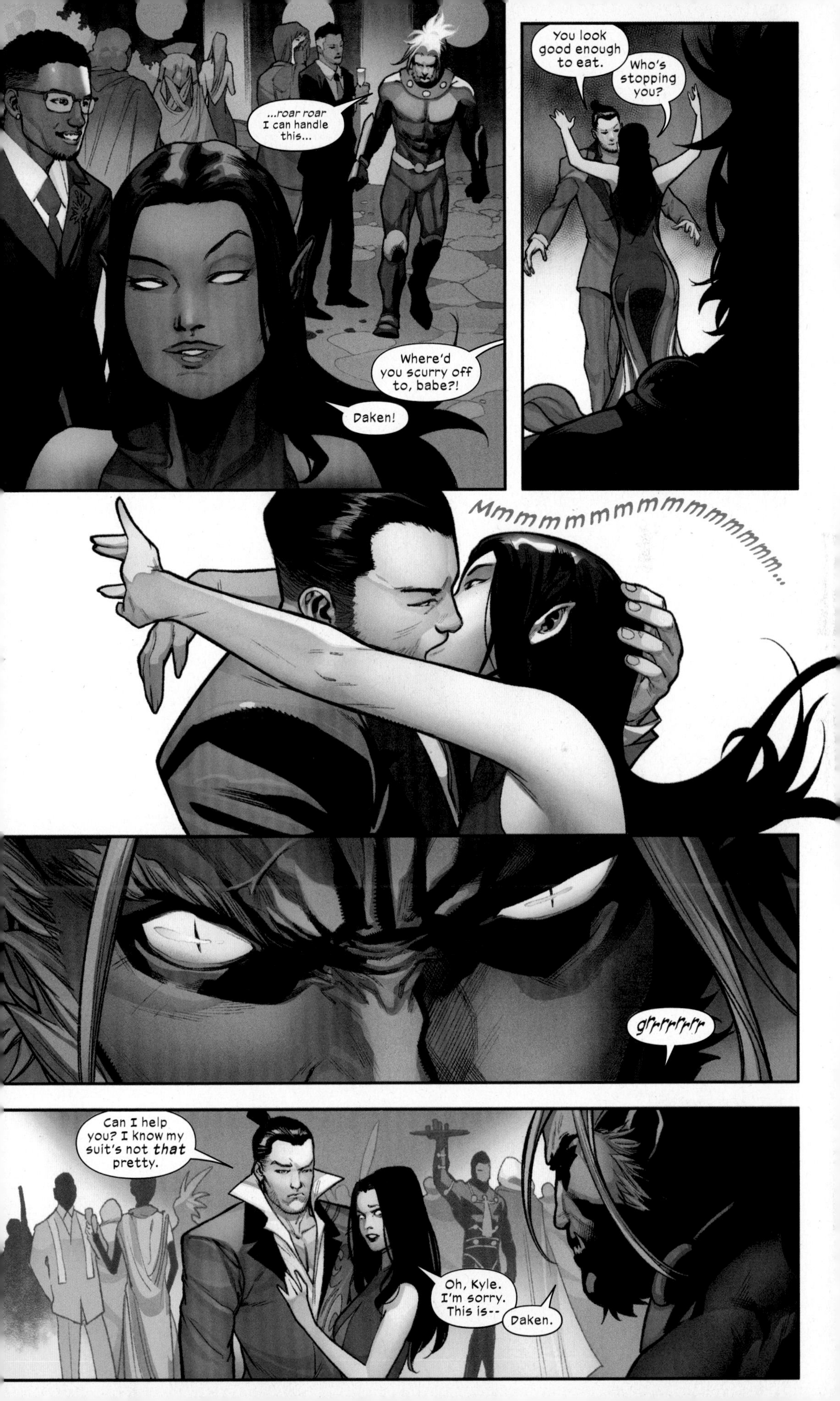
...roar roar I can handle this...
Where'd you scurry off to, babe?!
Daken!
You look good enough to eat.
Who's stopping you?
Mmmmmmmmmmmmmmm...
grrrrrrr
Can I help you? I know my suit's not *that* pretty.
Oh, Kyle. I'm sorry. This is--
Daken.

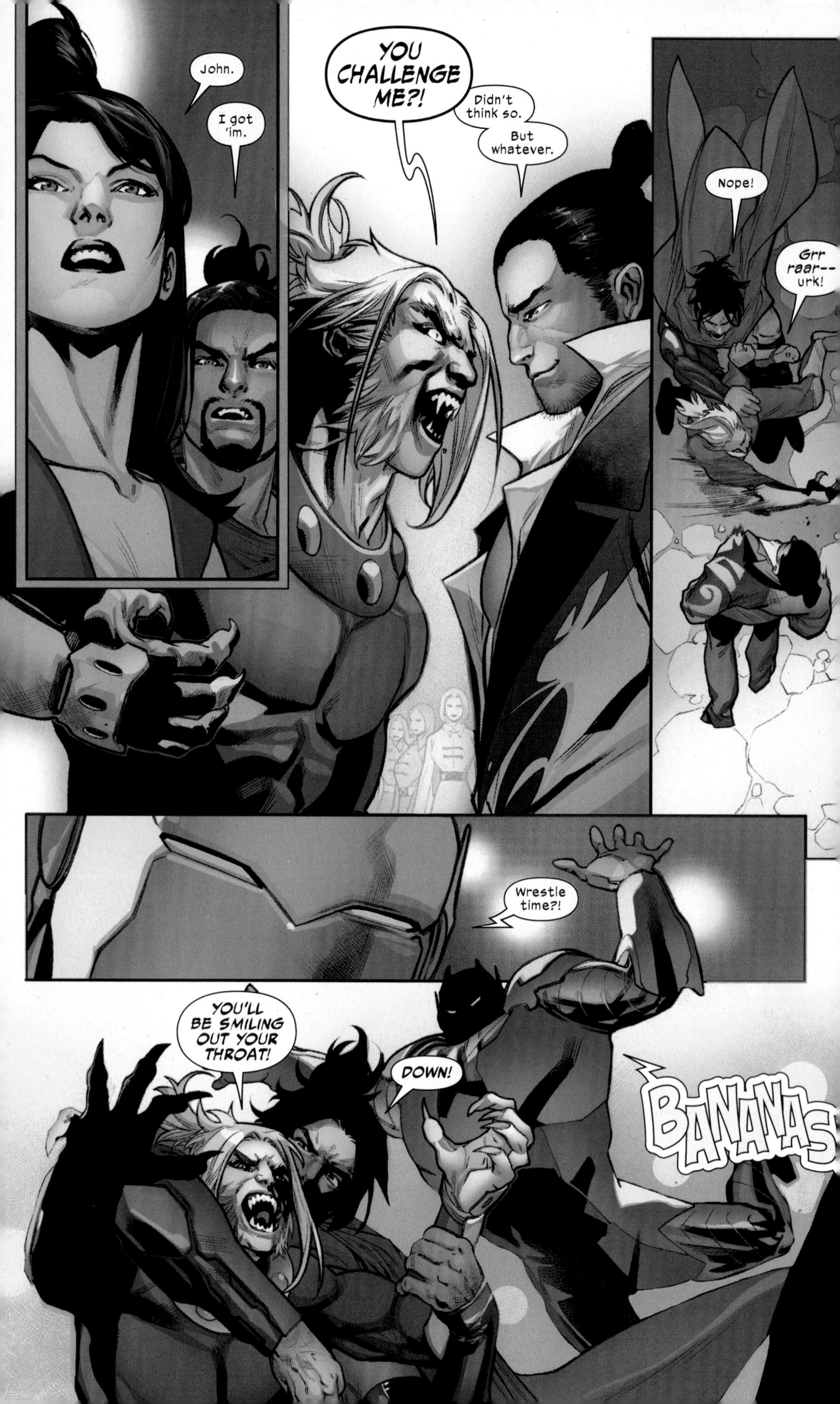
John.
I got 'im.
YOU CHALLENGE ME?!
Didn't think so.
But whatever.
Nope!
Grr raar--urk!
Wrestle time?!
YOU'LL BE SMILING OUT YOUR THROAT!
DOWN!
BANANAS

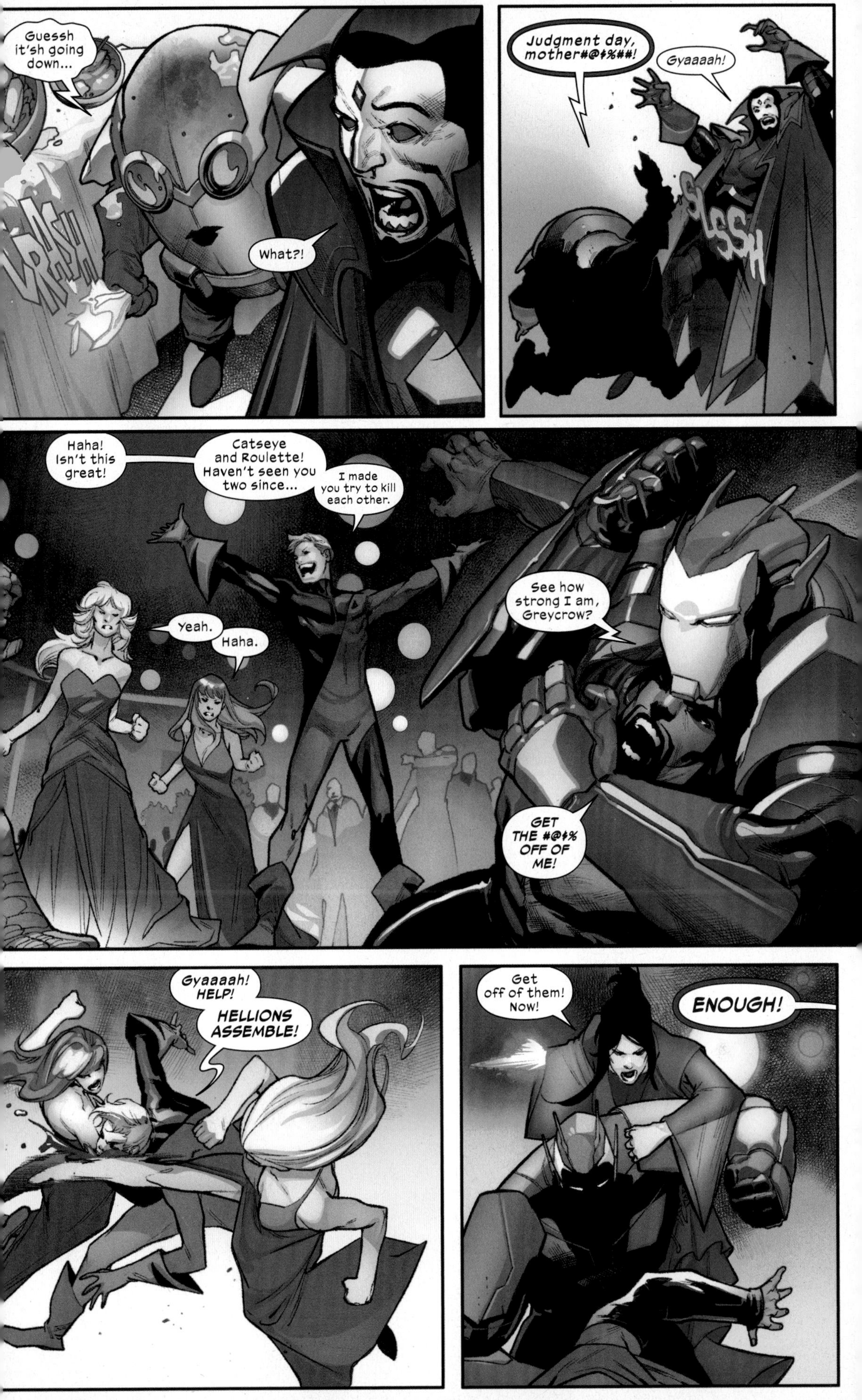

Guessh it'sh going down...
CRASH
What?!
Judgment day, mother#@$%##!
Gyaaaah!
SLSSH
Haha! Isn't this great!
Catseye and Roulette! Haven't seen you two since...
I made you try to kill each other.
Yeah.
Haha.
See how strong I am, Greycrow?
GET THE #@$% OFF OF ME!
Gyaaaah! HELP!
HELLIONS ASSEMBLE!
Get off of them! Now!
ENOUGH!

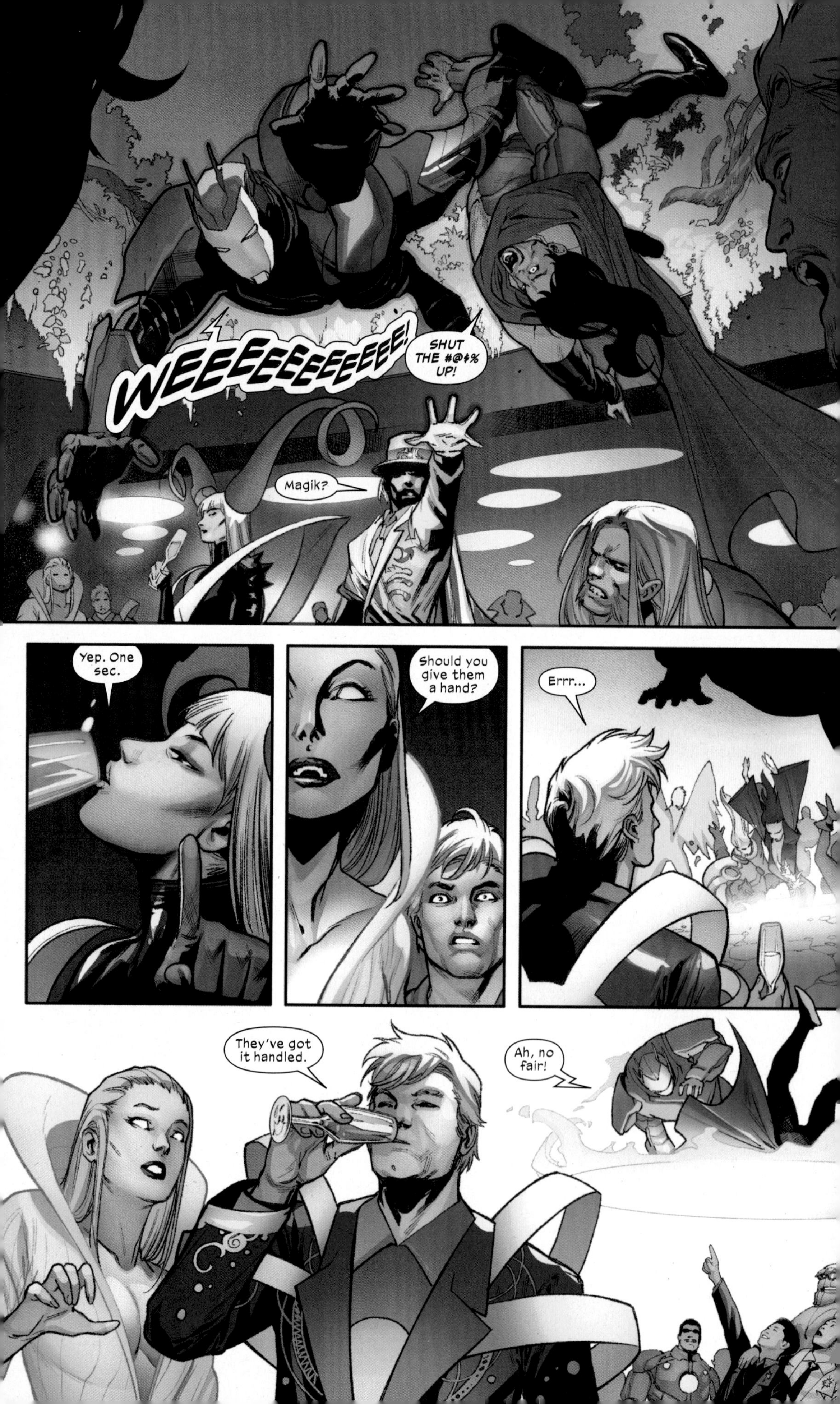
WEEEEEEEEEEEE!
SHUT THE #@$% UP!
Magik?
Yep. One sec.
Should you give them a hand?
Errr...
They've got it handled.
Ah, no fair!

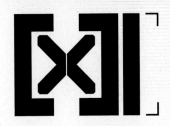

CUCKOO PSI-TRANSCRIPT (CONT.)

Celeste: Oooh, Magneto is ANGRY. He wants answers.

Sophie: A lot to sort through here.

Esme: Is there? Wild Child tried to slash his way out of a broken heart. Greycrow tried to stop him.

Mindee: Dumb, but kind of hot.

Celeste: He's a murderer.

Mindee: No one told his incredible hair.

Sophie: Why did the kid yell, "Bananas"?

Esme: He likes bananas.

Sophie: Cool.

Celeste: I blame Nanny.

Mindee: 100%.

Esme: It's like, girl, I know it's a party, but your kid is tearing the place up. Put the drink down.

Celeste: And don't try to murder Sinister in front of the humans. It's cringe.

Sophie: Yeah, do you think there was more to that? Maybe those two --

Esme: NO!

Celeste: STOP!

Sophie: I'M KIDDING. She's not his type.

Mindee: What is his type?

Sophie: Himself. What do you think all the cloning is about?

Celeste: SOPHIE!

Sophie: It's what I heard!

Celeste: Where is Phoebe?

Sophie/Mindee/Esme: PHOEBE!

Phoebe: I'M CHANGING!

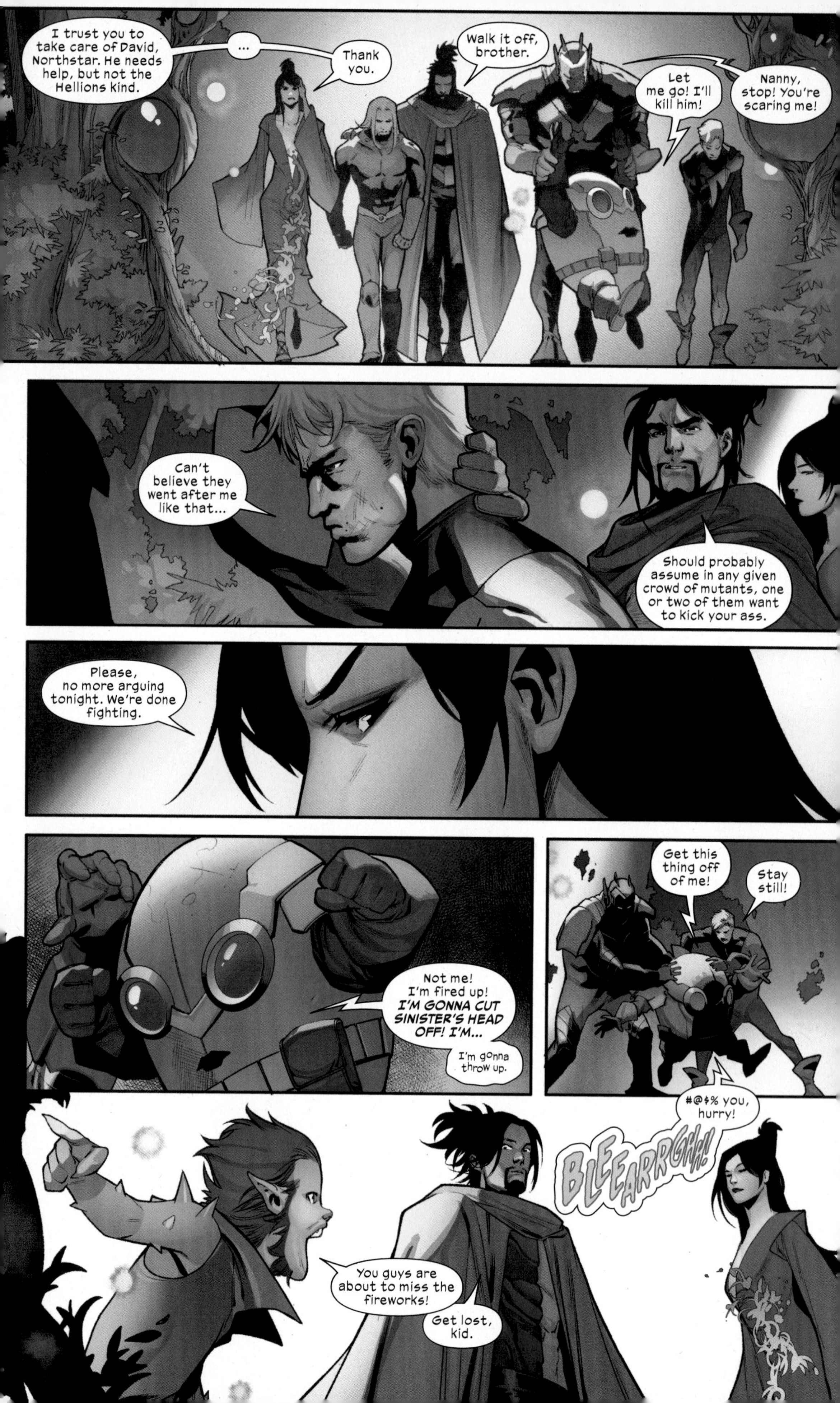

I trust you to take care of David, Northstar. He needs help, but not the Hellions kind.
...
Thank you.
Walk it off, brother.
Let me go! I'll kill him!
Nanny, stop! You're scaring me!
Can't believe they went after me like that...
Should probably assume in any given crowd of mutants, one or two of them want to kick your ass.
Please, no more arguing tonight. We're done fighting.
Not me! I'm fired up! I'M GONNA CUT SINISTER'S HEAD OFF! I'M...
I'm gonna throw up.
Get this thing off of me!
Stay still!
#@$% you, hurry!
BLEEARRGHH!
You guys are about to miss the fireworks!
Get lost, kid.

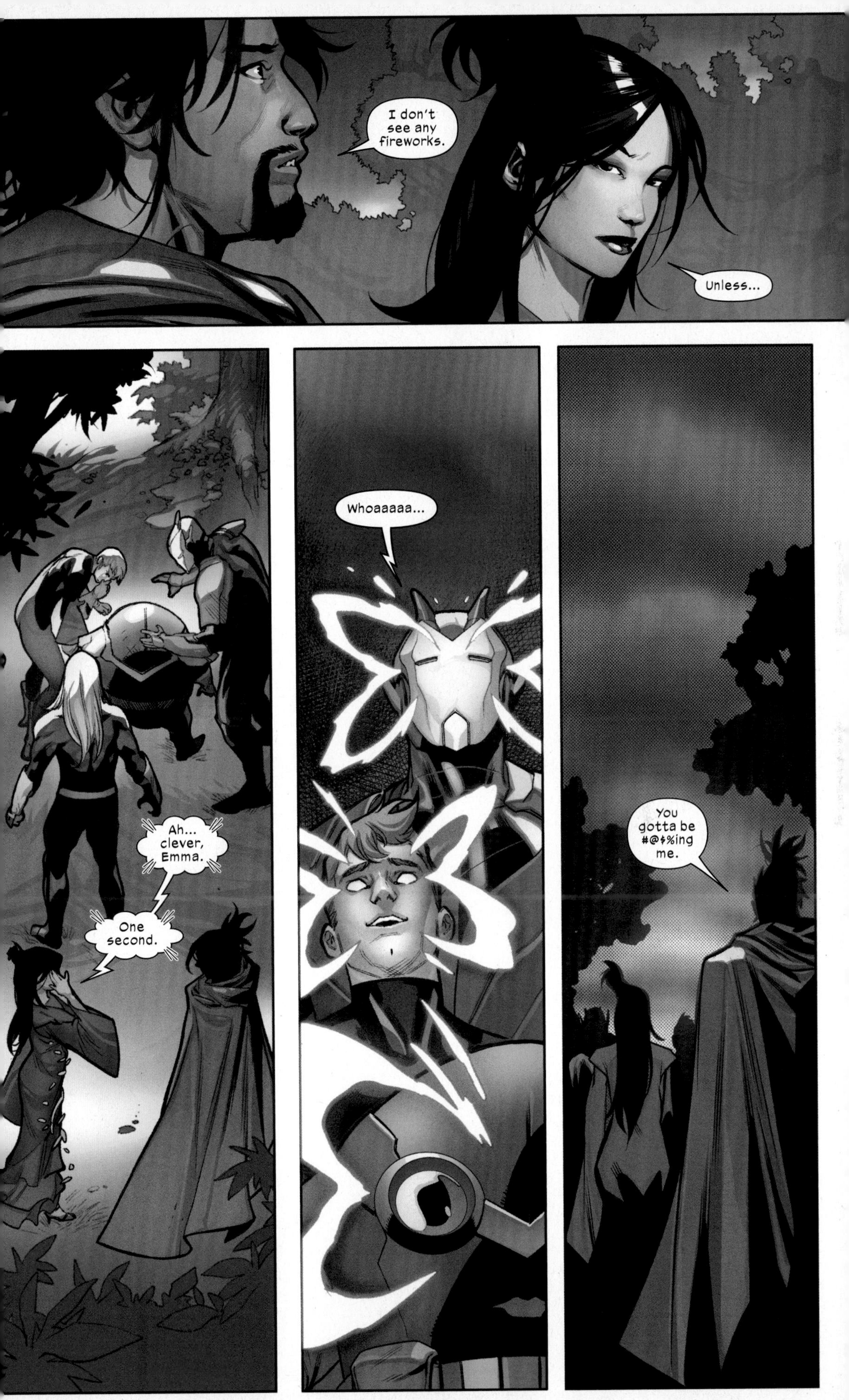
I don't see any fireworks.
Unless...
Ah... clever, Emma.
One second.
Whoaaaaa...
You gotta be #@$%ing me.

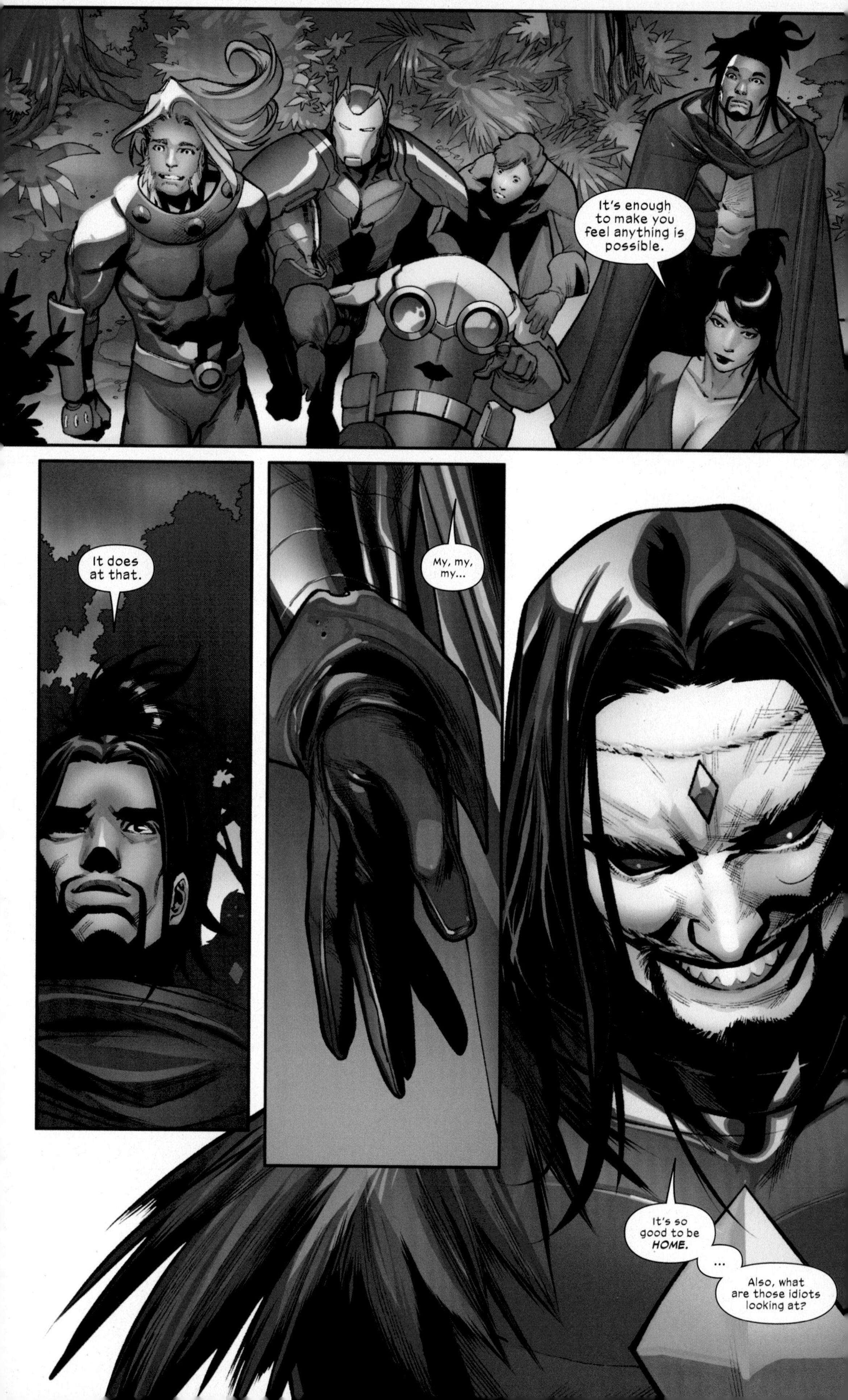
It's enough to make you feel anything is possible.
It does at that.
My, my, my...
It's so good to be HOME.
...
Also, what are those idiots looking at?

[reign_of_x]

[kra_]
[koa_]

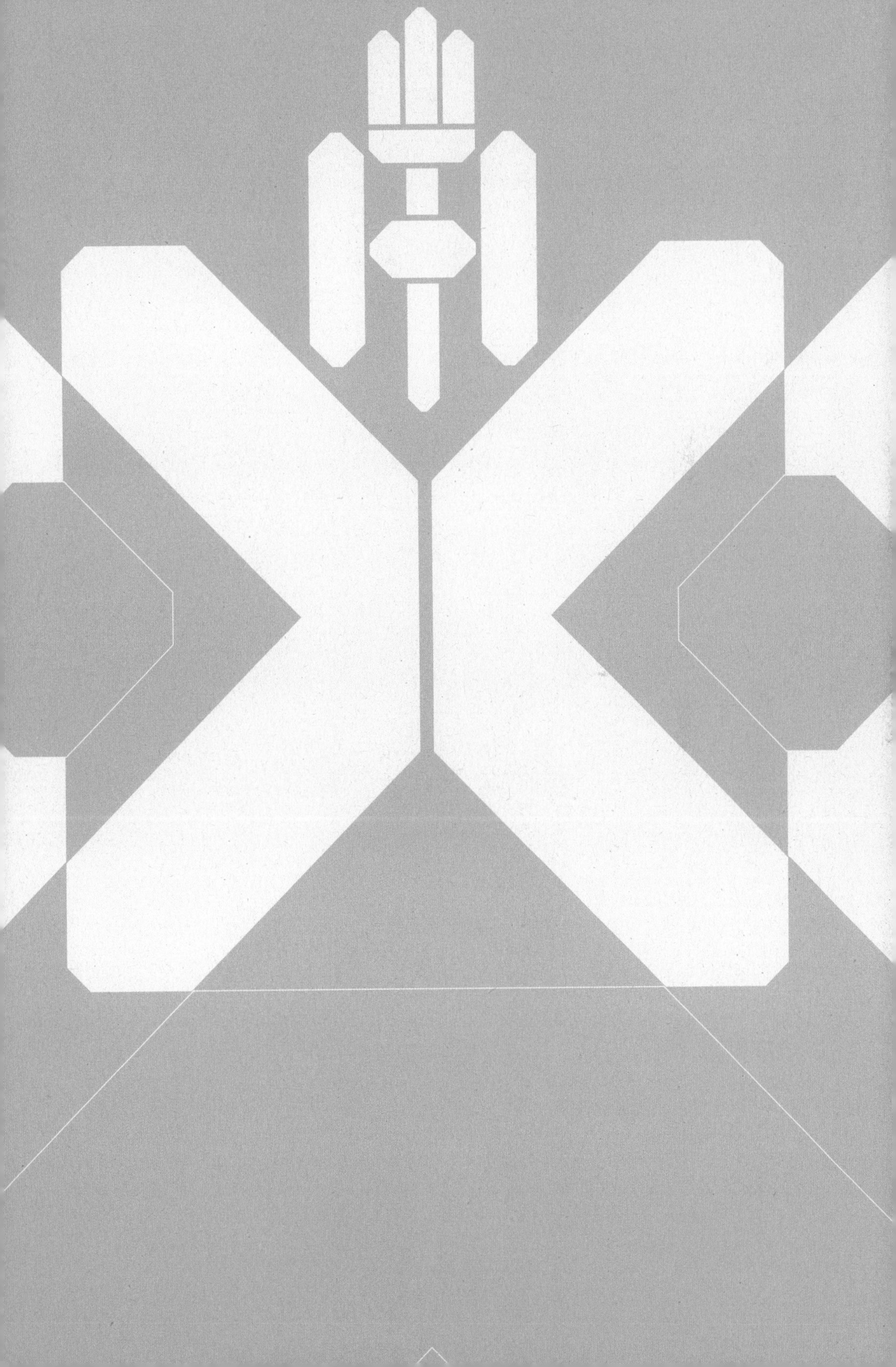

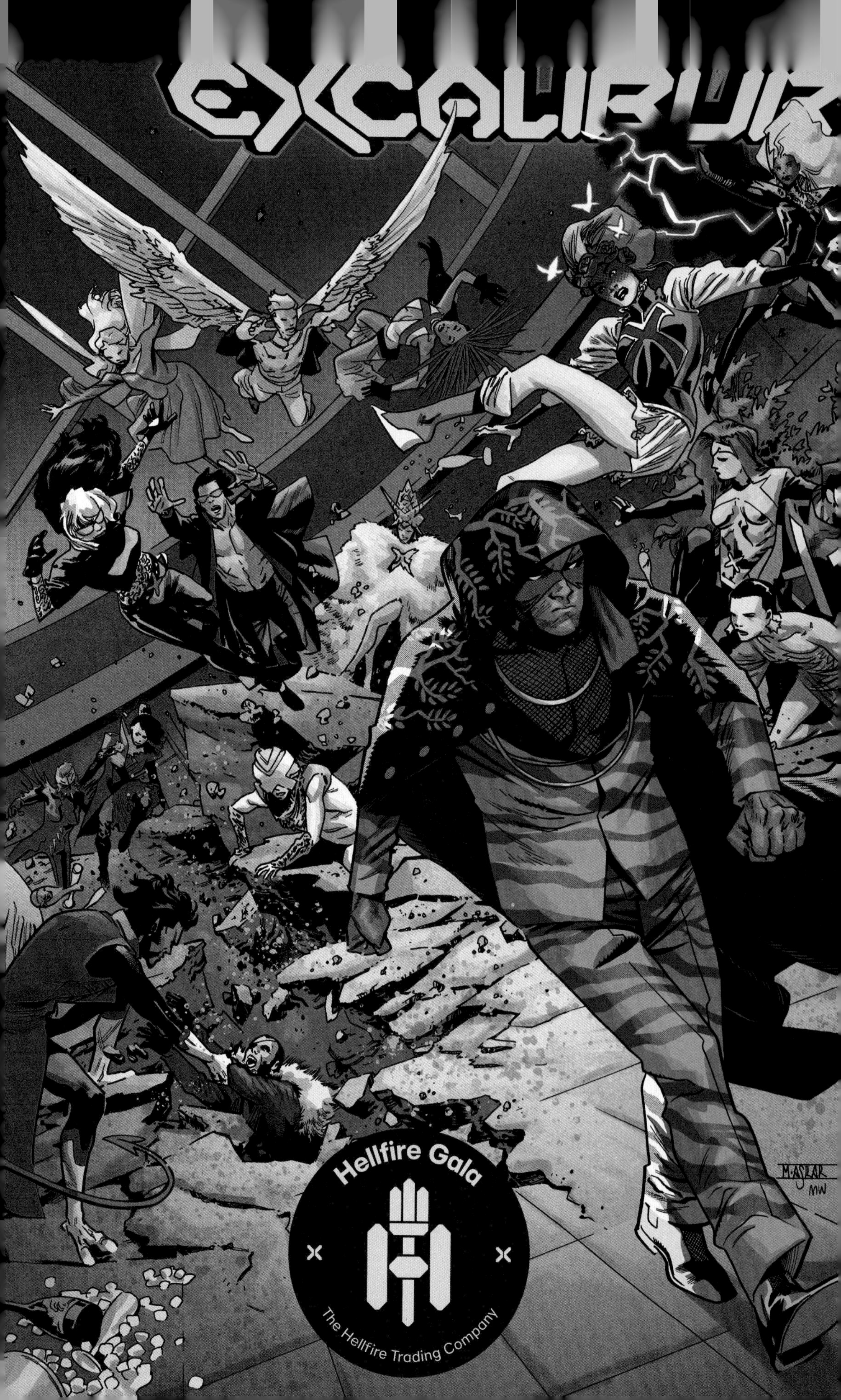
EXCALIBUR
Hellfire Gala
The Hellfire Trading Company
M.ASLAR
MW

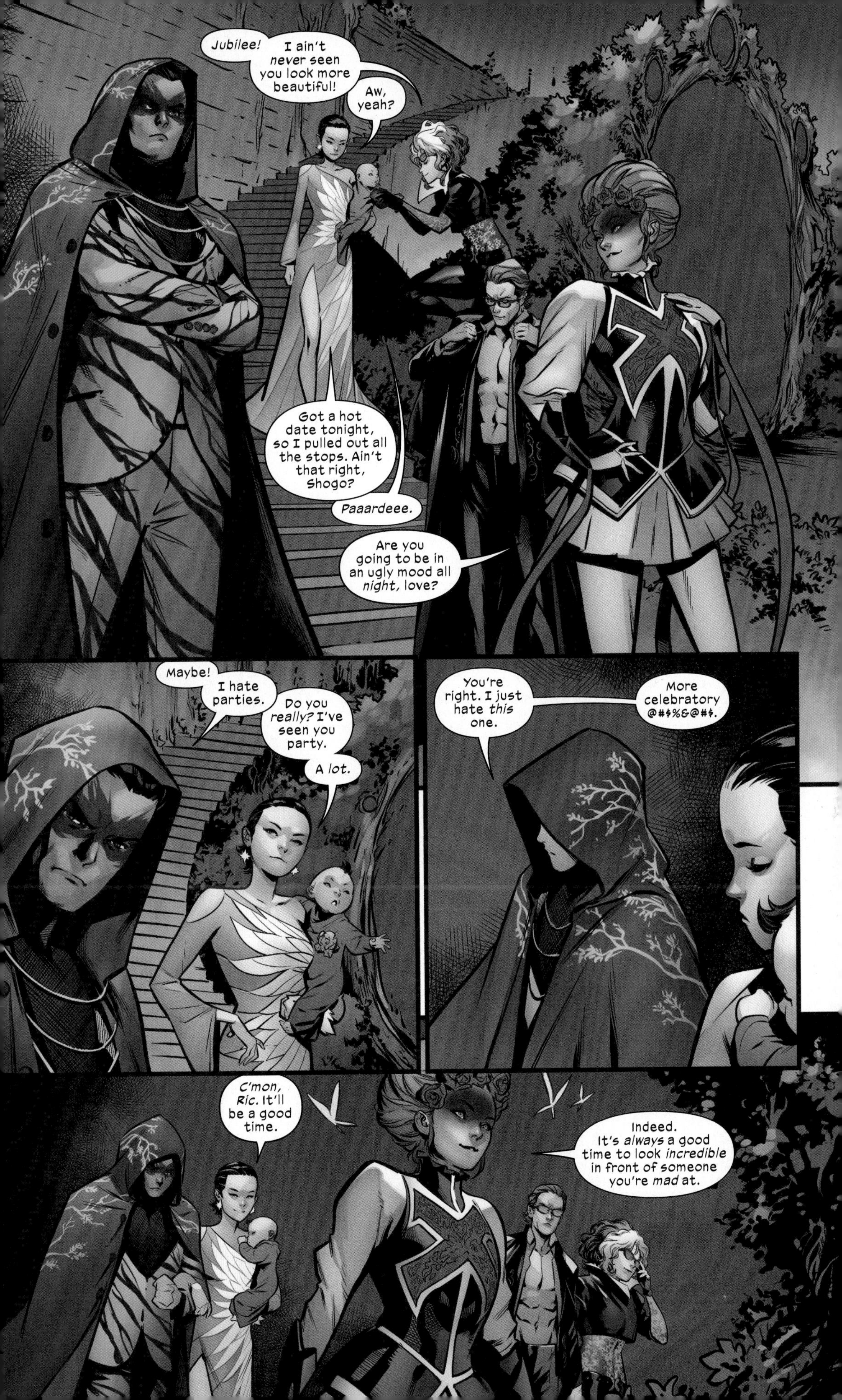

Jubilee!
I ain't never seen you look more beautiful!
Aw, yeah?
Got a hot date tonight, so I pulled out all the stops. Ain't that right, Shogo?
Paaardeee.
Are you going to be in an ugly mood all night, love?
Maybe!
I hate parties.
Do you really? I've seen you party.
A lot.
You're right. I just hate this one.
More celebratory @#$%&@#$.
C'mon, Ric. It'll be a good time.
Indeed. It's always a good time to look incredible in front of someone you're mad at.

[00_hellfire_gala_X]
[00_excalibur__21]

FIRE & BRIMSTONE

EXCALIBUR has been up to their elbows in mysterious and magical mutant affairs -- from facing the nefarious Coven Akkaba, determined to unseat Captain Britain, to a war in Otherworld that ended with the departure of one of their own. After all that... haven't they earned a night off?

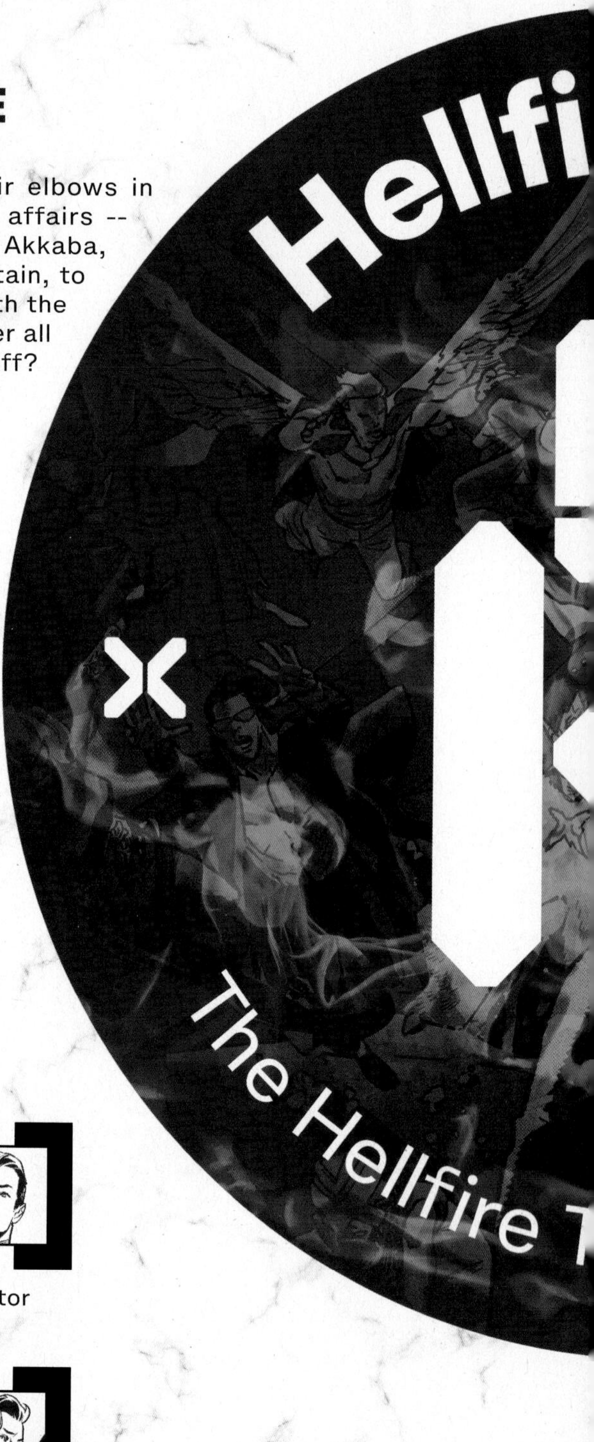

Hellfi
The Hellfire T

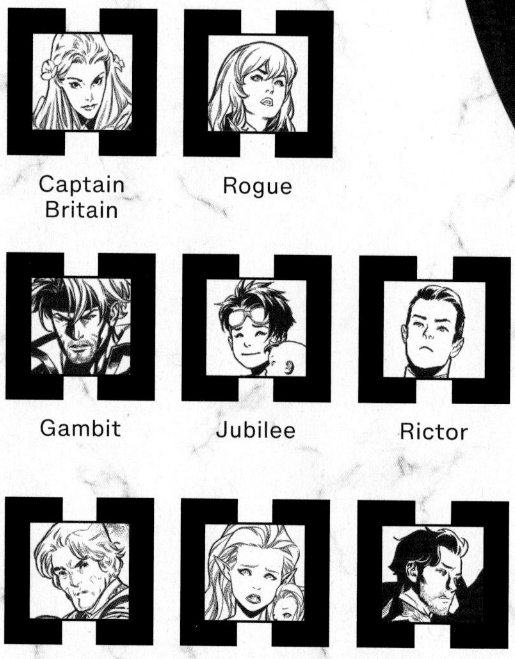

Captain Britain — Rogue

Gambit — Jubilee — Rictor

Brian Braddock — Meggan Braddock — Pete Wisdom

EXCALIBUR

[X_21]

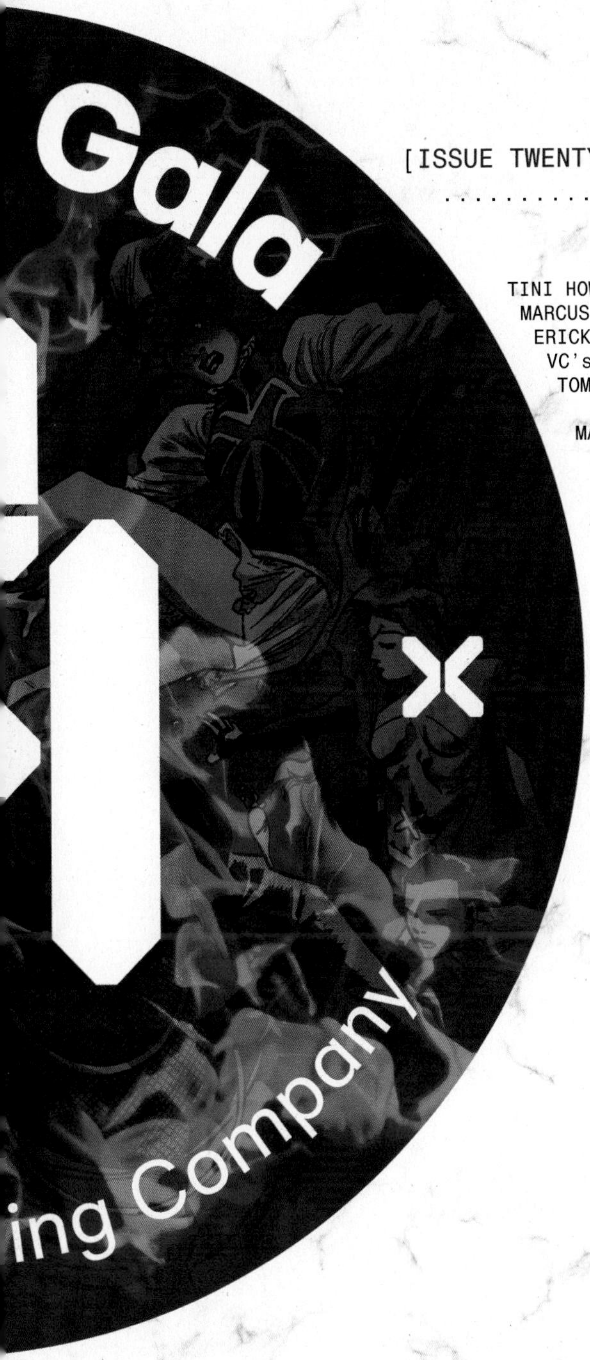
Gala
ing Company

[ISSUE TWENTY-ONE] ....
...............DON'T FEEL LIKE DANCIN'

TINI HOWARD ....[WRITER]
MARCUS TO ....[ARTIST]
ERICK ARCINIEGA ....[COLOR ARTIST]
VC's ARIANA MAHER ....[LETTERER]
TOM MULLER ....[DESIGN]

MAHMUD ASRAR & MATTHEW WILSON
......................[COVER ARTISTS]

MARCUS TO...........................
[EXCALIBUR DESIGN VARIANT COVER ARTIST]

RUSSELL DAUTERMAN..................
[ROGUE DESIGN VARIANT COVER ARTIST]

RUSSELL DAUTERMAN & MATTHEW WILSON
........[CONNECTING COVER ARTISTS]

JONATHAN HICKMAN........[HEAD OF X]
JAY BOWEN..............[PRODUCTION]
ANNALISE BISSA...[ASSOCIATE EDITOR]
JORDAN D. WHITE ....[EDITOR]
C.B. CEBULSKI......[EDITOR IN CHIEF]

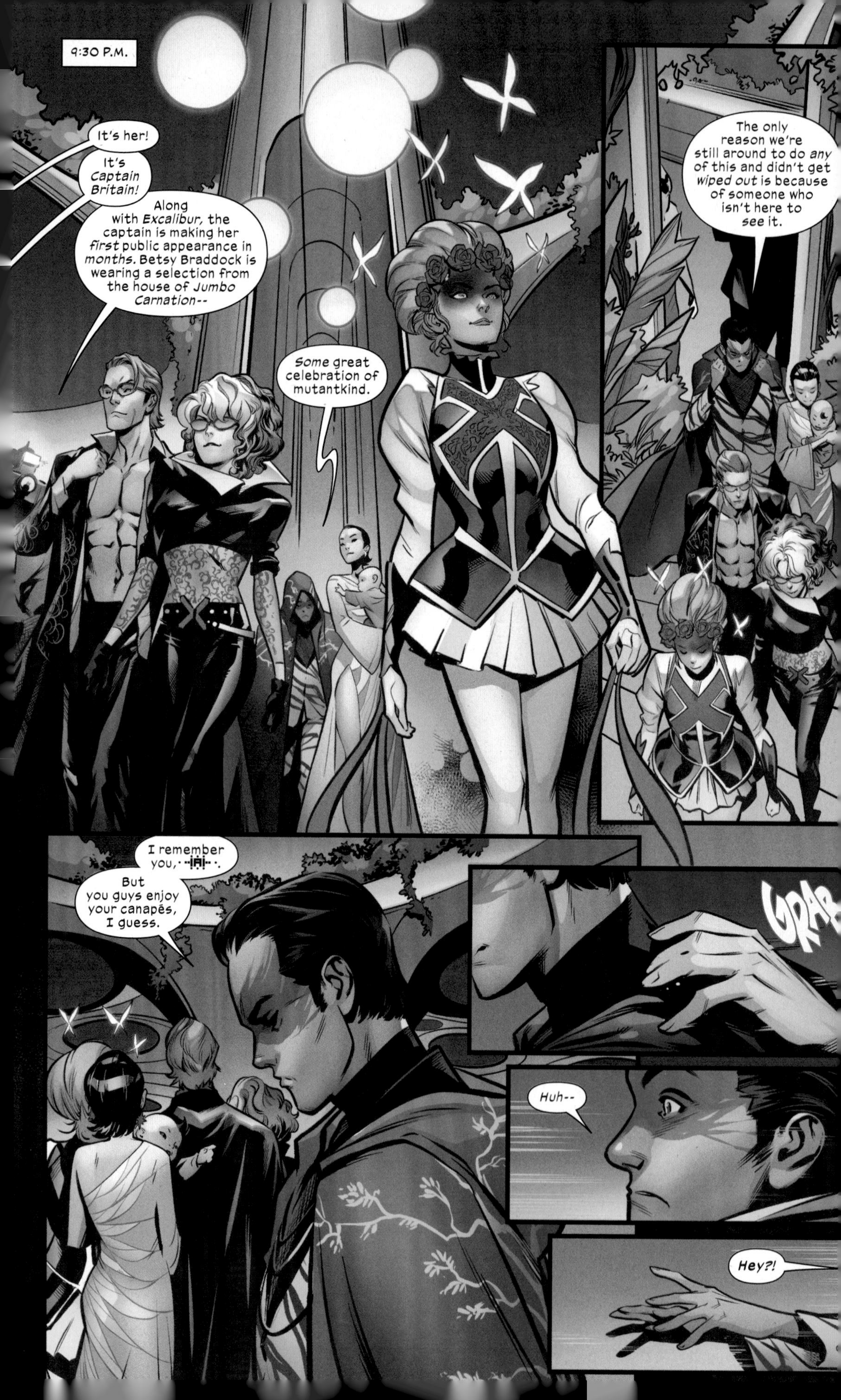
9:30 P.M.
It's her!
It's *Captain Britain!*
Along with *Excalibur,* the captain is making her *first* public appearance in *months.* Betsy Braddock is wearing a selection from the house of *Jumbo Carnation--*
Some great celebration of mutantkind.
The only reason we're still around to do *any* of this and didn't get *wiped out* is because of someone who isn't here to see it.
I remember you,
But you guys enjoy your canapés, I guess.
GRAB
Huh--
Hey?!

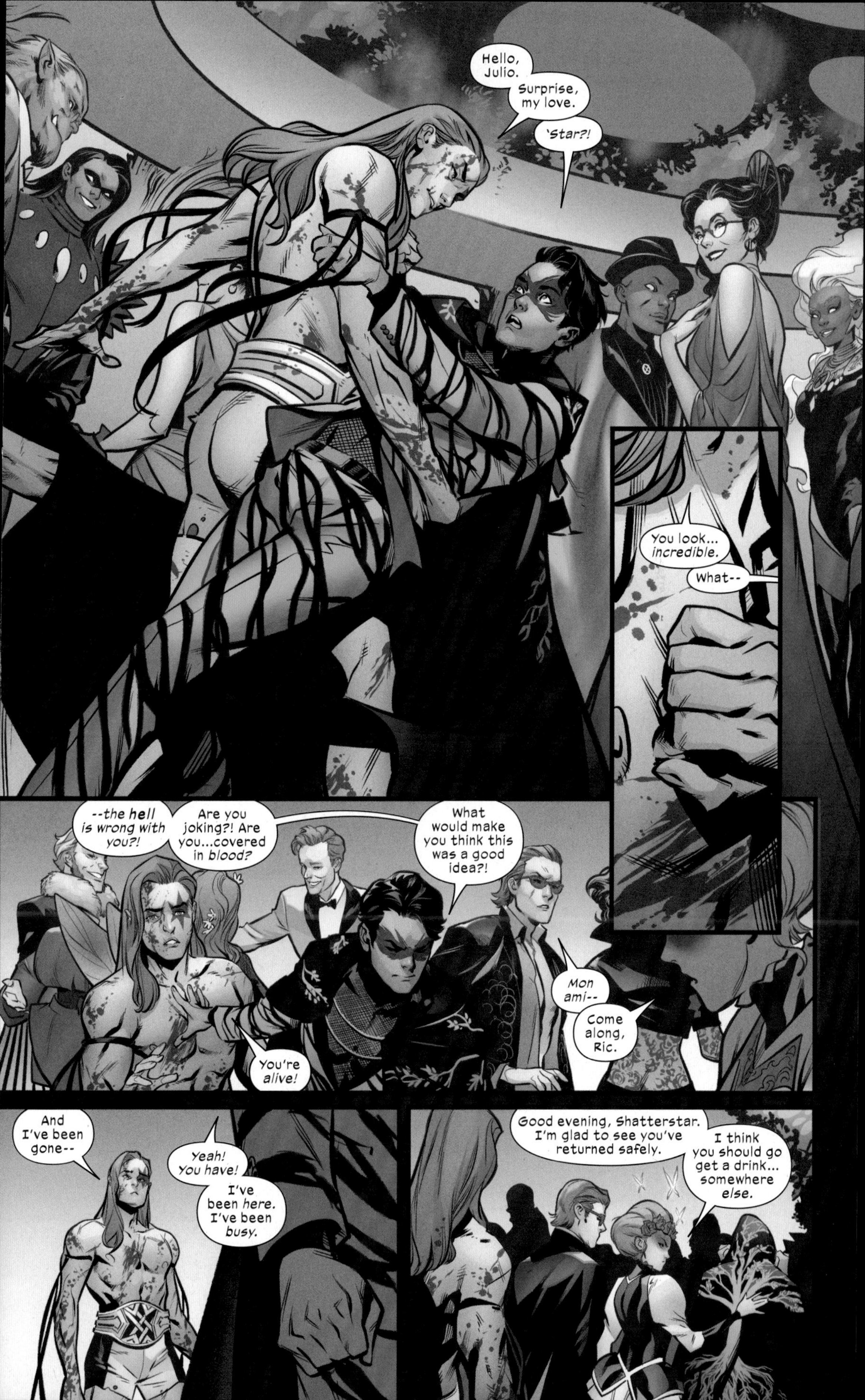
Hello, Julio.
Surprise, my love.
'Star?!
You look... *incredible.*
What--
--the *hell* is wrong with you?!
Are you joking?! Are you...covered in *blood?*
What would make you think this was a good idea?!
You're *alive!*
Mon ami--
Come along, Ric.
And I've been gone--
Yeah! You have!
I've been *here.* I've been *busy.*
Good evening, Shatterstar. I'm glad to see you've returned safely.
I think you should go get a drink... somewhere *else.*

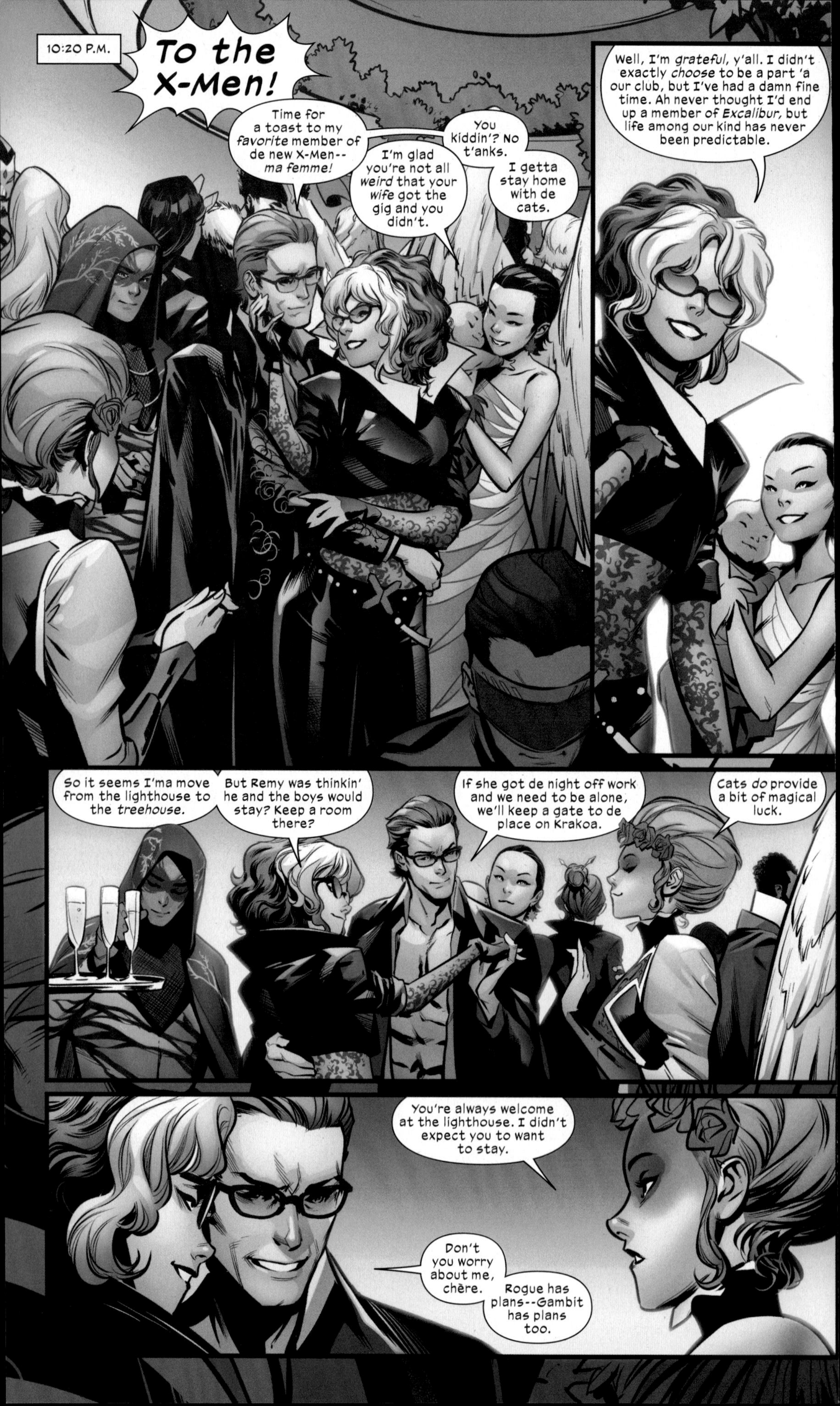

10:20 P.M.
To the X-Men!
Time for a toast to my *favorite* member of de new X-Men-- *ma femme!*
I'm glad you're not all *weird* that your *wife* got the gig and you didn't.
You kiddin'? No t'anks.
I getta stay home with de cats.
Well, I'm *grateful*, y'all. I didn't exactly *choose* to be a part 'a our club, but I've had a damn fine time. Ah never thought I'd end up a member of *Excalibur,* but life among our kind has never been predictable.
So it seems I'ma move from the lighthouse to the *treehouse.*
But Remy was thinkin' he and the boys would stay? Keep a room there?
If she got de night off work and we need to be alone, we'll keep a gate to de place on Krakoa.
Cats *do* provide a bit of magical luck.
You're always welcome at the lighthouse. I didn't expect you to want to stay.
Don't you worry about me, chère.
Rogue has plans--Gambit has plans too.

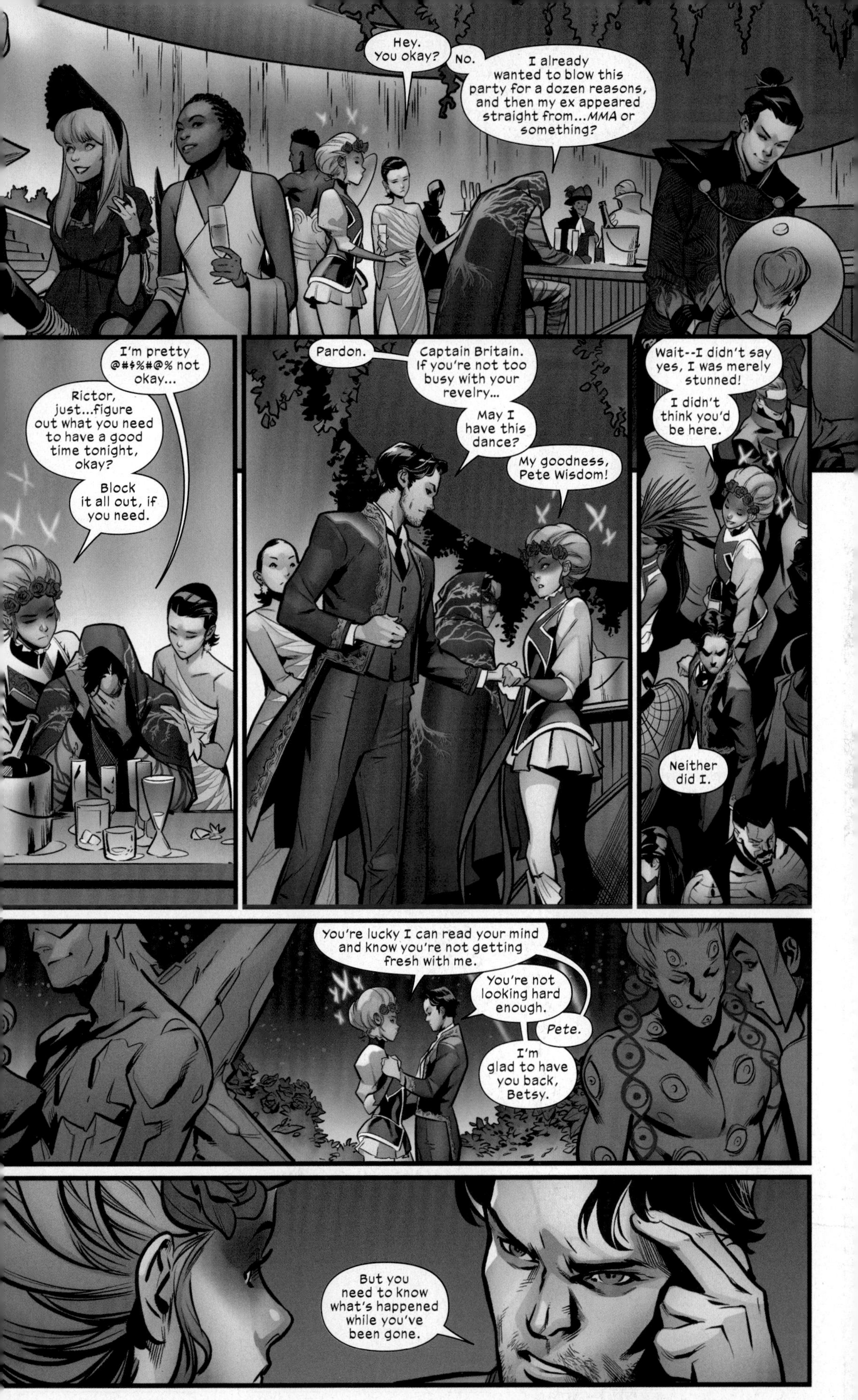
Hey. You okay?
No.
I already wanted to blow this party for a dozen reasons, and then my ex appeared straight from...MMA or something?
I'm pretty @#$%#@% not okay...
Rictor, just...figure out what you need to have a good time tonight, okay?
Block it all out, if you need.
Pardon.
Captain Britain. If you're not too busy with your revelry...
May I have this dance?
My goodness, Pete Wisdom!
Wait--I didn't say yes, I was merely stunned!
I didn't think you'd be here.
Neither did I.
You're lucky I can read your mind and know you're not getting fresh with me.
You're not looking hard enough.
Pete.
I'm glad to have you back, Betsy.
But you need to know what's happened while you've been gone.

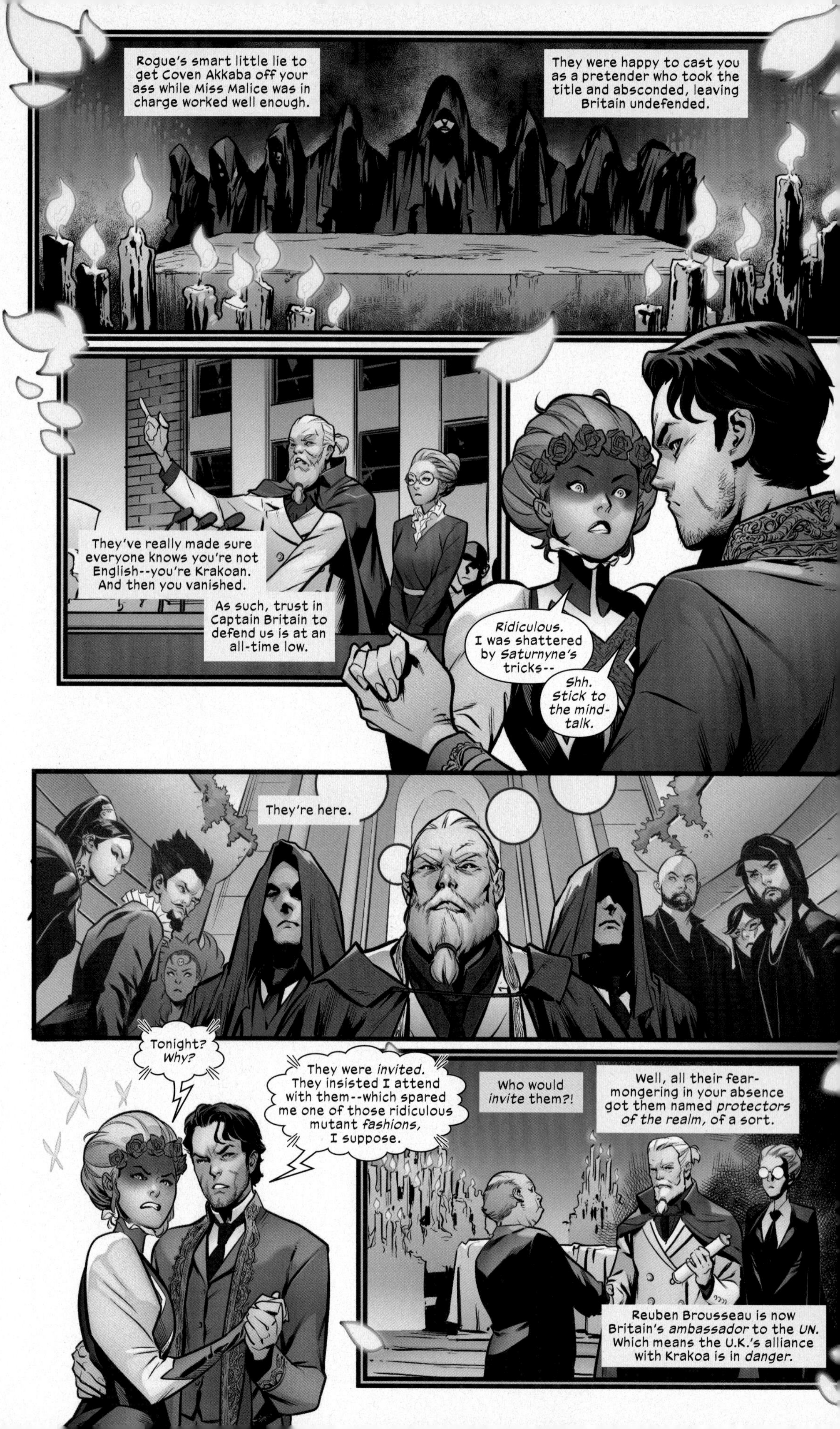
Rogue's smart little lie to get Coven Akkaba off your ass while Miss Malice was in charge worked well enough.
They were happy to cast you as a pretender who took the title and absconded, leaving Britain undefended.
They've really made sure everyone knows you're not English--you're Krakoan. And then you vanished.
As such, trust in Captain Britain to defend us is at an all-time low.
Ridiculous. I was shattered by *Saturnyne's* tricks--
Shh. Stick to the mind-talk.
They're here.
Tonight? *Why?*
They were *invited.* They insisted I attend with them--which spared me one of those ridiculous mutant *fashions,* I suppose.
Who would *invite* them?!
Well, all their fear-mongering in your absence got them named *protectors of the realm,* of a sort.
Reuben Brousseau is now Britain's *ambassador* to the *UN.* Which means the U.K.'s alliance with Krakoa is in *danger.*

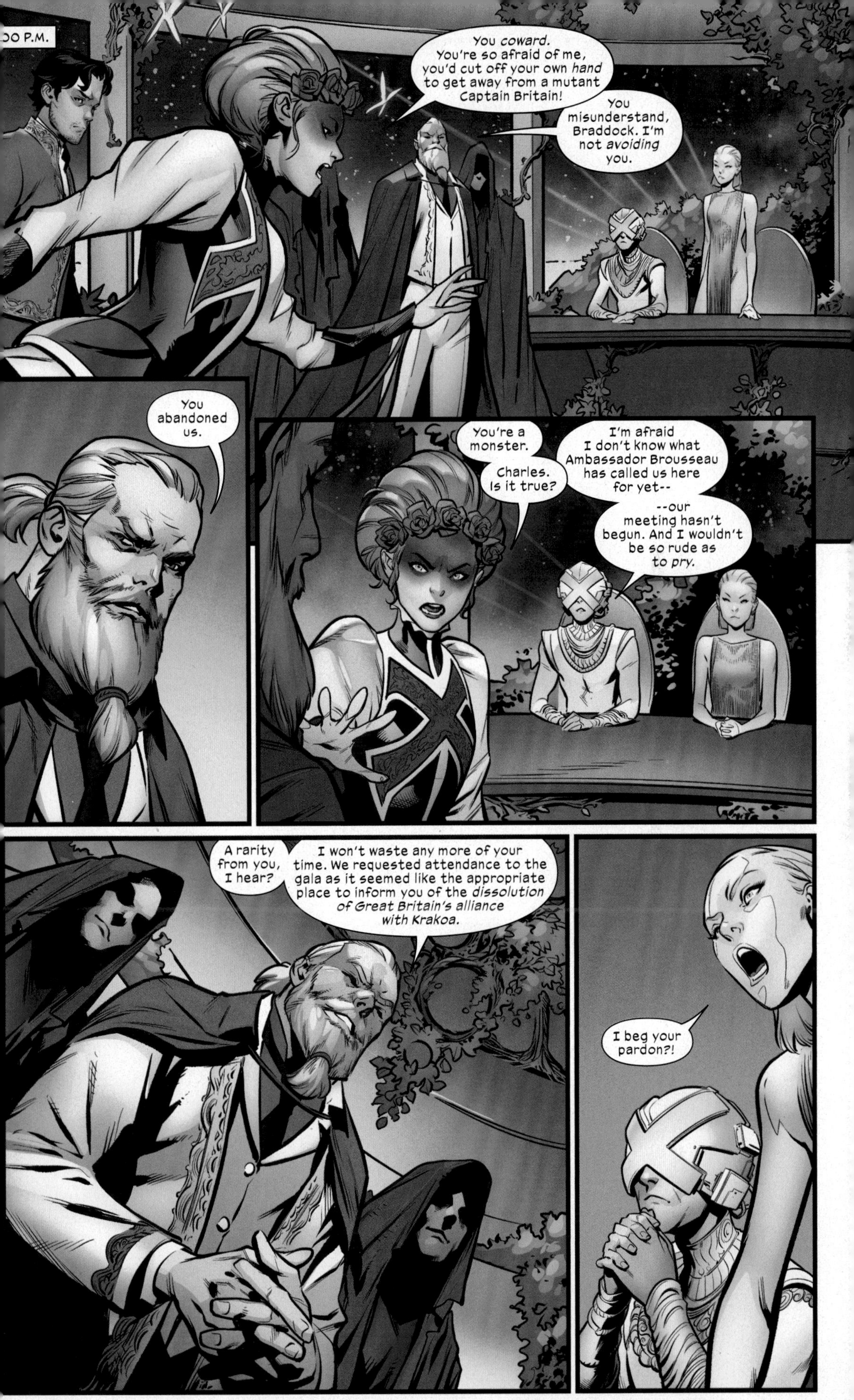

00 P.M.
You *coward*. You're so afraid of me, you'd cut off your own *hand* to get away from a mutant Captain Britain!
You misunderstand, Braddock. I'm not *avoiding* you.
You abandoned us.
You're a monster.
Charles. Is it true?
I'm afraid I don't know what Ambassador Brousseau has called us here for yet--
--our meeting hasn't begun. And I wouldn't be so rude as to *pry*.
A rarity from you, I hear?
I won't waste any more of your time. We requested attendance to the gala as it seemed like the appropriate place to inform you of the *dissolution of Great Britain's alliance with Krakoa*.
I beg your pardon?!

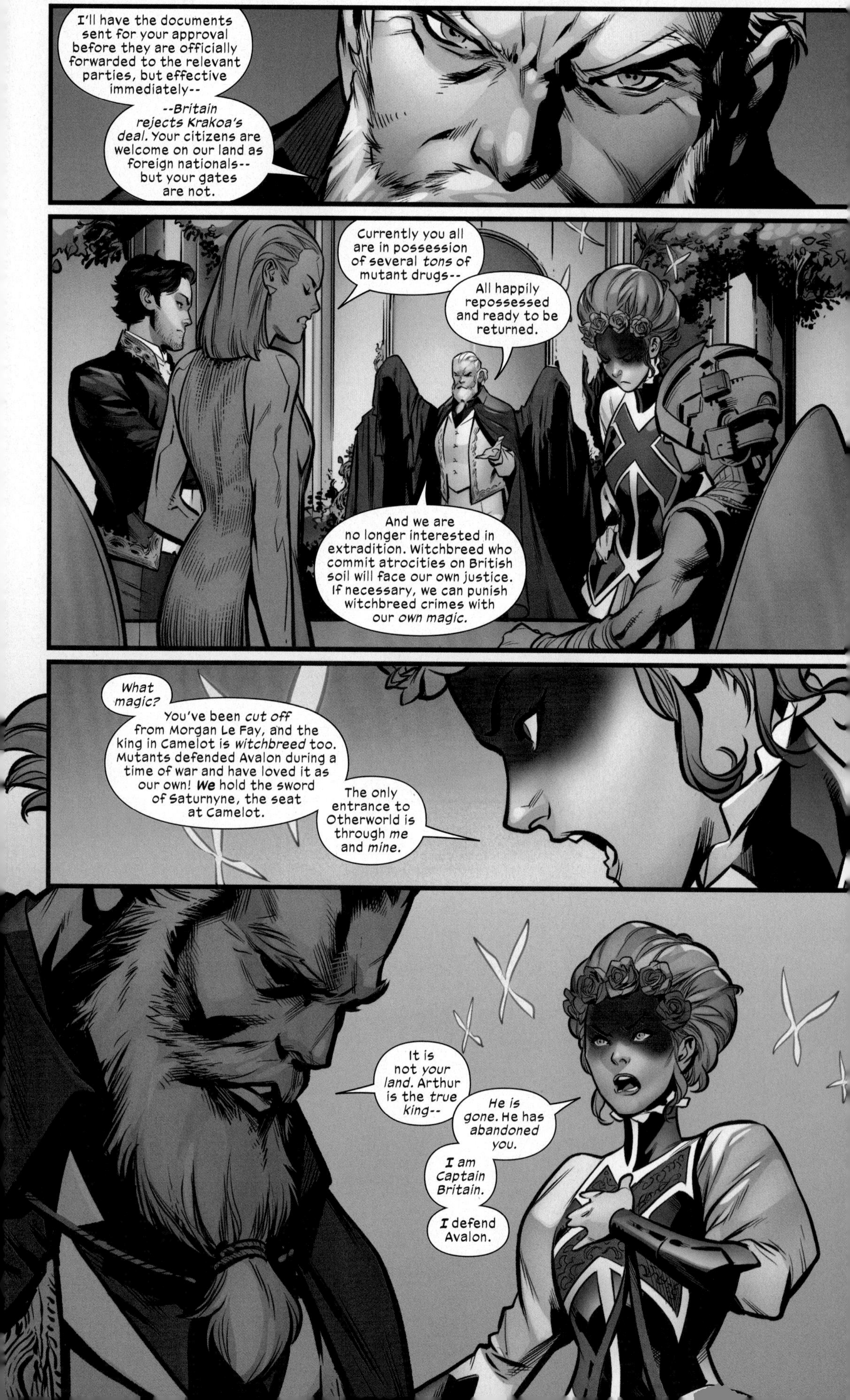
I'll have the documents sent for your approval before they are officially forwarded to the relevant parties, but effective immediately--
--*Britain rejects Krakoa's deal.* Your citizens are welcome on our land as foreign nationals--but your gates are not.
Currently you all are in possession of several *tons* of mutant drugs--
All happily repossessed and ready to be returned.
And we are no longer interested in extradition. Witchbreed who commit atrocities on British soil will face our own justice. If necessary, we can punish witchbreed crimes with our *own magic.*
What magic?
You've been *cut off* from Morgan Le Fay, and the king in Camelot is *witchbreed* too. Mutants defended Avalon during a time of war and have loved it as our own! ***We*** hold the sword of Saturnyne, the seat at Camelot.
The only entrance to Otherworld is through *me* and *mine.*
It is not *your land.* Arthur is the *true* king--
He is gone. He has abandoned you.
I am Captain Britain.
I defend Avalon.

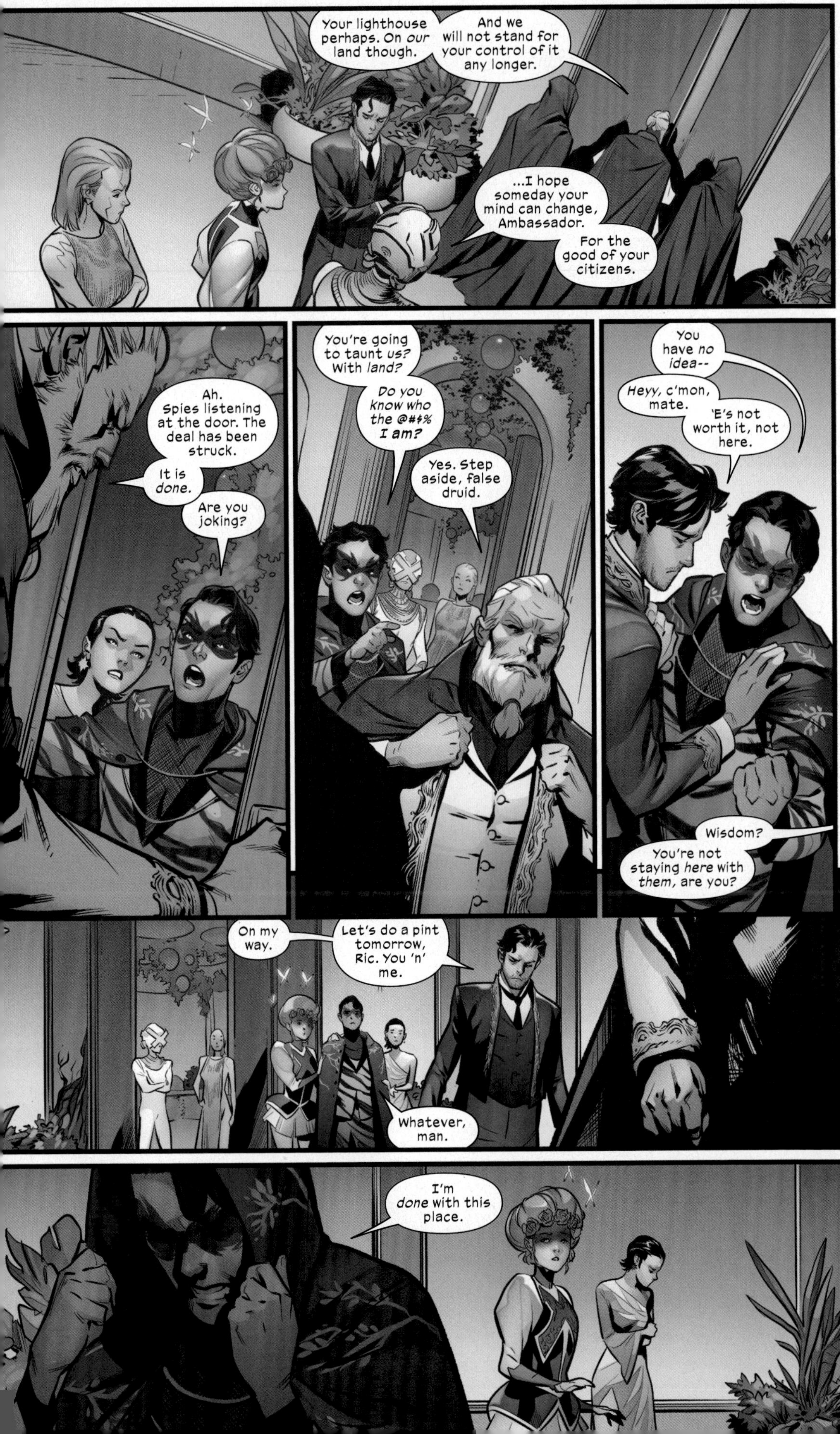

Your lighthouse perhaps. On *our* land though.
And we will not stand for your control of it any longer.
...I hope someday your mind can change, Ambassador.
For the good of your citizens.
Ah. Spies listening at the door. The deal has been struck.
It is *done.*
Are you joking?
You're going to taunt *us?* With *land?*
Do you know who the @#$% I am?
Yes. Step aside, false druid.
You have *no idea--*
Heyy, c'mon, mate.
'E's not worth it, not here.
Wisdom?
You're not staying *here* with *them,* are you?
On my way.
Let's do a pint tomorrow, Ric. You 'n' me.
Whatever, man.
I'm *done* with this place.

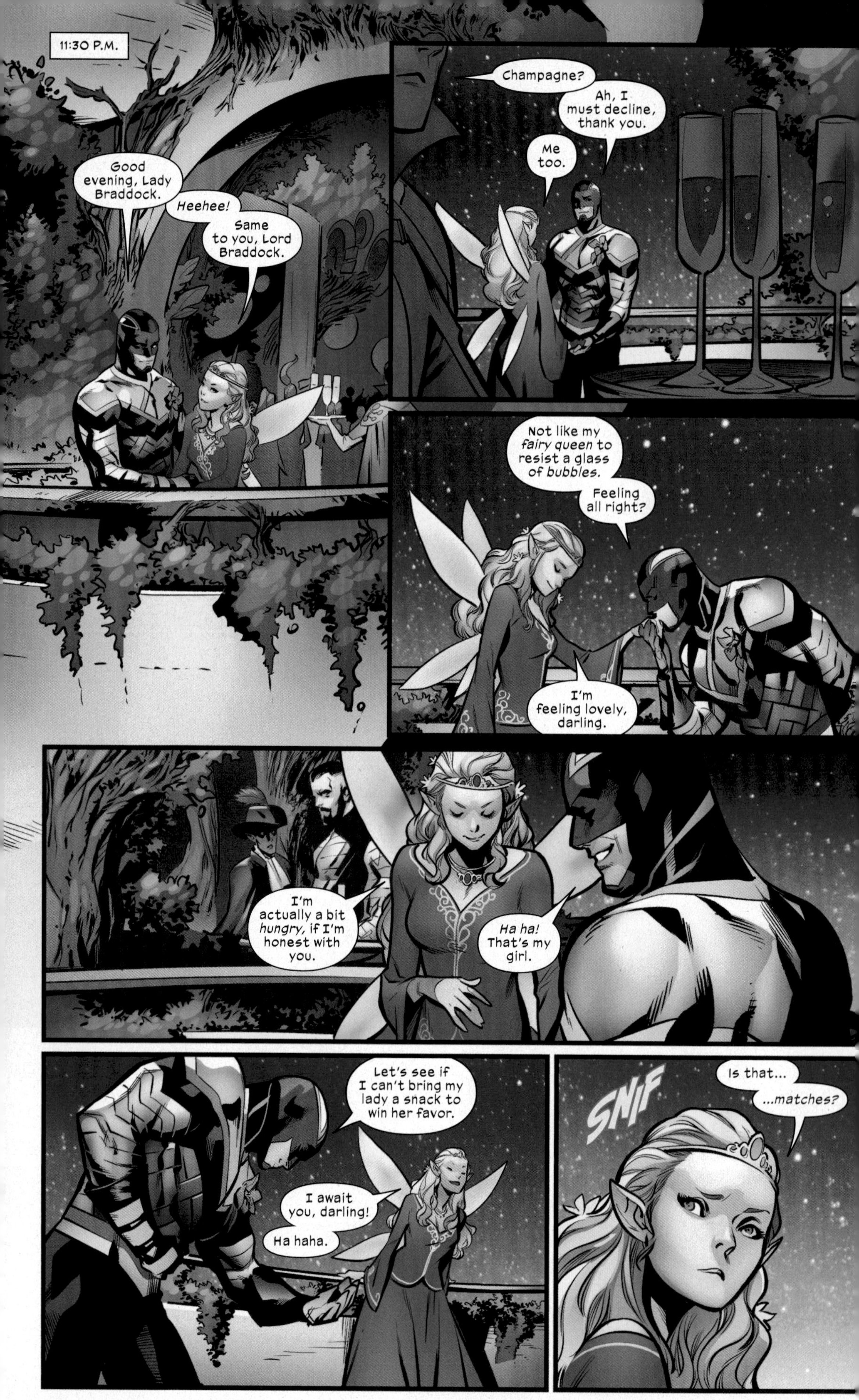
11:30 P.M.
Good evening, Lady Braddock.
Heehee!
Same to you, Lord Braddock.
Champagne?
Ah, I must decline, thank you.
Me too.
Not like my fairy queen to resist a glass of bubbles.
Feeling all right?
I'm feeling lovely, darling.
I'm actually a bit hungry, if I'm honest with you.
Ha ha! That's my girl.
Let's see if I can't bring my lady a snack to win her favor.
I await you, darling!
Ha haha.
SNIF
Is that...
...matches?

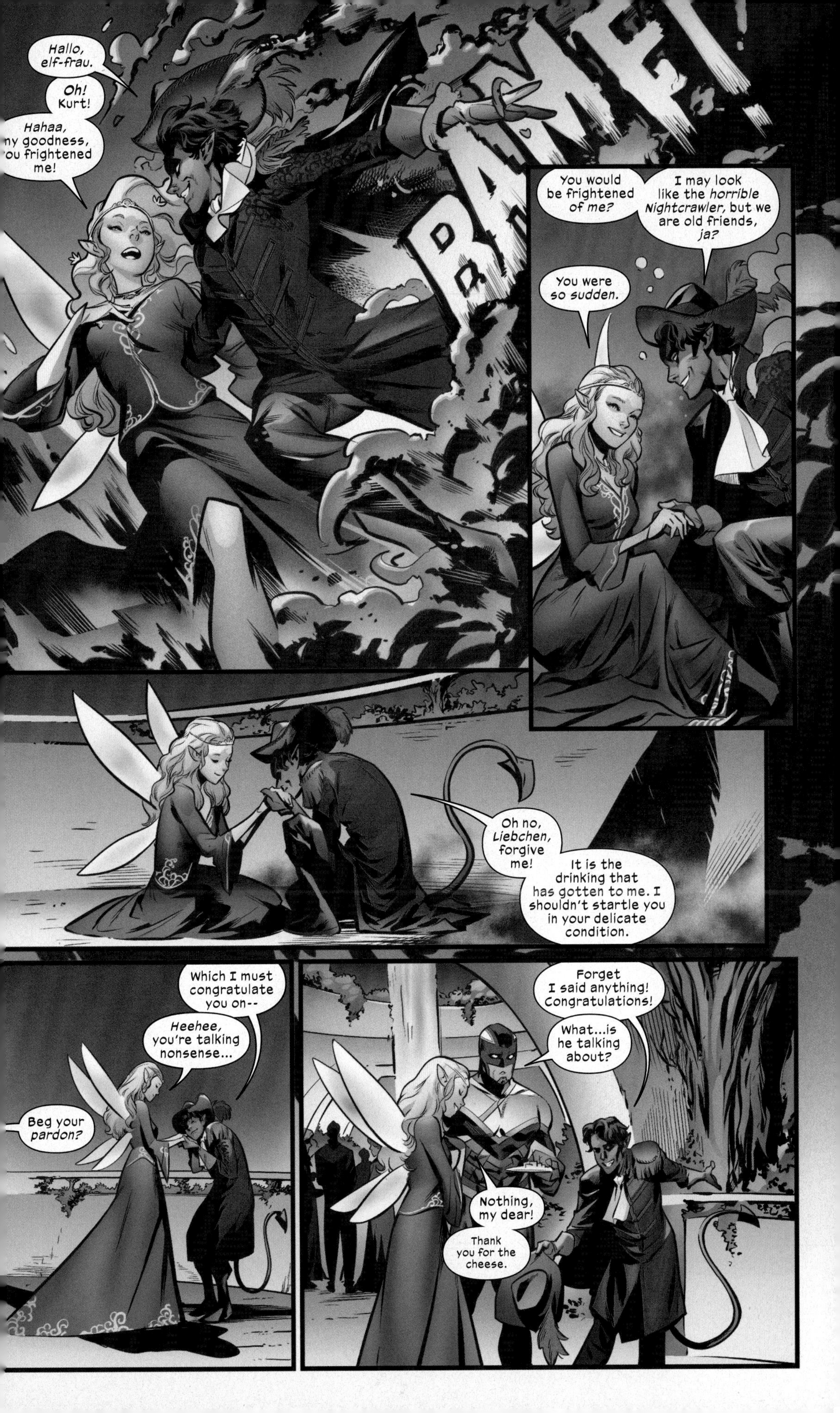
Hallo, elf-frau.
Oh! Kurt!
Hahaa, my goodness, you frightened me!
BAMF!
You would be frightened of me?
I may look like the horrible Nightcrawler, but we are old friends, ja?
You were so sudden.
Oh no, Liebchen, forgive me!
It is the drinking that has gotten to me. I shouldn't startle you in your delicate condition.
Which I must congratulate you on--
Heehee, you're talking nonsense...
Beg your pardon?
Forget I said anything! Congratulations!
What...is he talking about?
Nothing, my dear!
Thank you for the cheese.

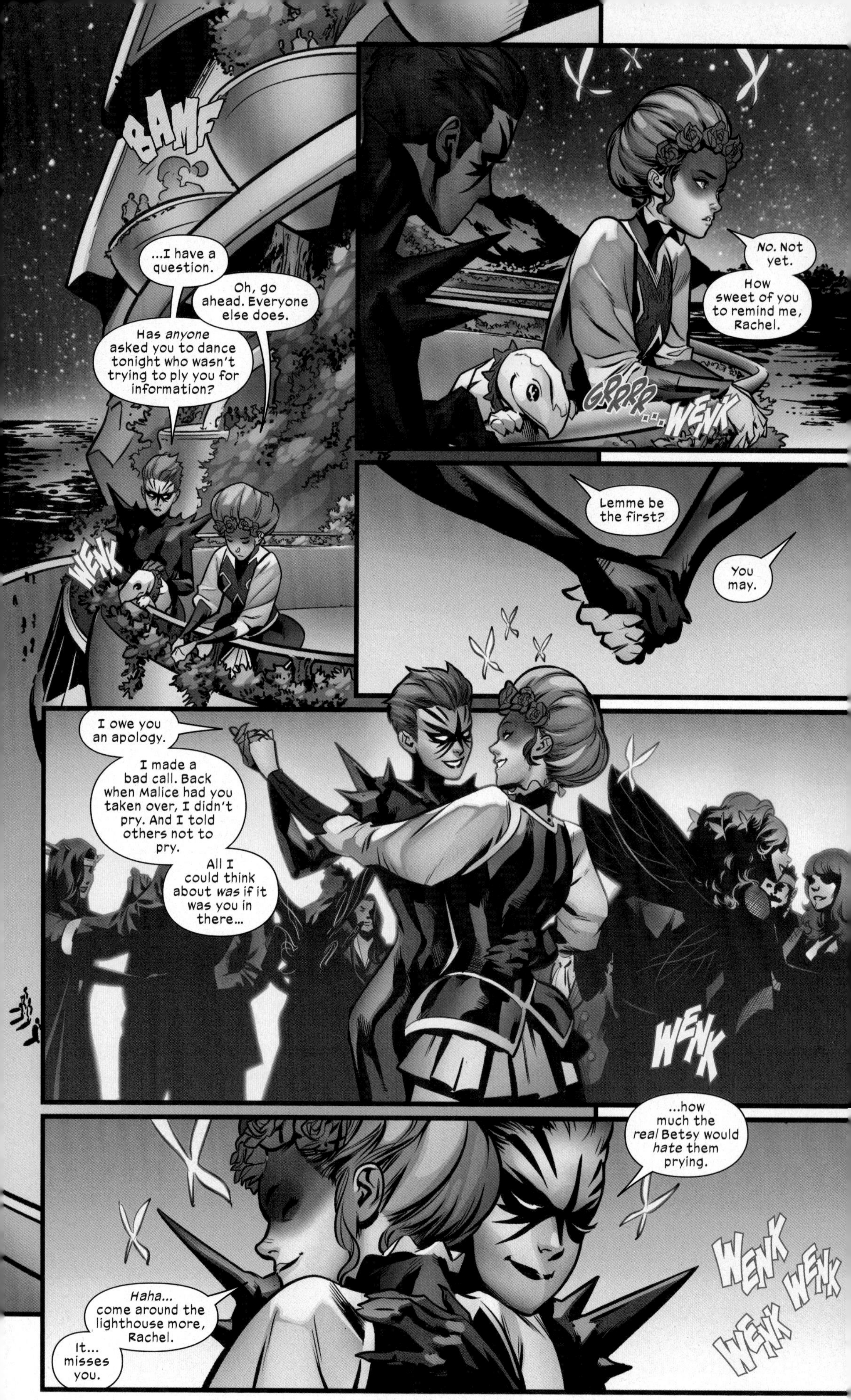
BAMF
...I have a question.
Oh, go ahead. Everyone else does.
Has *anyone* asked you to dance tonight who wasn't trying to ply you for information?
WENK
No. Not yet.
How sweet of you to remind me, Rachel.
GRRRR... WENK
Lemme be the first?
You may.
I owe you an apology.
I made a bad call. Back when Malice had you taken over, I didn't pry. And I told others not to pry.
All I could think about *was* if it was you in there...
WENK
...how much the *real* Betsy would *hate* them prying.
Haha... come around the lighthouse more, Rachel.
It... misses you.
WENK WENK WENK

COVEN AKKABA

"From *Lineage: An Examination of Traditional British Coven Structure* by Katherine Bushwick, (copyright *Dry Biscuit Publishing*). Page 368.

...Certain rogue covens are still literal believers in Murray's largely disproved "witch cult" hypothesis, which states that modern British covens are holdouts of pre-Roman druidic god and hero worship. In order to protect the highly guarded spiritual mysteries, formal ritual secrets are reserved for hidden initiations and careful lineages, so that all who know a mystery are named and known to the others and those they are taught by are named too. As such, many Covens maintain anonymous membership save for the high priest and priestess, who choose to make themselves known.

Despite this, certain Covens develop fringe and radical beliefs even within the lineage structure, and prodigious young practitioners can find themselves rapidly rising within the initiate degrees and in charge of their own covens before long, where the standard rules are often quickly abandoned.

Some Covens maintain the claim of the "witch cult" hypothesis, such as in the case of Coven Akkaba. The Coven has two leaders, like most British Covens, a High Priestess[1] and High Priest[2], though they claim several degrees of ranking and hidden knowledge past the traditional three and more than a few uncompromising, rather heretical beliefs.

Namely, while most Covens keep the name of their patron goddess a mystery, Coven Akkaba openly worships the mythological Morgan Le Fay and claims direct and physical contact with her. High Priestess Marianna Stern openly decries the typical practice of "embodying the goddess," saying instead "Our goddess has a body. Why in the hell would we waste our time with a goddess who couldn't even manifest that?"

---

1. Sublime High Priestess of the Ninth Degree Marianna Stern
(Initiated by Queen Lady Rosamund & Coven Scandia.)

2. Sublime High Priest of the Ninth Degree Reuben Brousseau
(Initiated by Lady Brigid & Derfel of Coven Modred.)

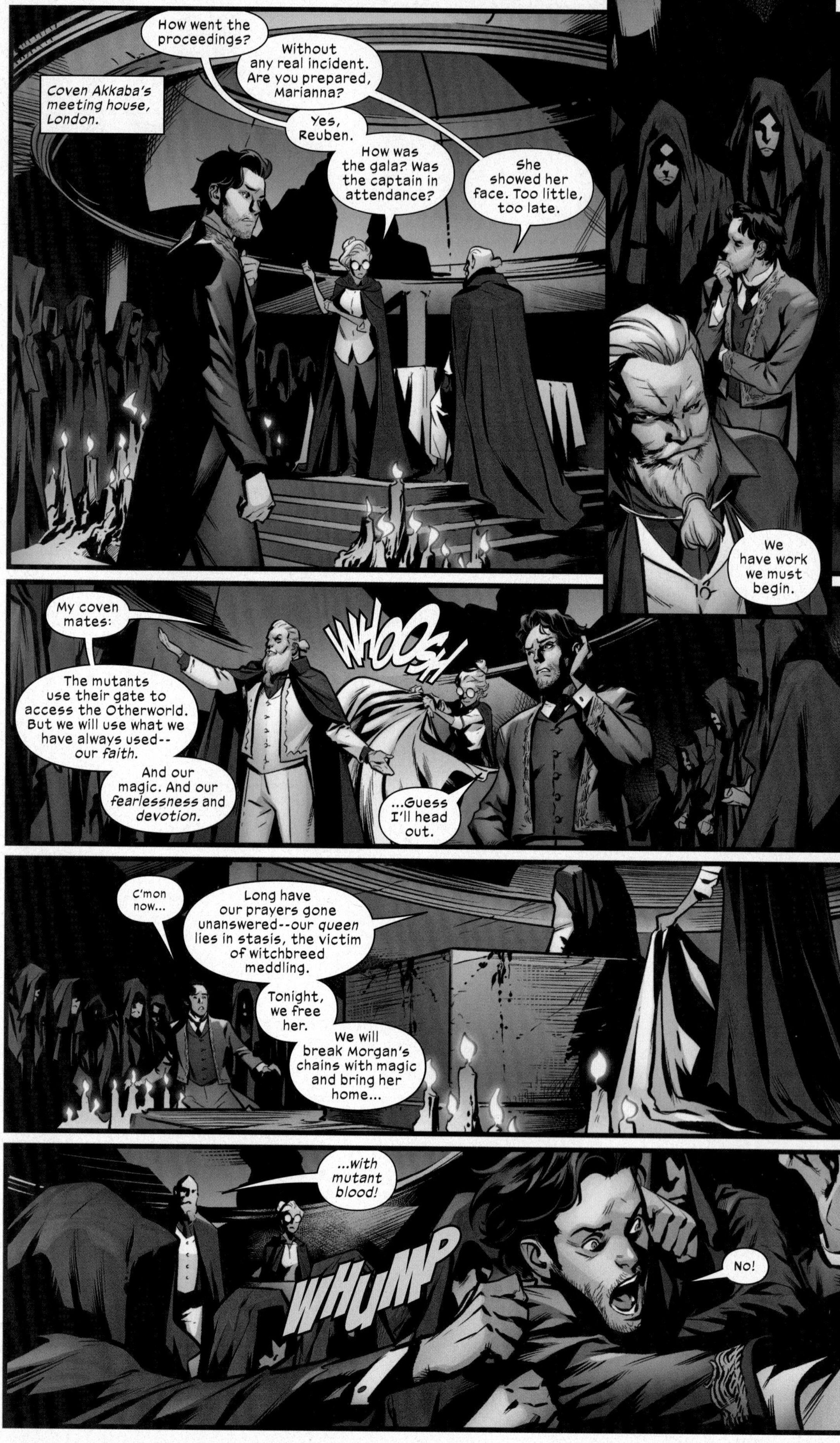

Coven Akkaba's meeting house, London.
How went the proceedings?
Without any real incident. Are you prepared, Marianna?
Yes, Reuben.
How was the gala? Was the captain in attendance?
She showed her face. Too little, too late.
We have work we must begin.
My coven mates:
The mutants use their gate to access the Otherworld. But we will use what we have always used--our *faith.*
And our magic. And our *fearlessness* and *devotion.*
WHOOSH
...Guess I'll head out.
C'mon now...
Long have our prayers gone unanswered--our *queen* lies in stasis, the victim of witchbreed meddling.
Tonight, we free her.
We will break Morgan's chains with magic and bring her home...
...with mutant blood!
WHUMP
No!

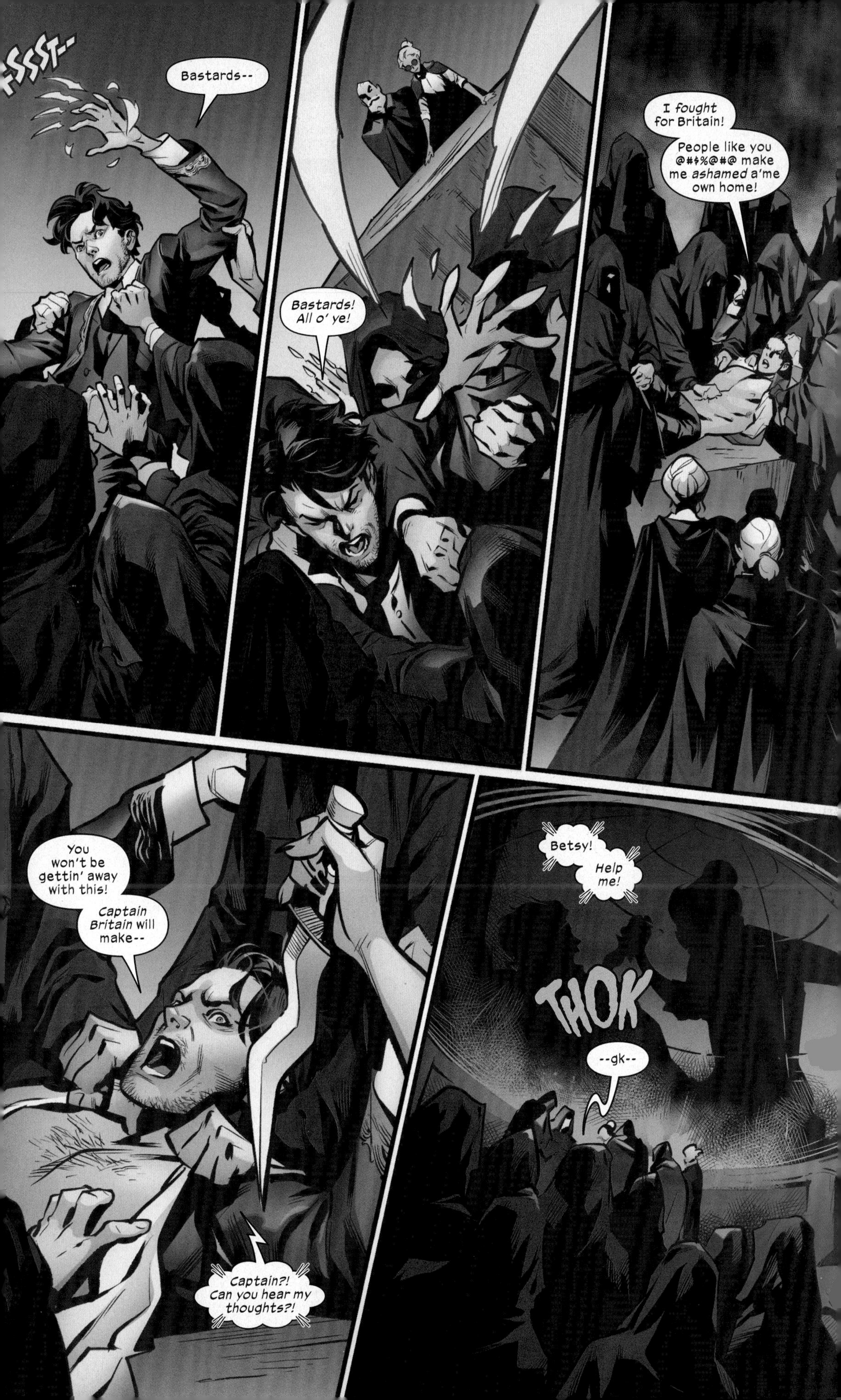
FSSST--
Bastards--
Bastards! All o' ye!
I fought for Britain!
People like you @#$%@#@ make me ashamed a'me own home!
You won't be gettin' away with this!
Captain Britain will make--
Captain?! Can you hear my thoughts?!
Betsy!
Help me!
THOK
--gk--

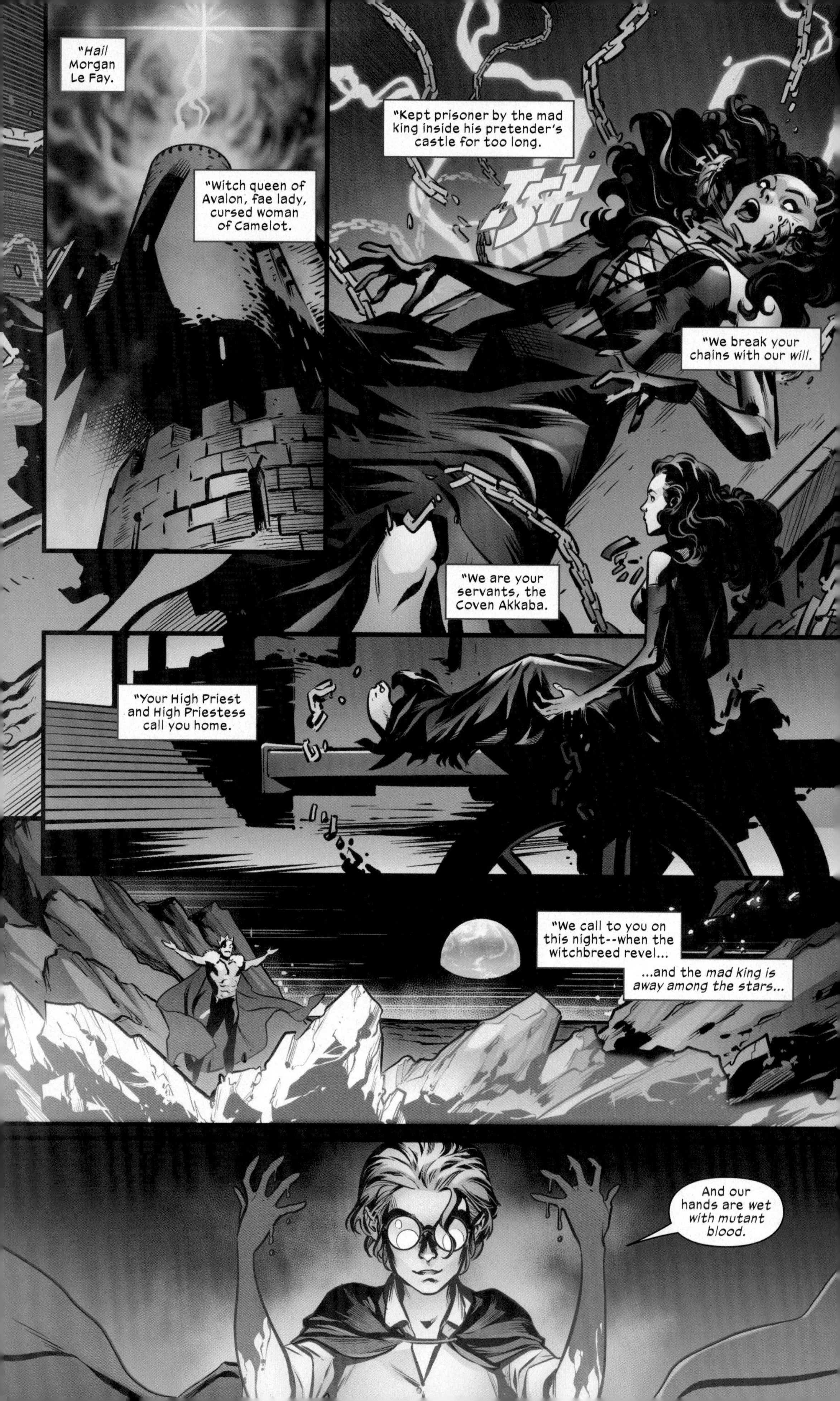
"Hail Morgan Le Fay.
"Witch queen of Avalon, fae lady, cursed woman of Camelot.
"Kept prisoner by the mad king inside his pretender's castle for too long.
"We break your chains with our *will*.
"We are your servants, the Coven Akkaba.
"Your High Priest and High Priestess call you home.
"We call to you on this night--when the witchbreed revel...
...and the *mad king* is *away among the stars*...
And our hands are *wet with mutant* blood.

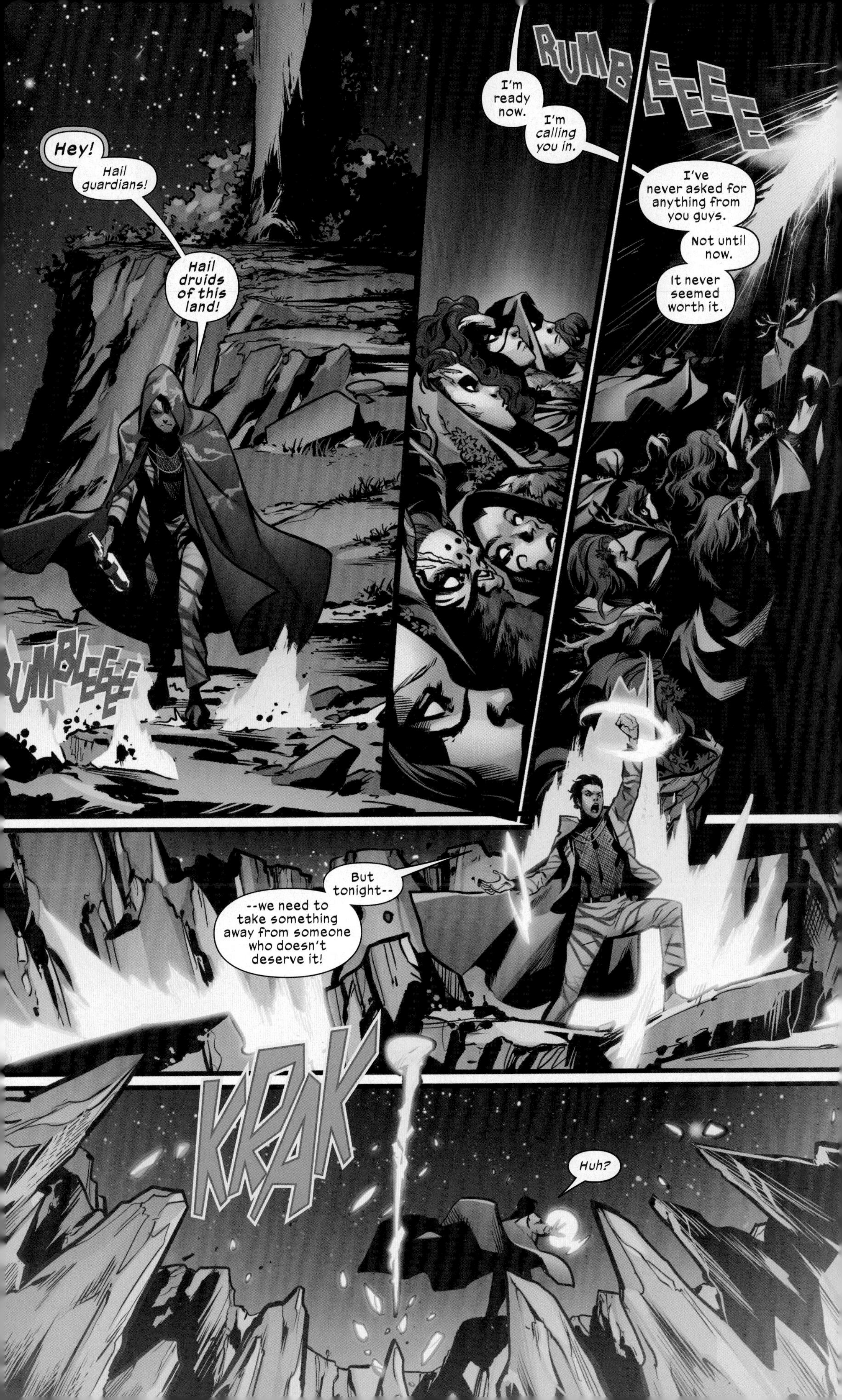
Hey!
Hail guardians!
Hail druids of this land!
RUMBLEEEE
RUMBLEEEE
I'm ready now.
I'm calling you in.
I've never asked for anything from you guys.
Not until now.
It never seemed worth it.
But tonight--
--we need to take something away from someone who doesn't deserve it!
KRAK
Huh?

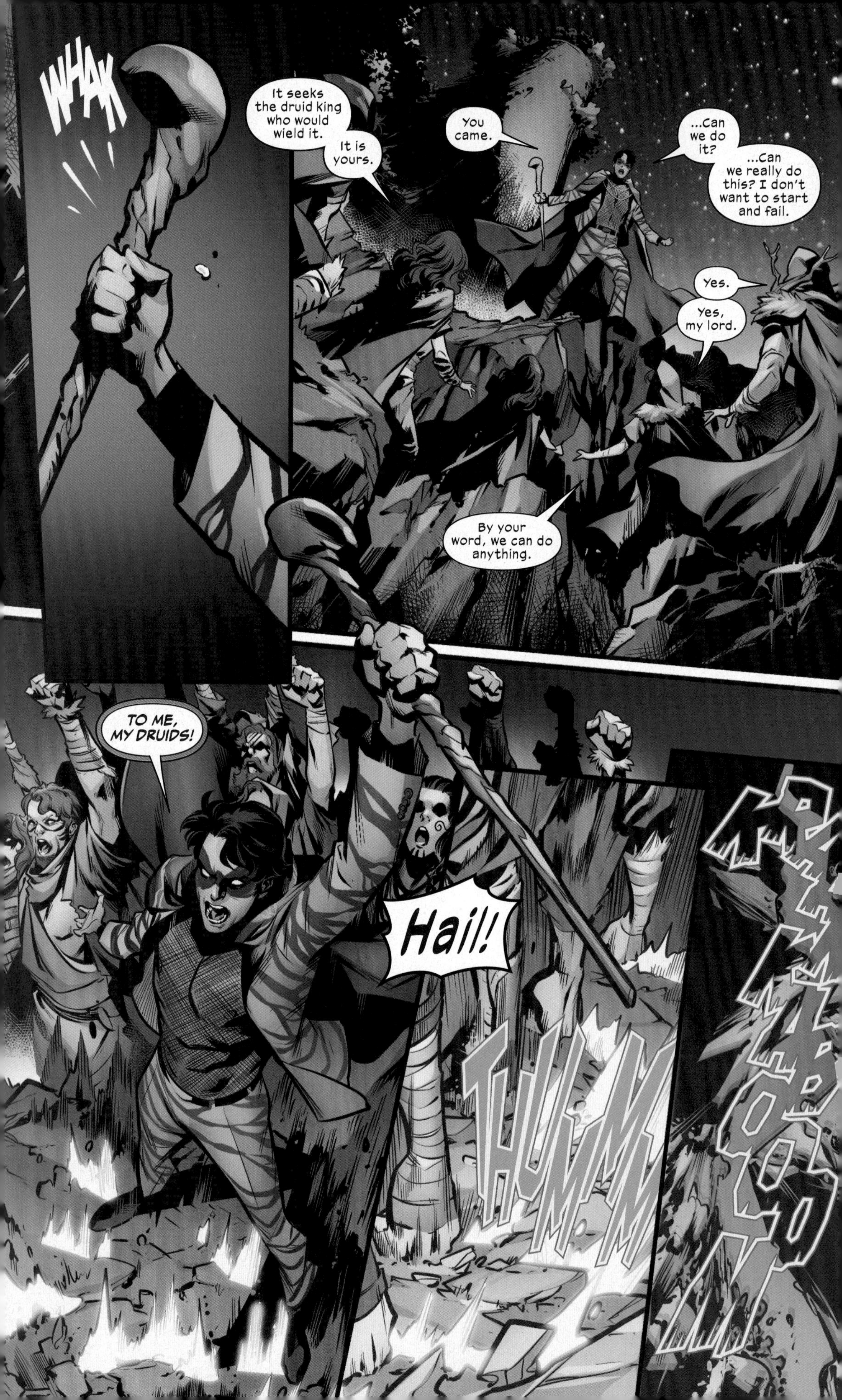
WHAK
It seeks the druid king who would wield it.
It is yours.
You came.
...Can we do it?
...Can we really do this? I don't want to start and fail.
Yes.
Yes, my lord.
By your word, we can do anything.
TO ME, MY DRUIDS!
Hail!
THUMM

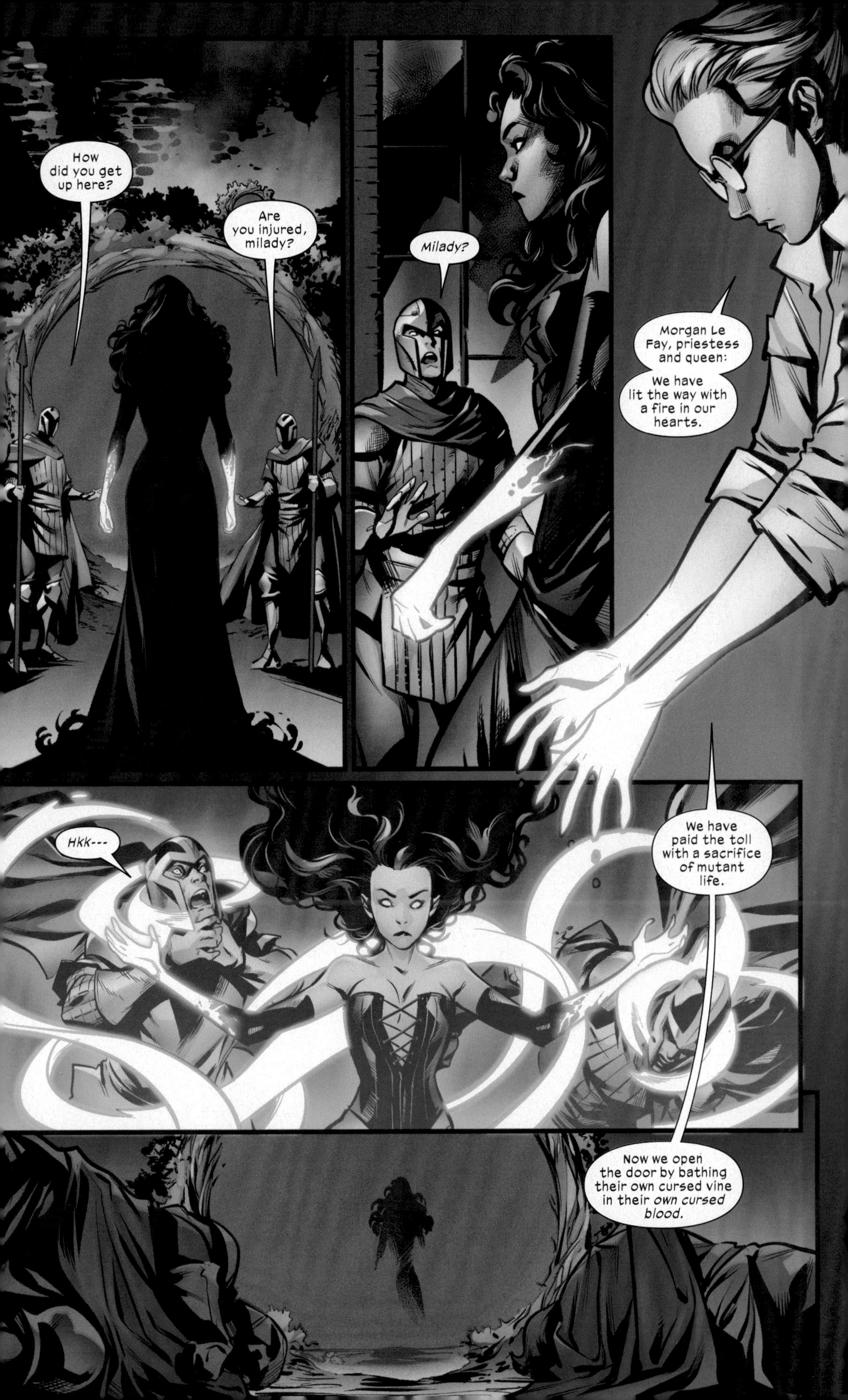
How did you get up here?
Are you injured, milady?
Milady?
Morgan Le Fay, priestess and queen:
We have lit the way with a fire in our hearts.
Hkk---
We have paid the toll with a sacrifice of mutant life.
Now we open the door by bathing their own cursed vine in their *own cursed blood.*

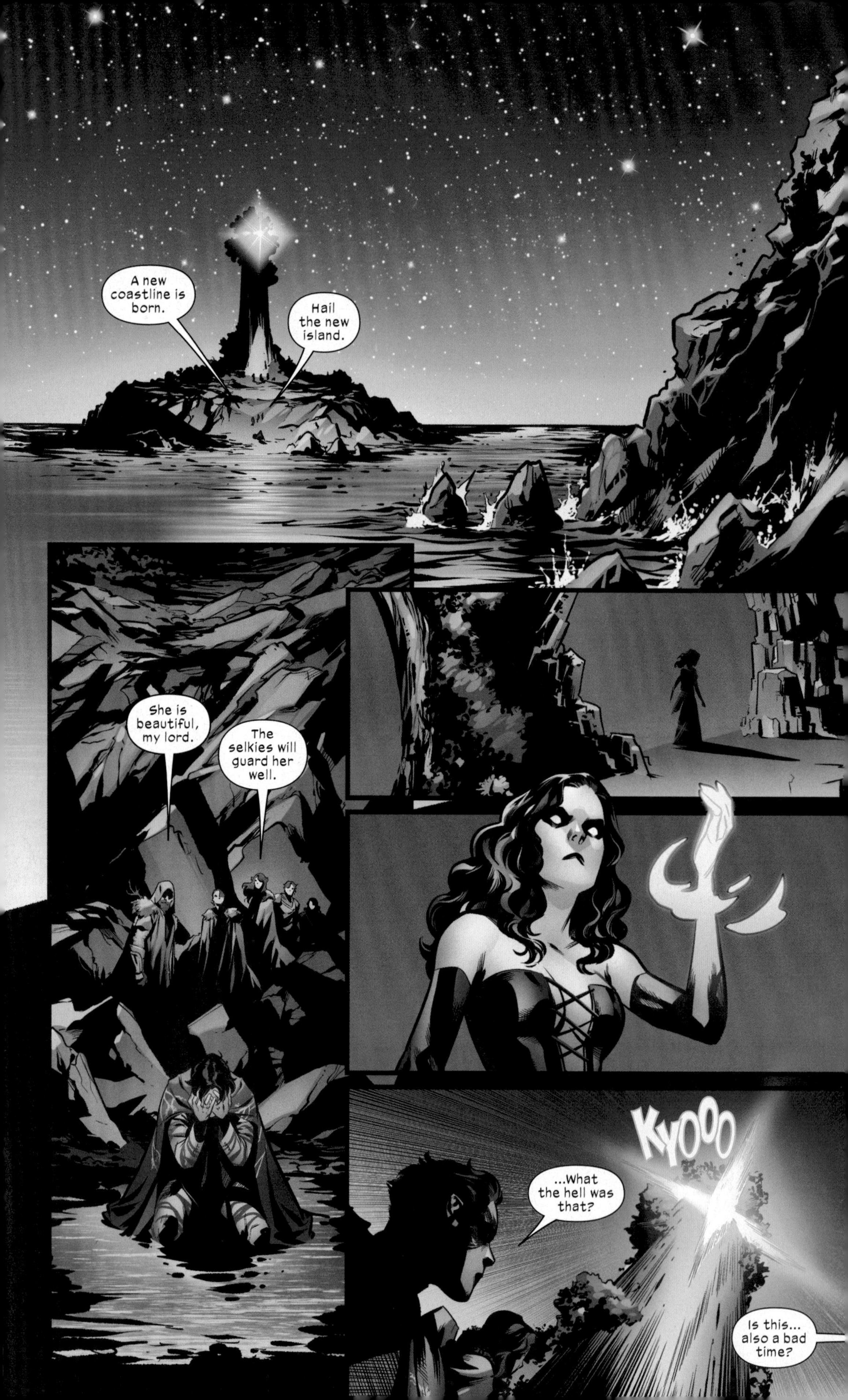
A new coastline is born.
Hail the new island.
She is beautiful, my lord.
The selkies will guard her well.
KYOOO
...What the hell was that?
Is this... also a bad time?

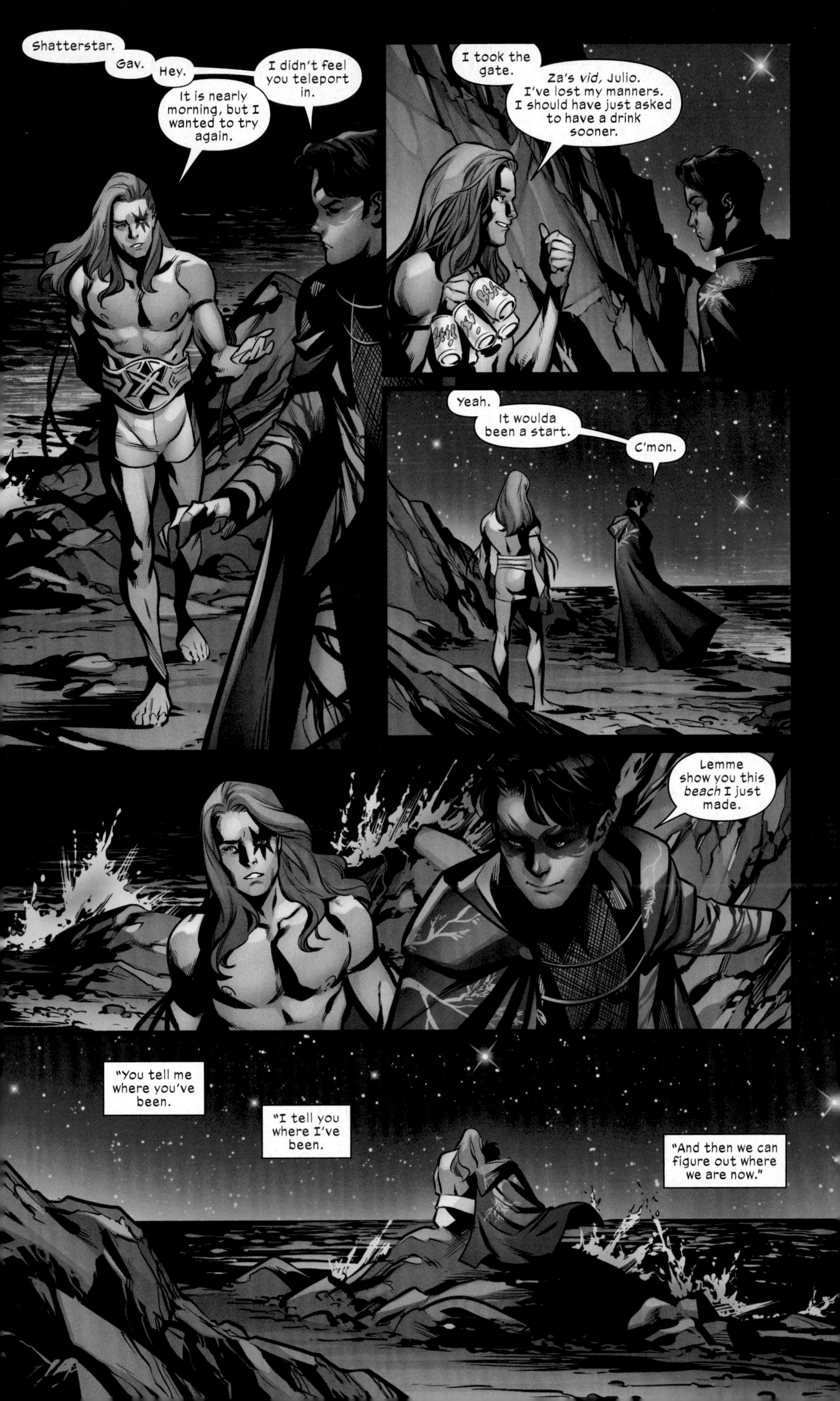
Shatterstar.
Gav.
Hey.
I didn't feel you teleport in.
It is nearly morning, but I wanted to try again.
I took the gate.
Za's *vid,* Julio. I've lost my manners. I should have just asked to have a drink sooner.
Yeah.
It woulda been a start.
C'mon.
Lemme show you this *beach* I just made.
"You tell me where you've been.
"I tell you where I've been.
"And then we can figure out where we are now."

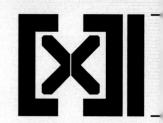

BRADDOCK ISLE

SIZE: ~0.14 km2

RELATIVE LOCATION: Southwest England, between Cornwall and the Isles of Scilly.

ADJACENT BODIES OF WATER: Celtic Sea, Atlantic Ocean.

NATIONALITY: Krakoan. [DISPUTED]

POINTS OF INTEREST: Braddock Lighthouse.

LEADERSHIP: Sui generis, Krakoan protectorate. [Unconfirmed]

POPULATION: Under 10, primarily mutant.

CHARACTERISTICS: A recently formed rocky islet that does not typically support vegetation, Krakoan flowers have taken to the land hardily, building their signature architectural structures to additional heights. At times of extremely low tide, the island is occasionally still reachable by land.

[reign_of_x]

[kra_]
[koa_]

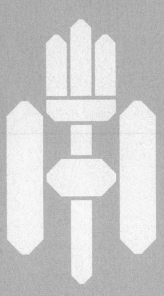

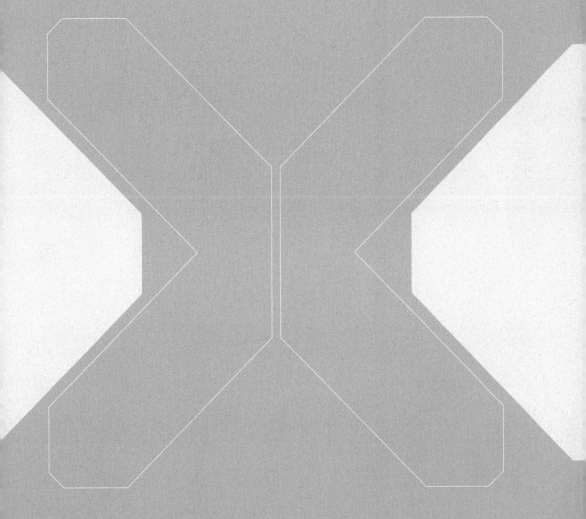

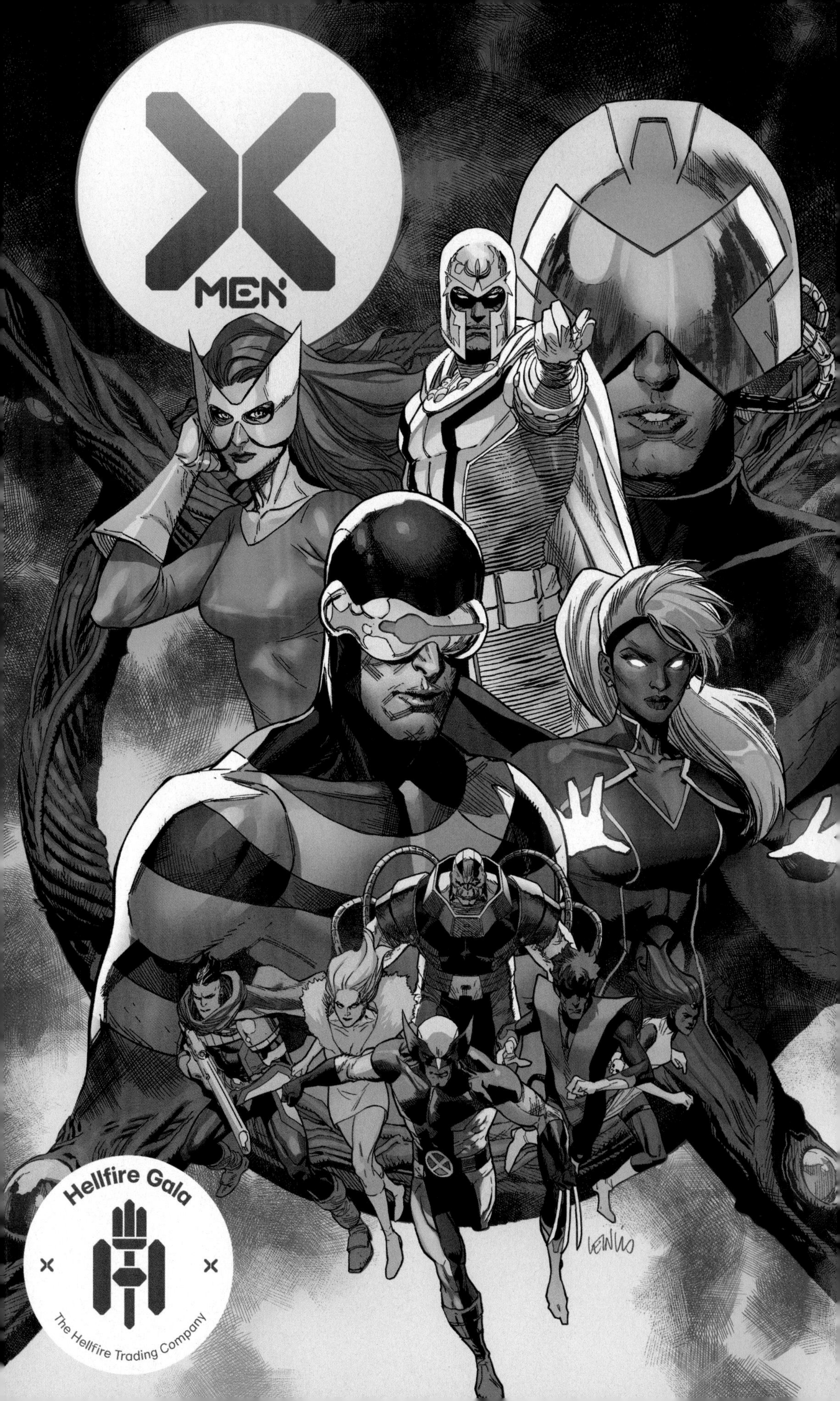
X MEN
Hellfire Gala
The Hellfire Trading Company

Yes. And be sure to make your return *often* and the pour *generous.*

I fear it may be the only way we two get through this night.

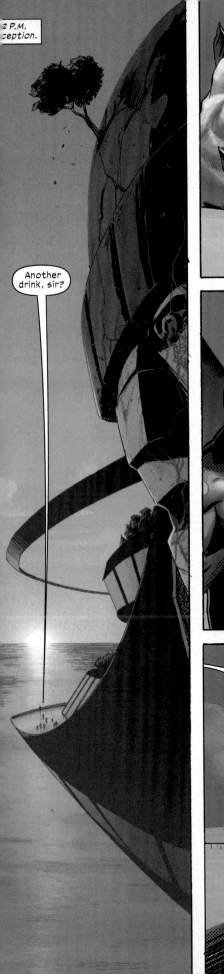

Another drink, sir?

Understood. Can I bring you anything else, sir? Something to nibble on?

Cheese, perhaps?

We can handle it from here, Jamie.

Ah...

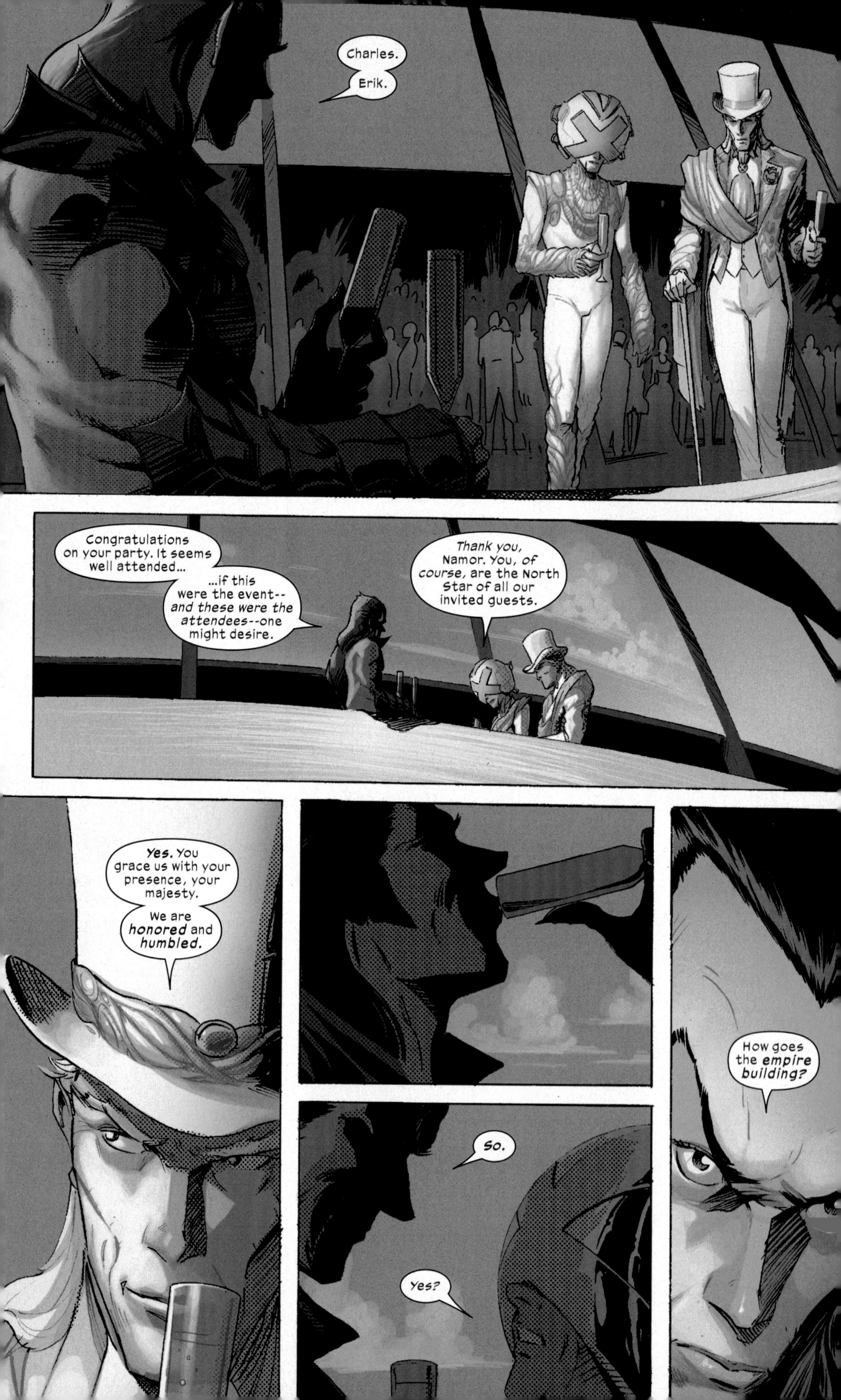
Charles.
Erik.
Congratulations on your party. It seems well attended...
...if this were the event--and these were the attendees--one might desire.
Thank you, Namor. You, of course, are the North Star of all our invited guests.
Yes. You grace us with your presence, your majesty.
We are honored and humbled.
How goes the empire building?
So.
Yes?

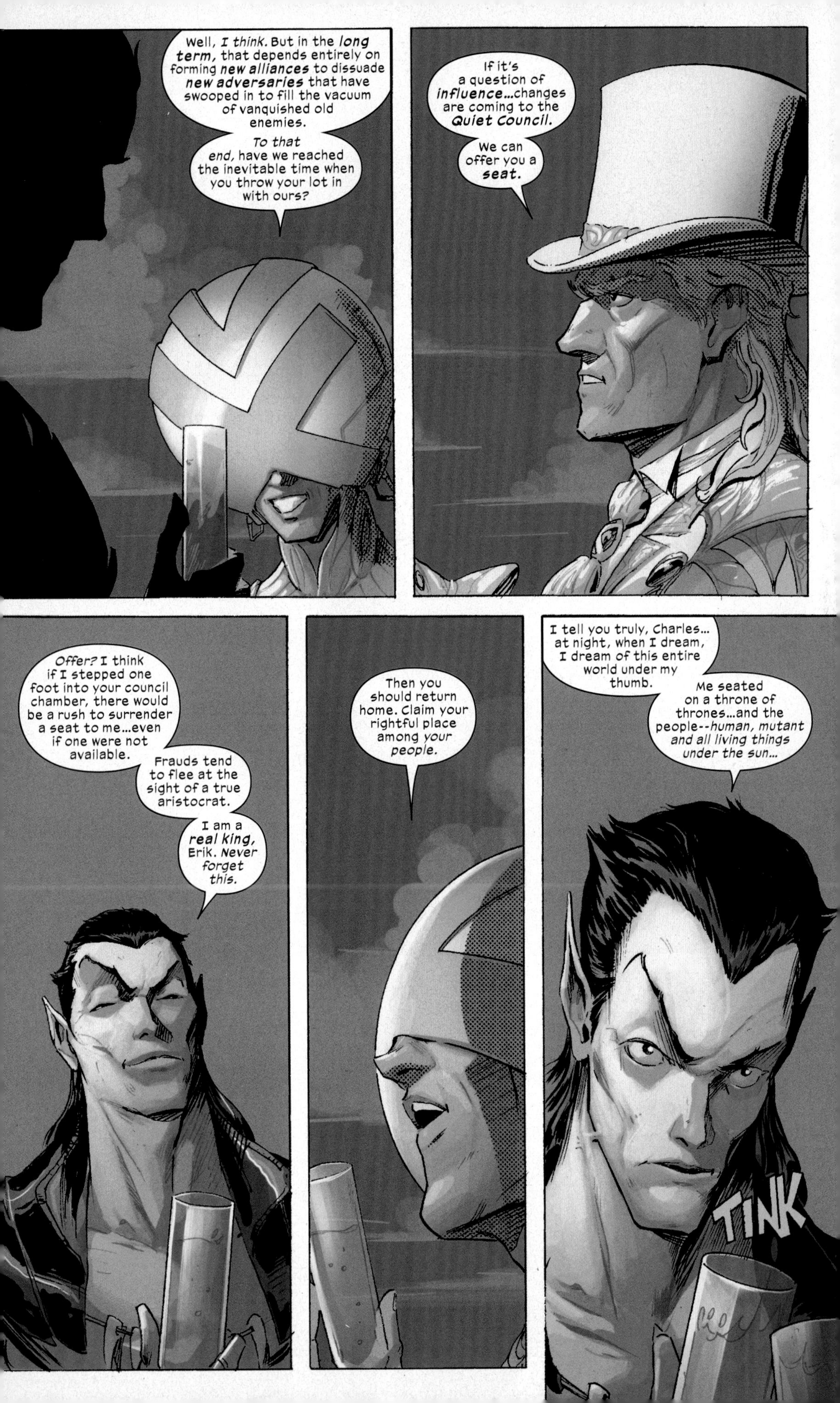
Well, *I think.* But in the *long term,* that depends entirely on forming ***new alliances*** to dissuade ***new adversaries*** that have swooped in to fill the vacuum of vanquished old enemies.
To that end, have we reached the inevitable time when you throw your lot in with ours?
If it's a question of ***influence***...changes are coming to the ***Quiet Council.***
We can offer you a ***seat.***
Offer? I think if I stepped one foot into your council chamber, there would be a rush to surrender a seat to me...even if one were not available.
Frauds tend to flee at the sight of a true aristocrat.
I am a ***real king,*** Erik. *Never* forget this.
Then you should return home. Claim your rightful place among *your people.*
I tell you truly, Charles... at night, when I dream, I dream of this entire world under my thumb.
Me seated on a throne of thrones...and the people--*human, mutant and all living things under the sun...*
TINK

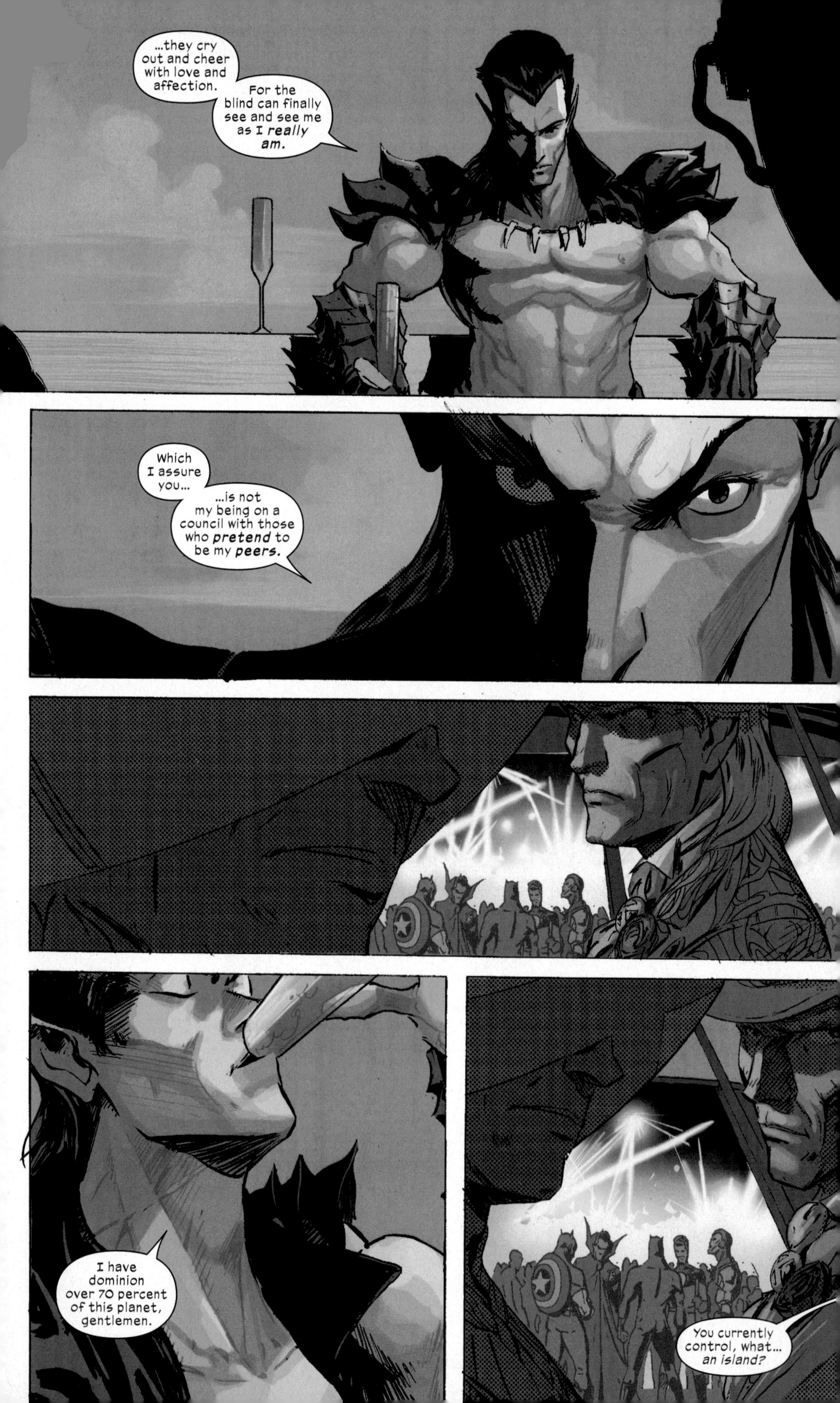
...they cry out and cheer with love and affection.
For the blind can finally see and see me as I *really am.*
Which I assure you...
...is not my being on a council with those who *pretend* to be my *peers.*
I have dominion over 70 percent of this planet, gentlemen.
You currently control, what... *an island?*

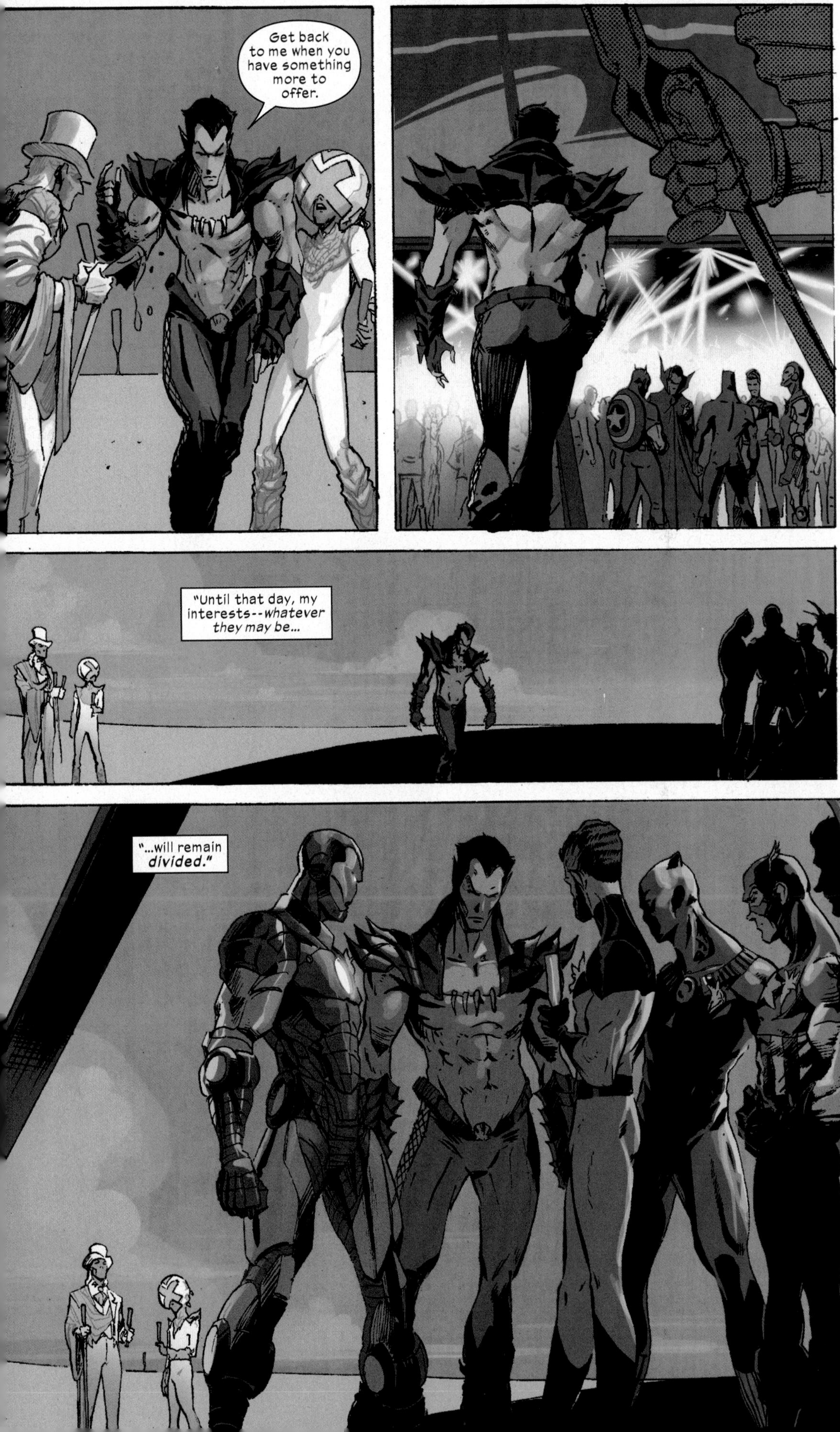
Get back to me when you have something more to offer.
"Until that day, my interests--*whatever* they may be...
"...will remain *divided.*"

[00_hellfire_gala_X]
[00_x-men__21]

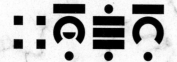

END OF AN ERA

At the first Krakoan Hellfire Gala, the mutant world is in flux. While an election is about to be held to select the X-MEN, the heroes of Krakoa, the new team is far from the only change coming...

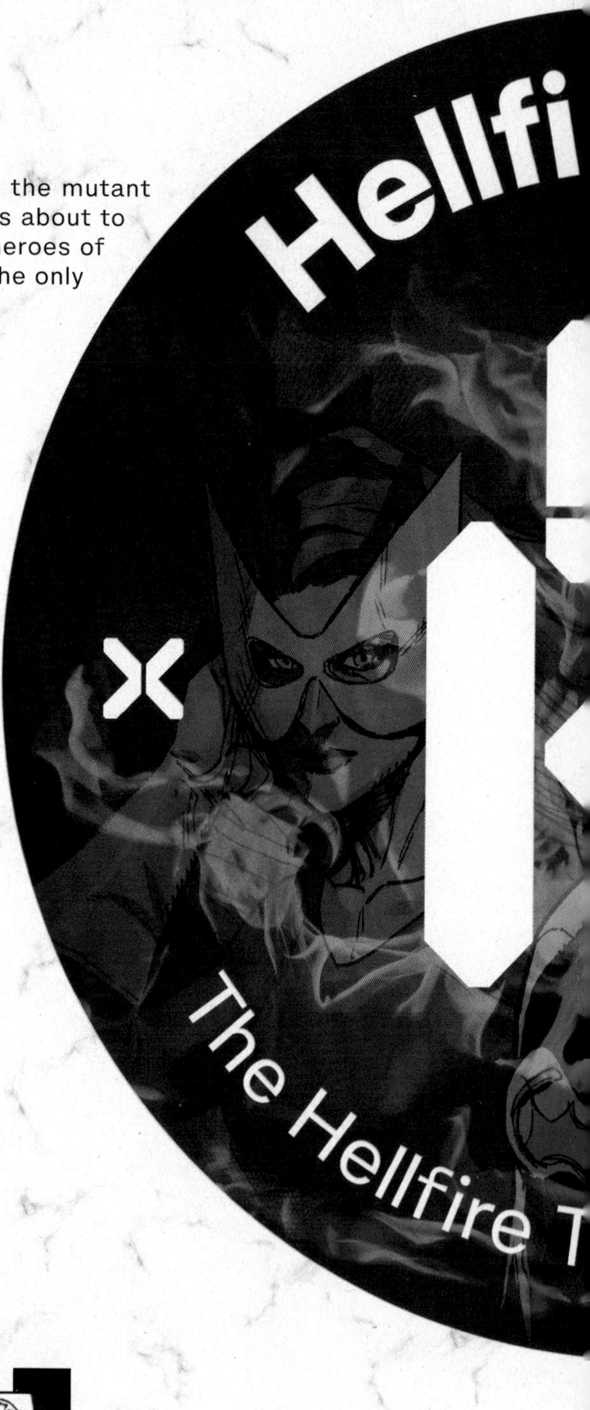

Hellfi
X
The Hellfire T

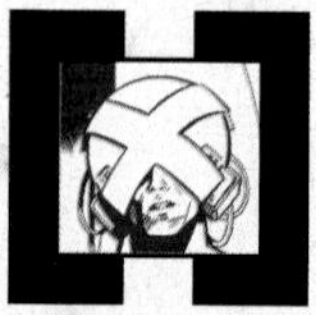
Professor X

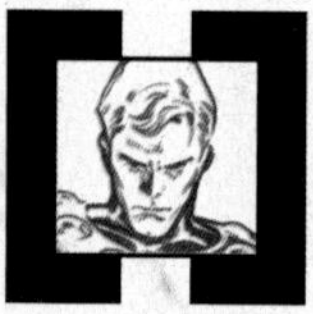
Magneto

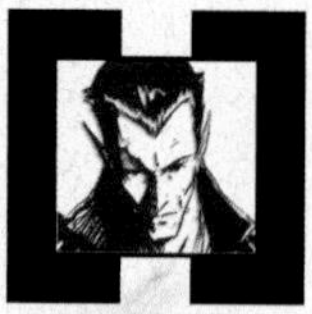
Namor

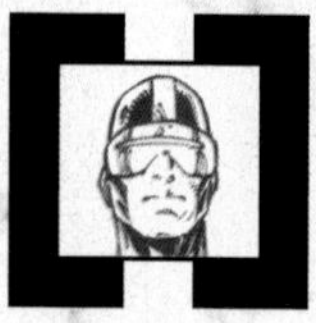
Cyclops

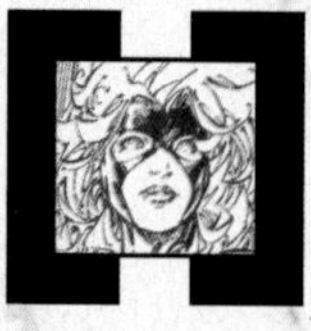
Jean Grey

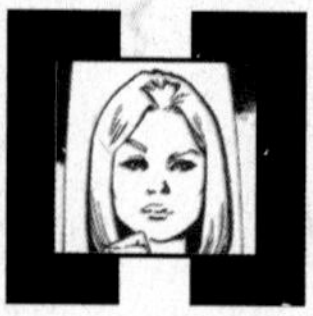
Emma Frost

[00_hellfire_gala_X]
[00_x-men__21]

X-MEN

[X_21]

[ISSUE TWENTY-ONE] ....
..........................THE BEGINNING

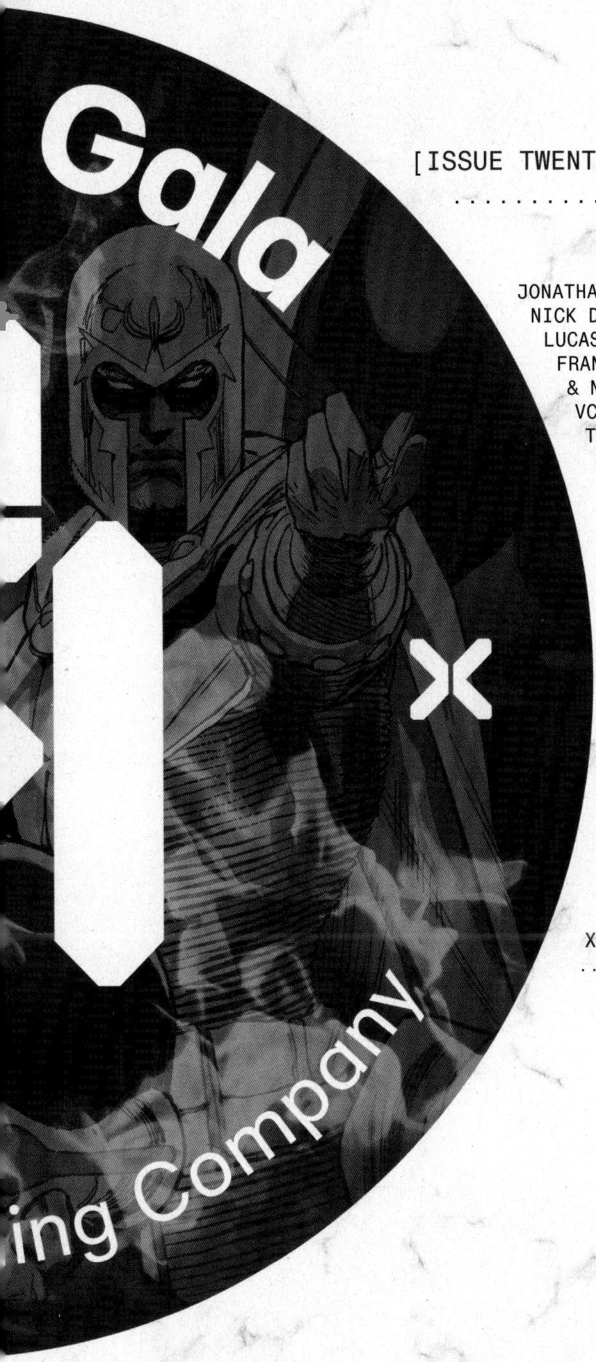
Gala
X
ing Company

JONATHAN HICKMAN ....[WRITER]
NICK DRAGOTTA, RUSSELL DAUTERMAN,
LUCAS WERNECK & SARA PICHELLI ...[ARTISTS]
FRANK MARTIN, MATTHEW WILSON, SUNNY GHO
& NOLAN WOODARD ....[COLOR ARTISTS]
VC's CLAYTON COWLES..........[LETTERER]
TOM MULLER....................[DESIGN]

LEINIL FRANCIS YU & SUNNY GHO
.....................[COVER ARTISTS]

LUKAS WERNECK ....
[X-MEN DESIGN VARIANT COVER ARTIST]

RUSSELL DAUTERMAN..................
.........[MARVEL GIRL DESIGN VARIANT
COVER ARTIST]

RUSSELL DAUTERMAN & MATTHEW WILSON
.........[CONNECTING COVER ARTISTS]

JONATHAN HICKMAN ....[HEAD OF X]
JAY BOWEN ....[PRODUCTION]
ANNALISE BISSA ....[ASSOCIATE EDITOR]
JORDAN D. WHITE ....[EDITOR]
C.B. CEBULSKI ....[EDITOR IN CHIEF]

X-MEN CREATED BY
..................STAN LEE & JACK KIRBY

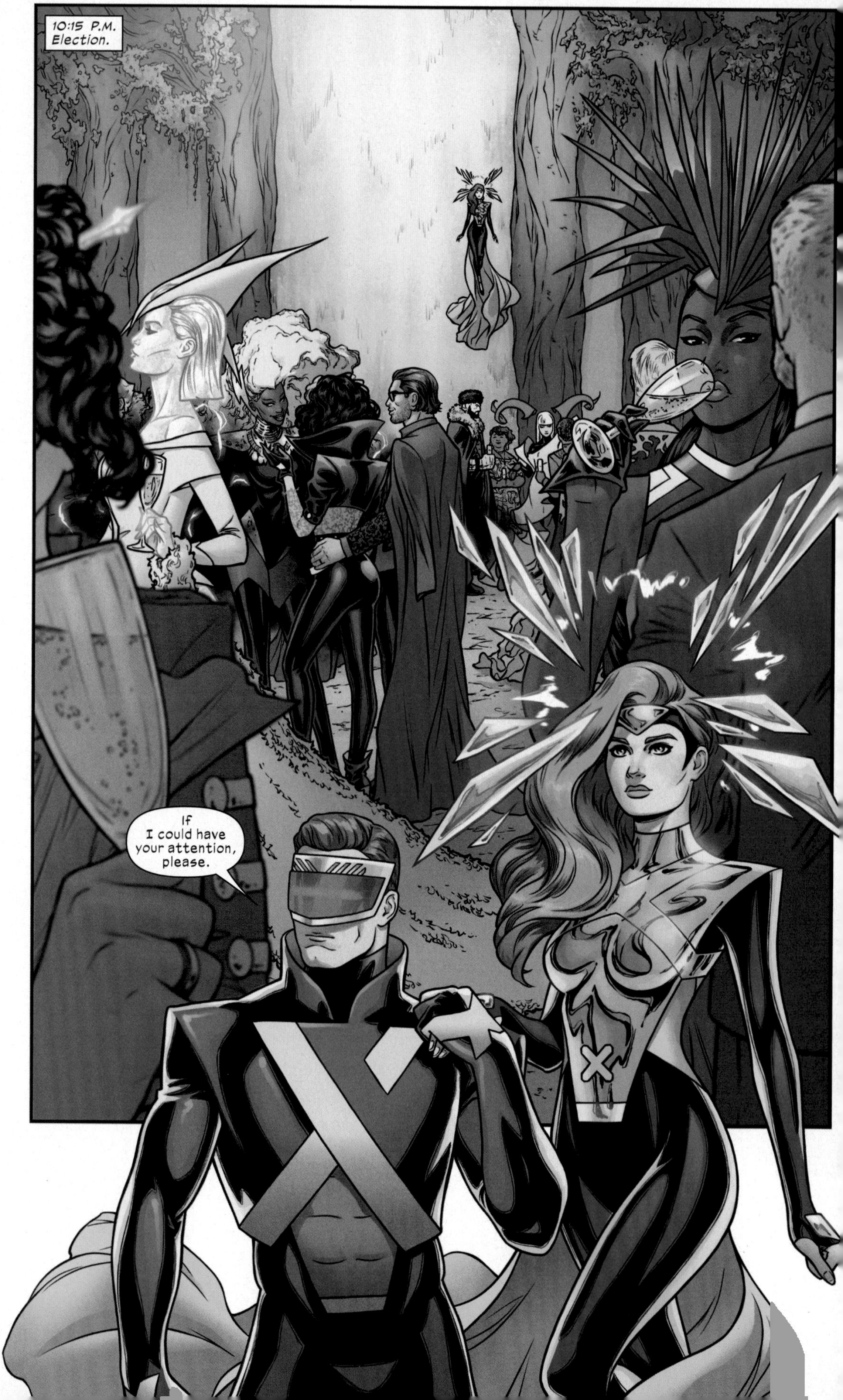
10:15 P.M.
Election.
If I could have your attention, please.

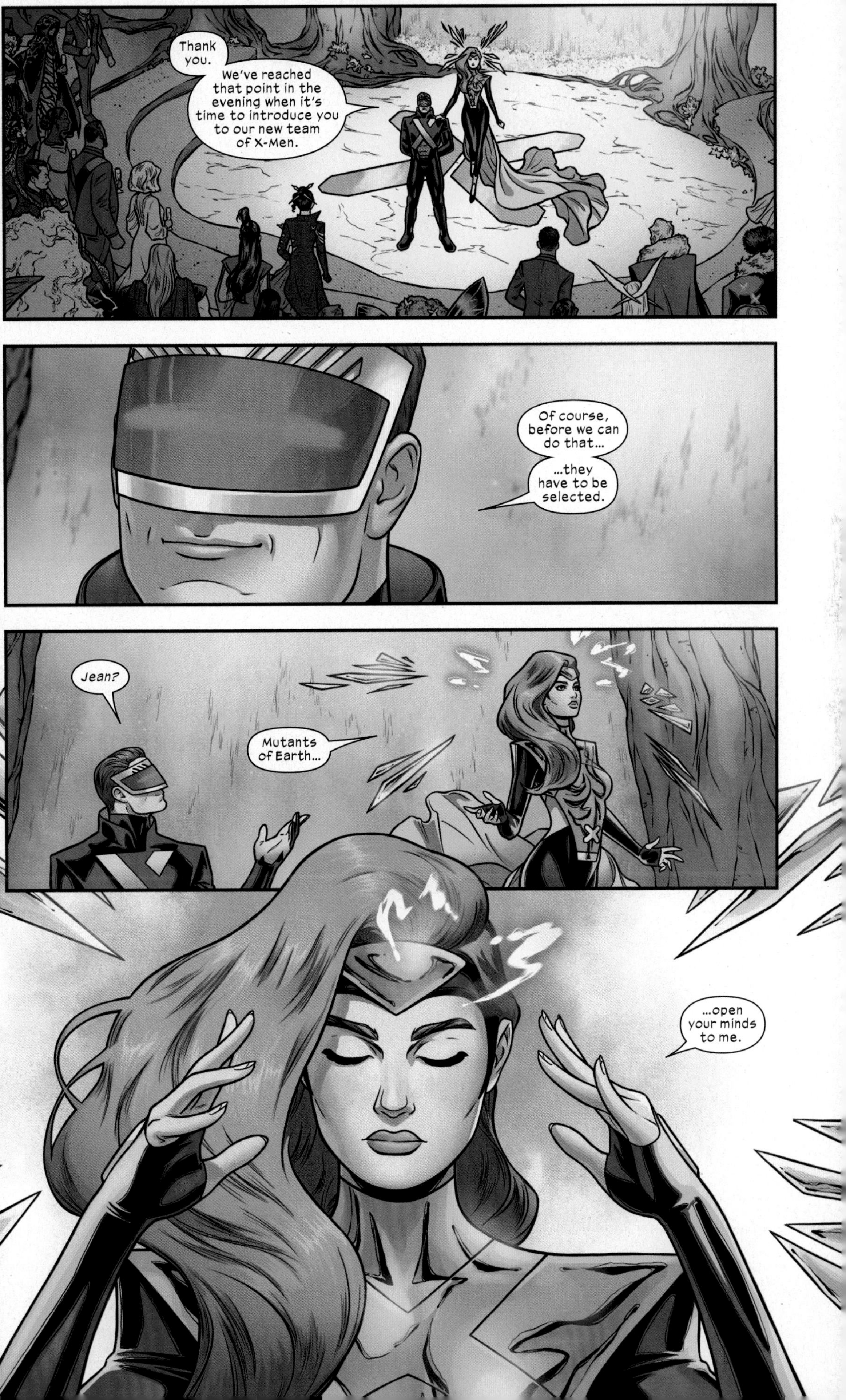
Thank you.
We've reached that point in the evening when it's time to introduce you to our new team of X-Men.
Of course, before we can do that...
...they have to be selected.
Jean?
Mutants of Earth...
...open your minds to me.

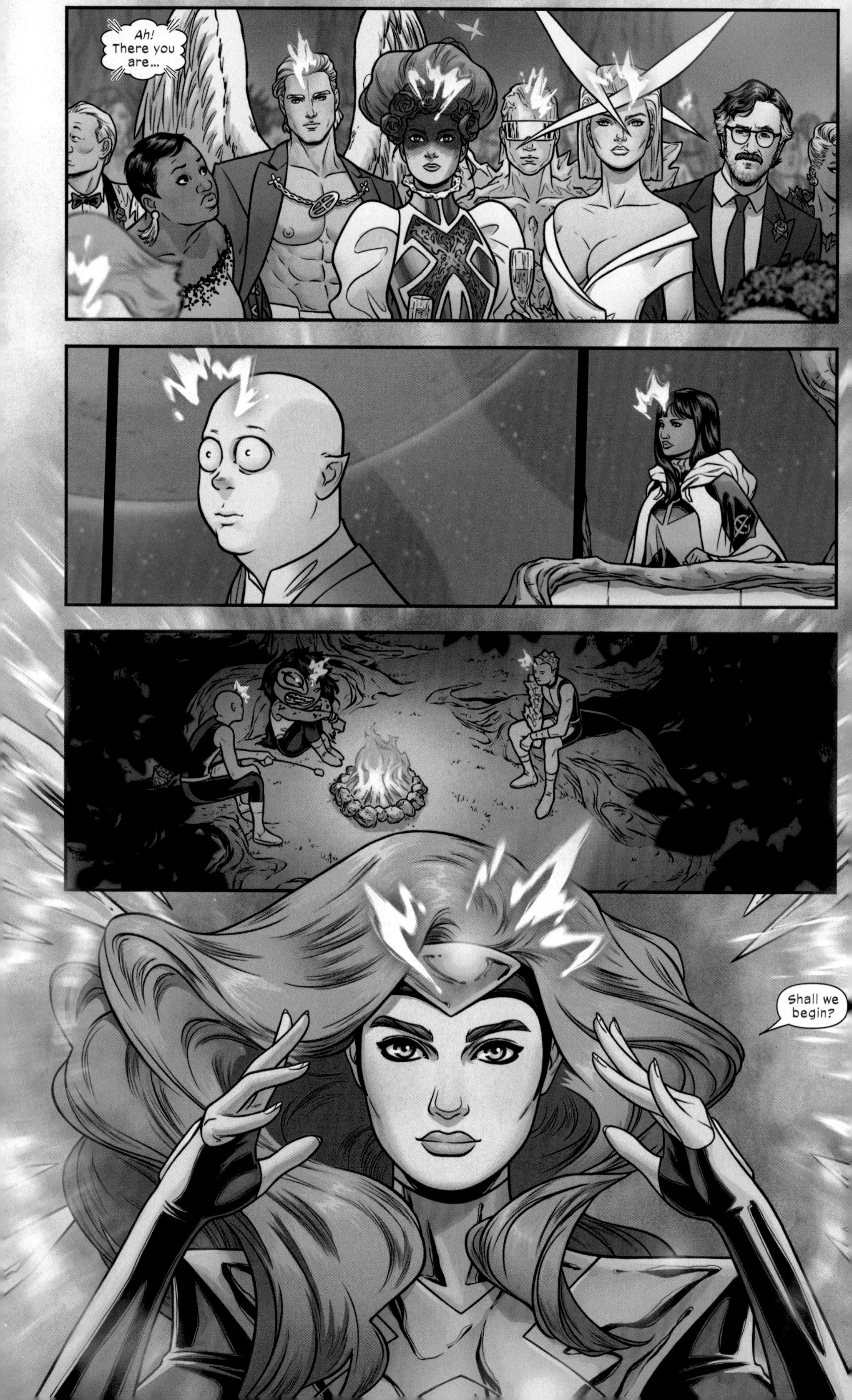
Ah! There you are...
Shall we begin?

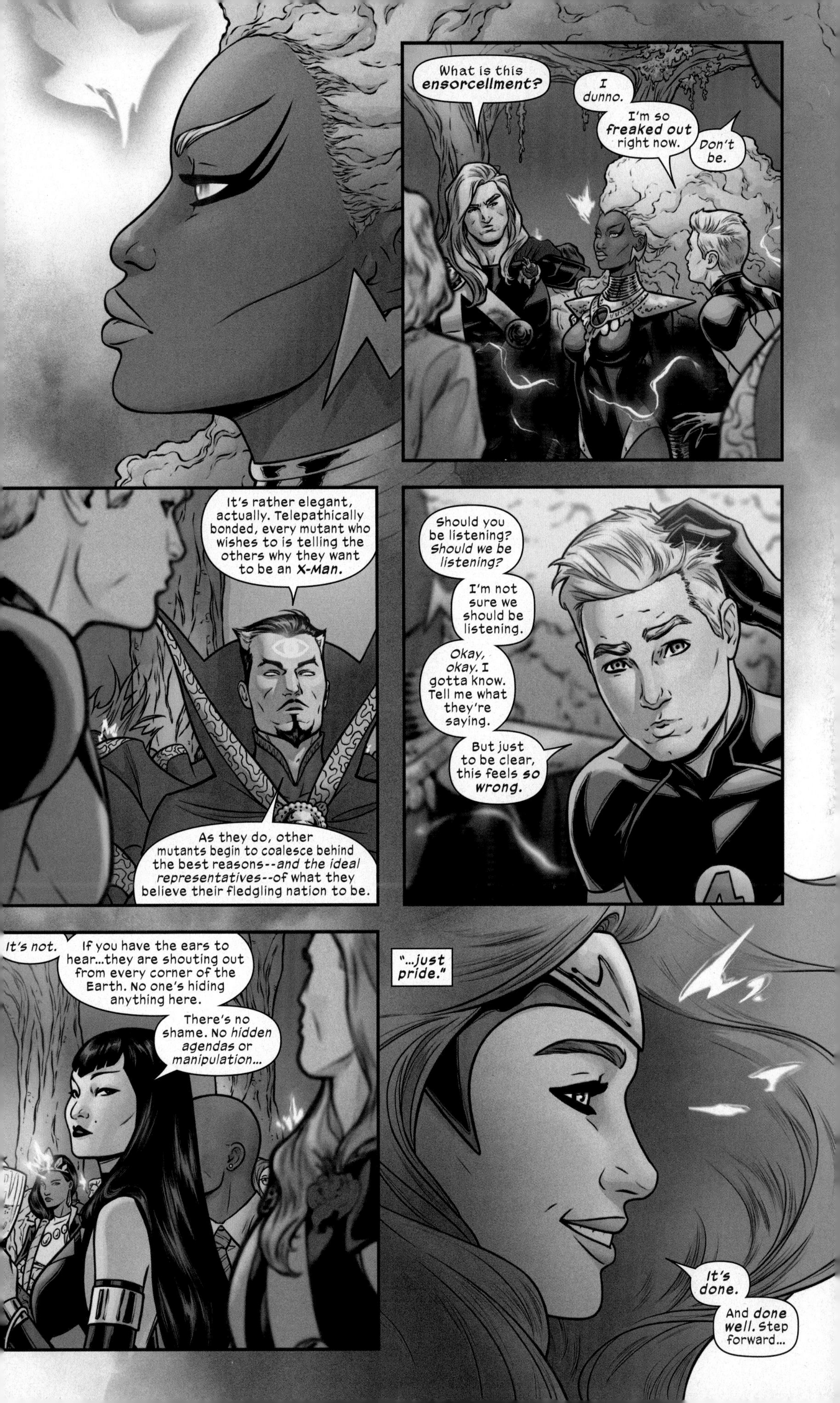
What is this ensorcellment?
I dunno.
I'm so freaked out right now.
Don't be.
It's rather elegant, actually. Telepathically bonded, every mutant who wishes to is telling the others why they want to be an X-Man.
As they do, other mutants begin to coalesce behind the best reasons--and the ideal representatives--of what they believe their fledgling nation to be.
Should you be listening? Should we be listening?
I'm not sure we should be listening.
Okay, okay. I gotta know. Tell me what they're saying.
But just to be clear, this feels so wrong.
It's not.
If you have the ears to hear...they are shouting out from every corner of the Earth. No one's hiding anything here.
There's no shame. No hidden agendas or manipulation...
"...just pride."
It's done.
And done well. Step forward...

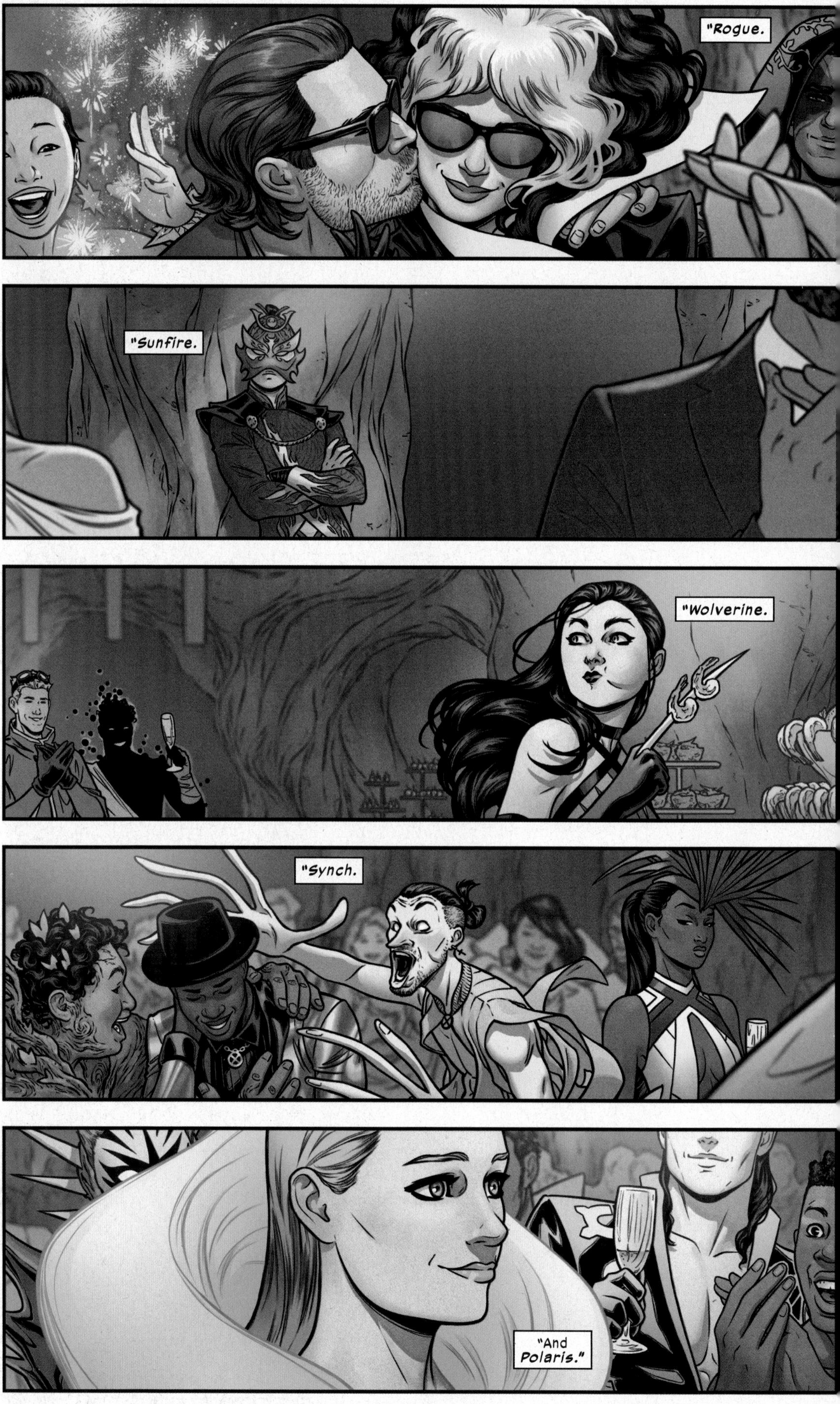
"Rogue.
"Sunfire.
"Wolverine.
"Synch.
"And Polaris."

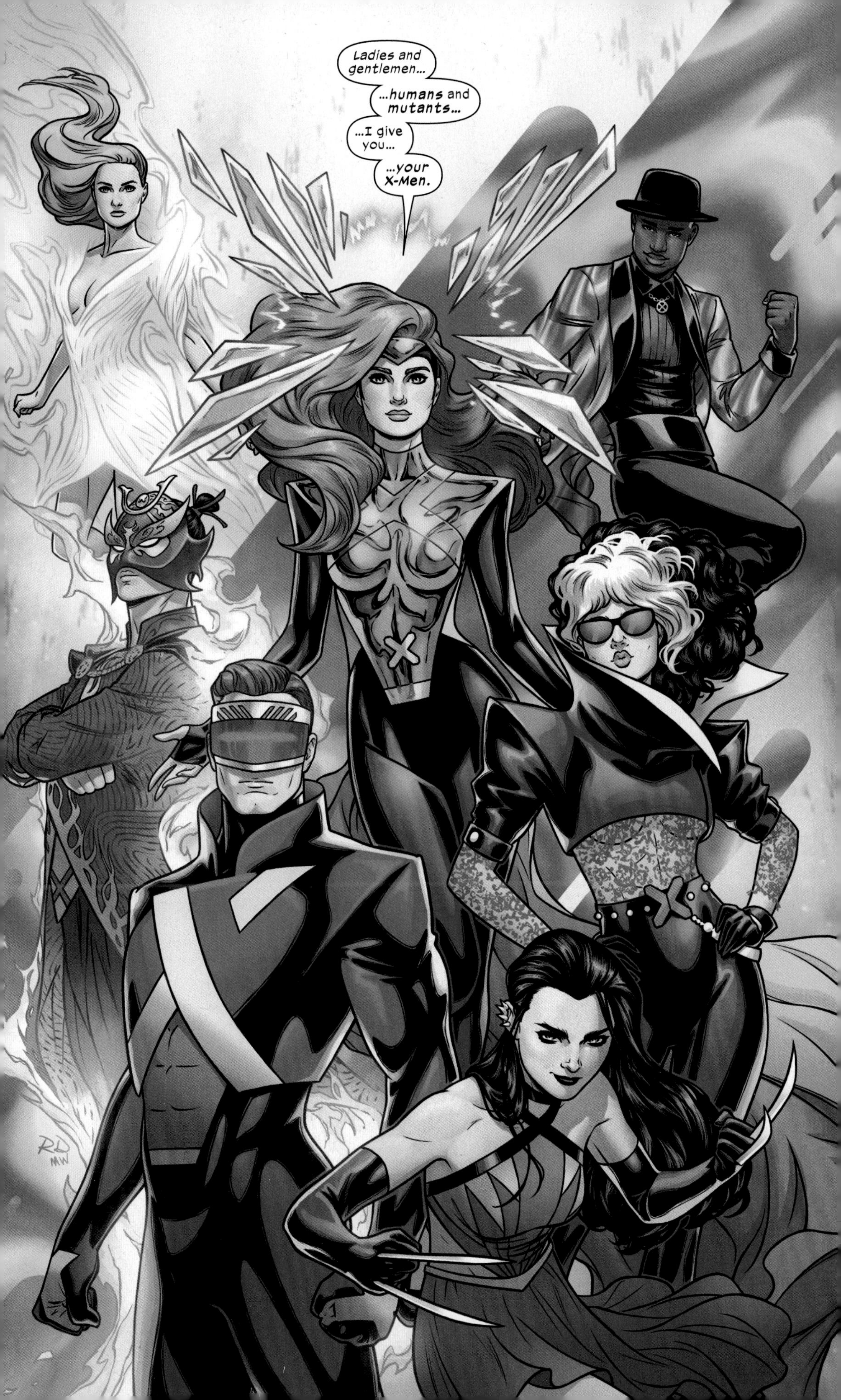

Ladies and gentlemen...
...humans and mutants...
...I give you...
...your X-Men.
RD MW

THE RED DIAMOND
[All the best news and gossip from Bar Sinister]

SINISTER SECRET #51
This Quiet Council member isn't actually fooling anyone, they're fooling everyone. Wear a mask long enough and eventually it starts wearing you. Such a shame, not being able to let things go.

SINISTER SECRET #52
She doesn't have it yet, but one way or another, this mutant always, always, always gets what she wants. Will it be given to her, or will it have to be taken? Doesn't matter -- the real question is: What's in the box? Could it be diamonds or something far more valuable?

SINISTER SECRET #53
I bet you'd like to know how this fittest-of-all mutant is handling the second genesis of his external life. Sorry, you'll have to wait to find out.

SINISTER SECRET #54
Seducer made an honest man of the island's favorite boy, but what unspoken secrets are coursing through the nervous system of the favorite boy's island friend? Are you listening? I know that you are.

SINISTER SECRET #55
Regarding secrets and secret alliances -- and the shadow play that is the great game of nations -- just how many ruling councils are there now circling the sun? I'll never tell, but if you say two, you're definitely too low.

SINISTER SECRET #56

And speaking of things that come in twos, two empty seats on the Quiet Council are two too many. Look for there to be moves made in the filling of those empty seats, regardless of how many favors have to be called in or how many unwise alliances are formed. Just remember: When everyone has a secret, no one can be trusted.

SINISTER SECRET #57

For far too long, they shared an existence. Now the one has become two. The first is a shattered captain of a demanding queen, and the second, a sinister sword under a sinister thumb. How long will the second stay there? How many more sinister demands will be too many? No one knows, but I think we're getting close.

SINISTER SECRET #58

It's still the early days of the Vescoran excavation of blight worlds, but an unknown material of immeasurable worth has begun appearing in the Crooked Market. So far, the Mad Jasper has snatched up every piece as soon as it's available for trade, but don't you worry -- our confederacy of capes is set on acquiring some. By hook or crook.

SINISTER SECRET #59

Promotions are hard to come by when everyone is a resurrected immortal, but sometimes a change has to be made when an unexpected variable is added to the equation. Heroes and their do-gooder ways -- always an inconvenience for a practical mutant.

SINISTER SECRETS REVEALED! [Reposted]

We don't hear this word spoken often, so when we do, it's best to pay attention, because when you square that circle, what took a long time to build can come crumbling down rather quickly.

[Inferno]

SINISTER SECRET #60

What sinister someone has been hard at work studying the vile helix of a vile world? *Pssst!* It's me! *Shhhhhhhh!*

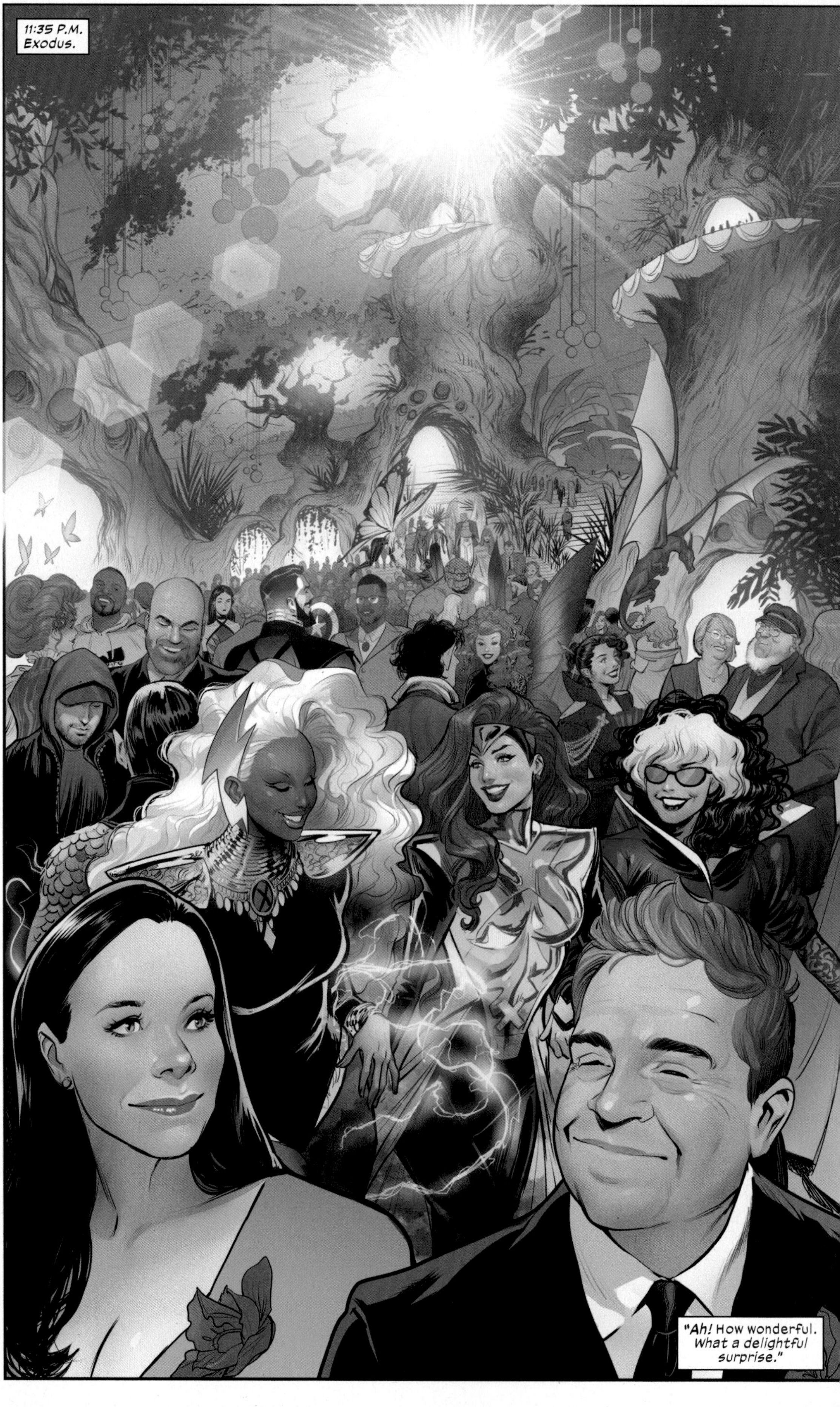
11:35 P.M.
Exodus.
"Ah! How wonderful. What a delightful surprise."

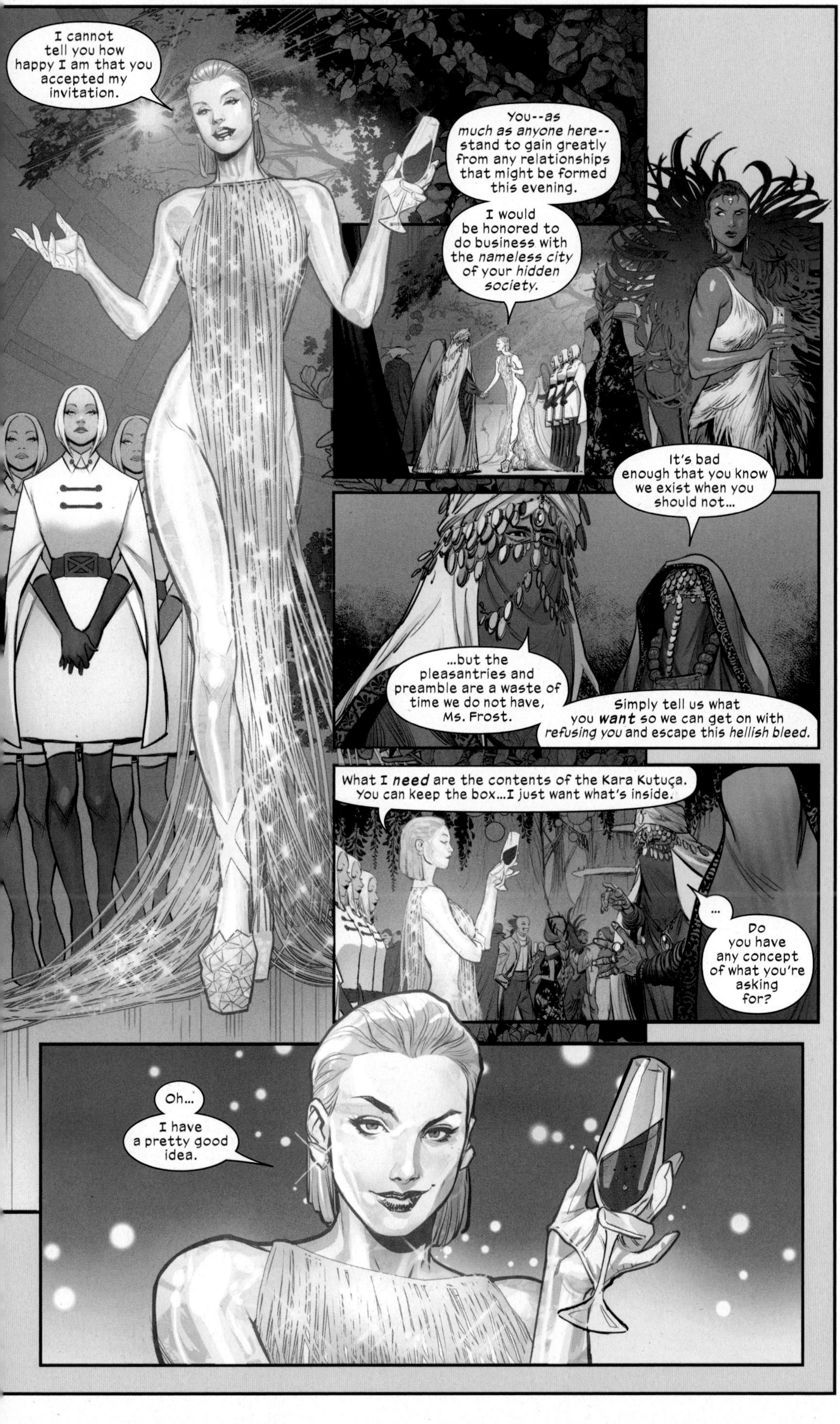
I cannot tell you how happy I am that you accepted my invitation.
You--as much as anyone here--stand to gain greatly from any relationships that might be formed this evening.
I would be honored to do business with the nameless city of your hidden society.
It's bad enough that you know we exist when you should not...
...but the pleasantries and preamble are a waste of time we do not have, Ms. Frost.
Simply tell us what you want so we can get on with refusing you and escape this hellish bleed.
What I need are the contents of the Kara Kutuça. You can keep the box...I just want what's inside.
...
Do you have any concept of what you're asking for?
Oh...
I have a pretty good idea.

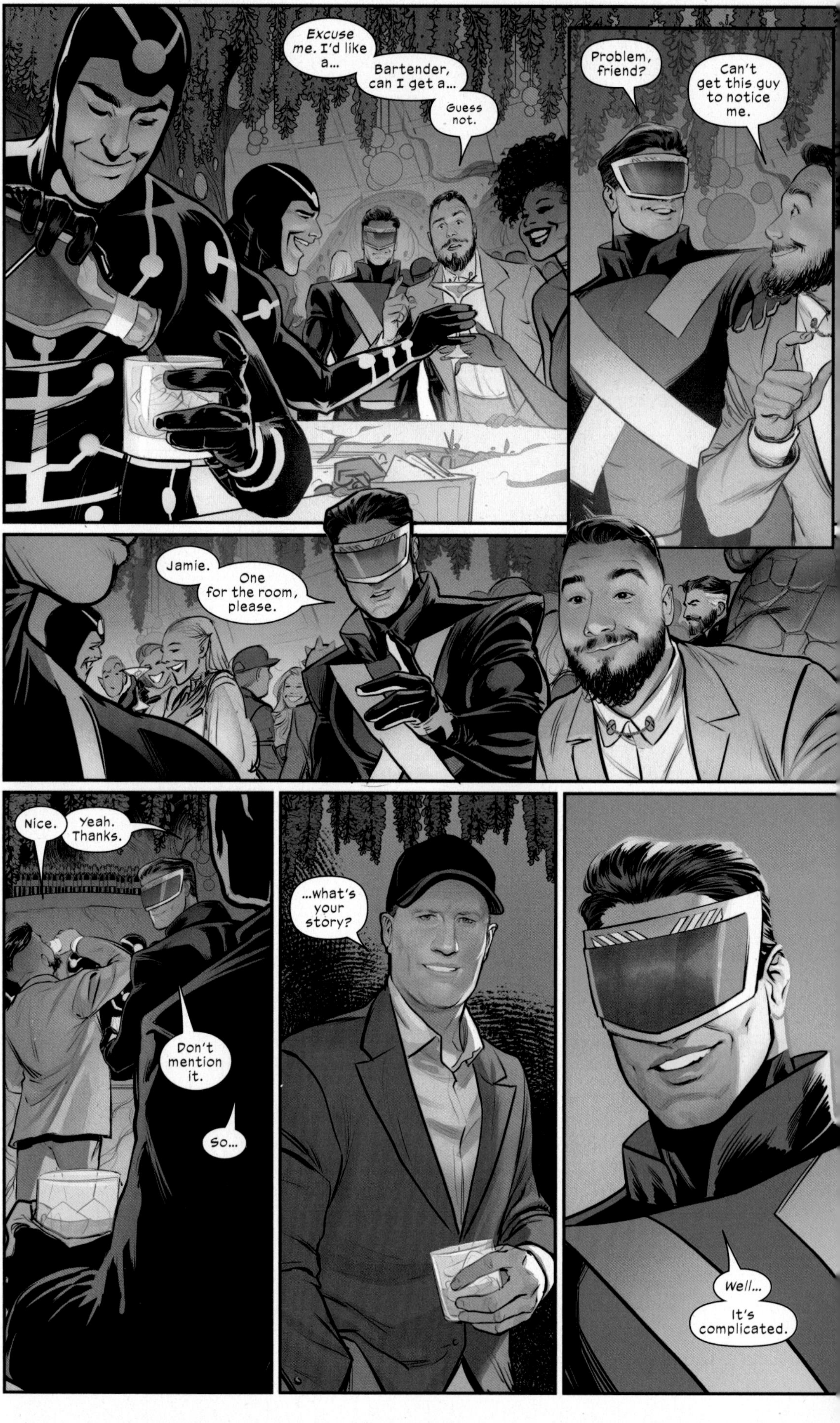

Excuse me. I'd like a...
Bartender, can I get a...
Guess not.
Problem, friend?
Can't get this guy to notice me.
Jamie.
One for the room, please.
Nice.
Yeah. Thanks.
Don't mention it.
So...
...what's your story?
Well...
It's complicated.

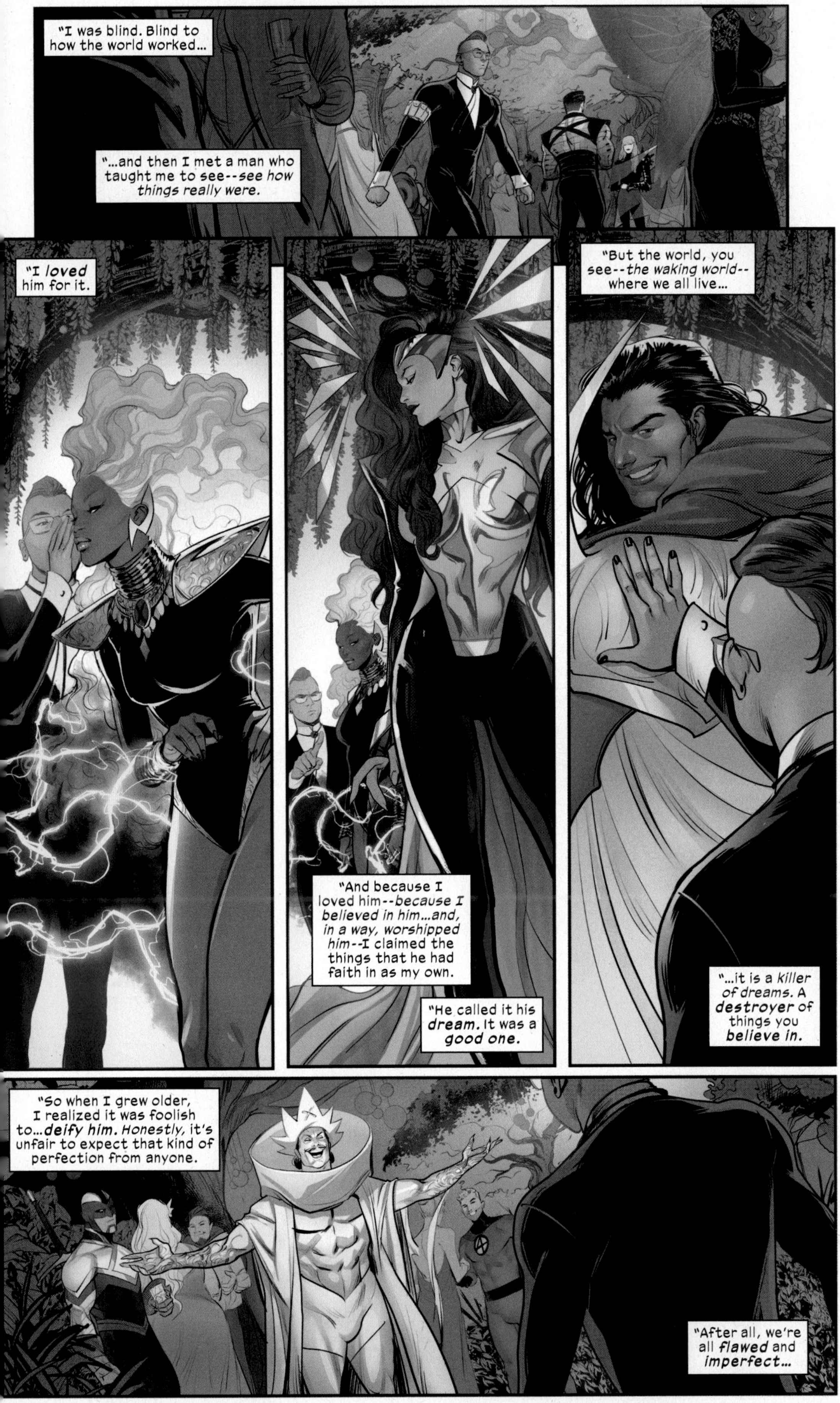
"I was blind. Blind to how the world worked...
"...and then I met a man who taught me to see--*see how things really were.*
"I *loved* him for it.
"And because I loved him--*because I believed in him...and, in a way, worshipped him*--I claimed the things that he had faith in as my own.
"He called it his ***dream.*** It was a ***good one.***
"But the world, you see--*the waking world*--where we all live...
"...it is a *killer of dreams.* A ***destroyer*** of things you ***believe in.***
"So when I grew older, I realized it was foolish to...***deify him.*** *Honestly,* it's unfair to expect that kind of perfection from anyone.
"After all, we're all ***flawed*** and ***imperfect...***

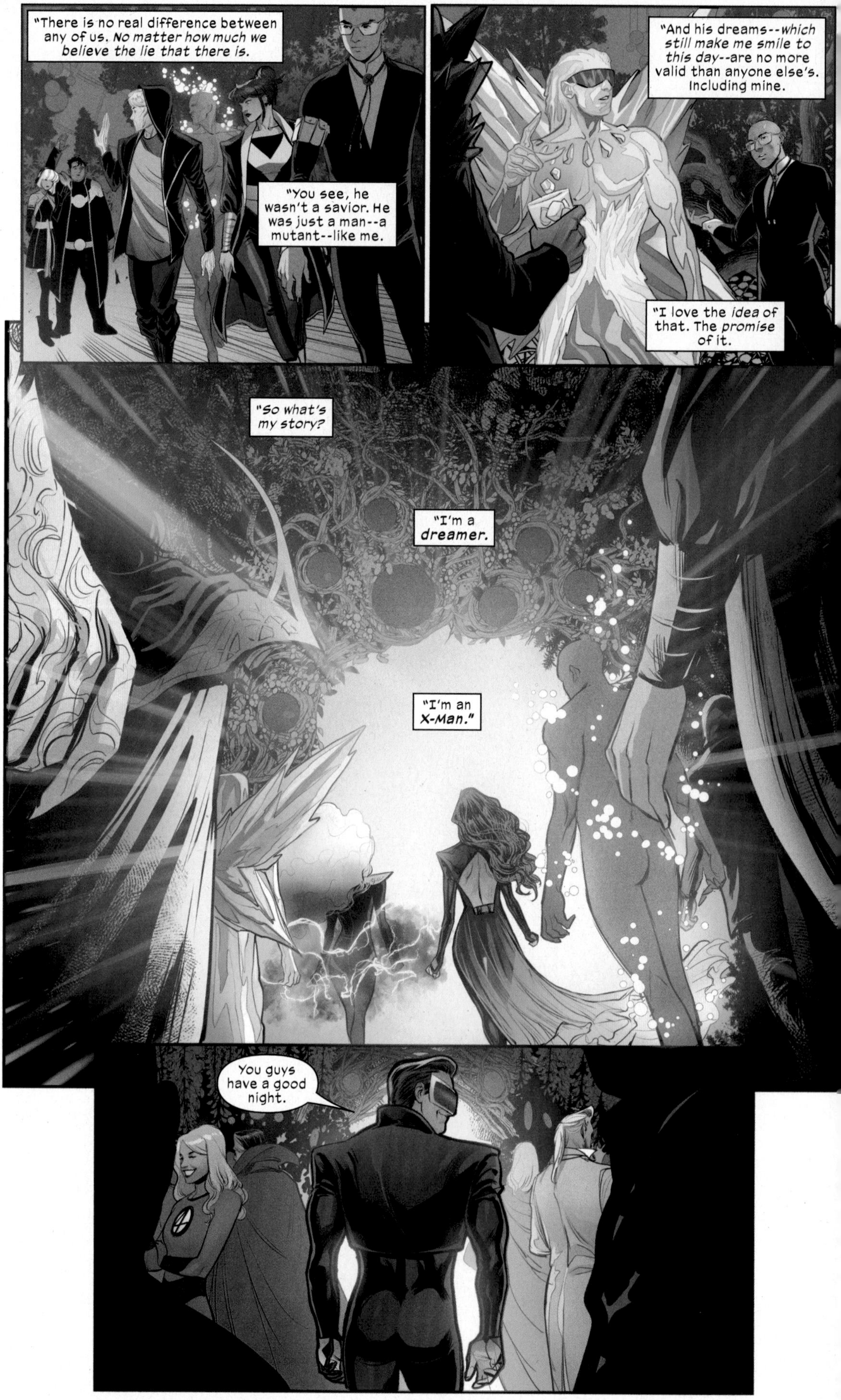
"There is no real difference between any of us. *No matter how much we believe the lie that there is.*
"You see, he wasn't a savior. He was just a man--a mutant--like me.
"And his dreams--*which still make me smile to this day*--are no more valid than anyone else's. Including mine.
"I love the *idea* of that. The *promise* of it.
"So what's my story?
"I'm a *dreamer.*
"I'm an *X-Man.*"
You guys have a good night.

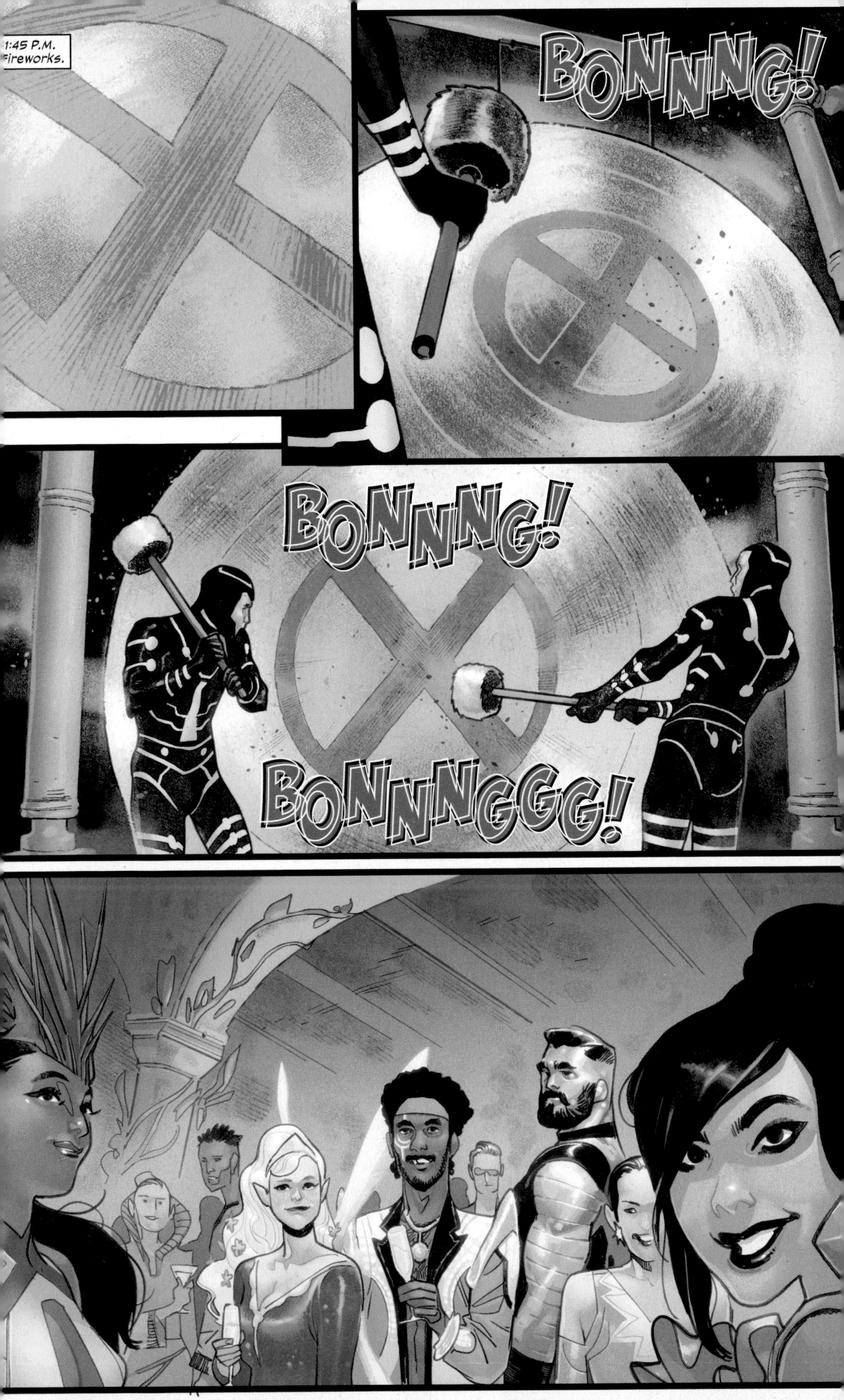

1:45 P.M.
Fireworks.
BONNNG!
BONNNG!
BONNNGGG!

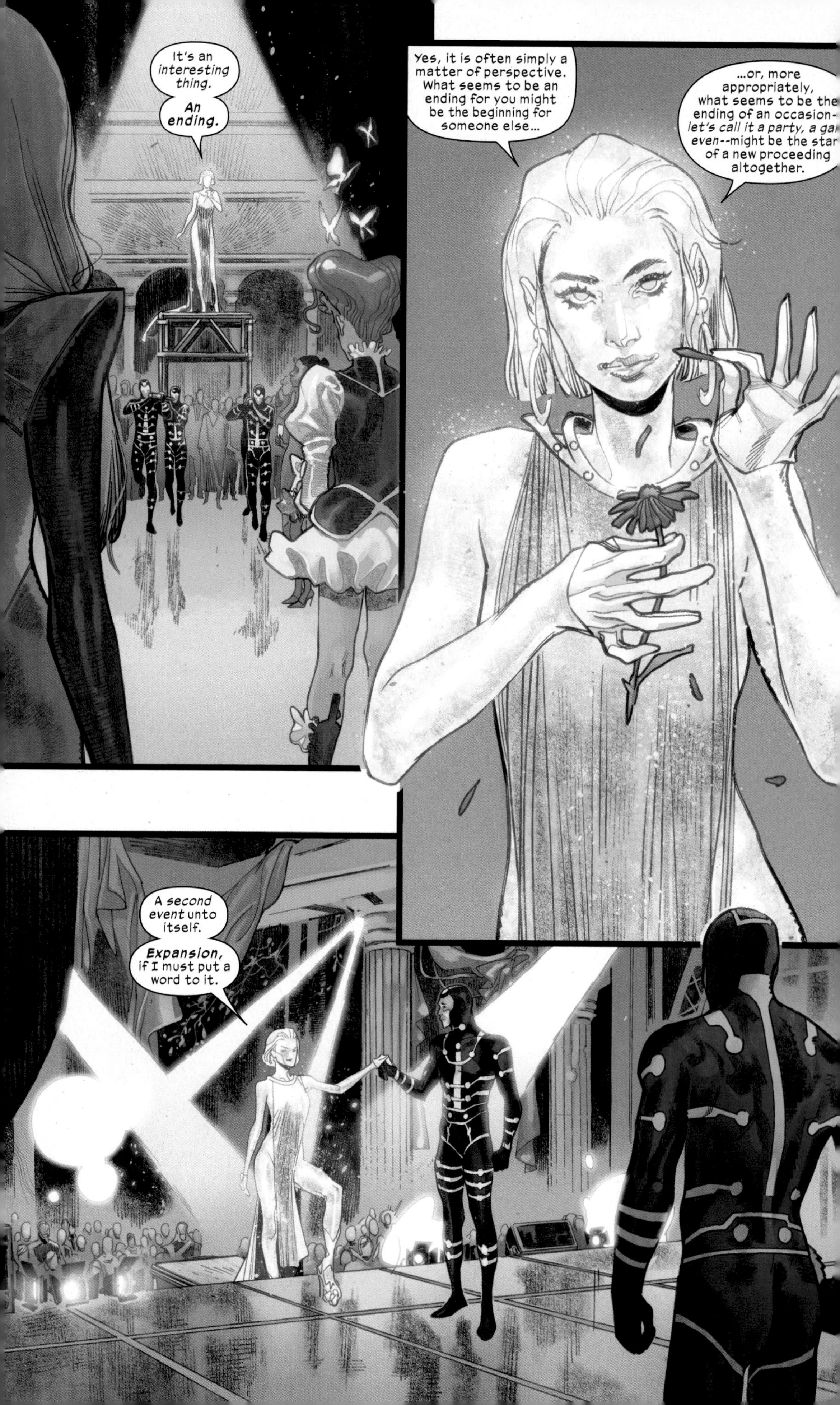
It's an interesting thing.
An ending.
Yes, it is often simply a matter of perspective. What seems to be an ending for you might be the beginning for someone else...
...or, more appropriately, what seems to be the ending of an occasion-let's call it a party, a ga even--might be the star of a new proceeding altogether.
A second event unto itself.
Expansion, if I must put a word to it.

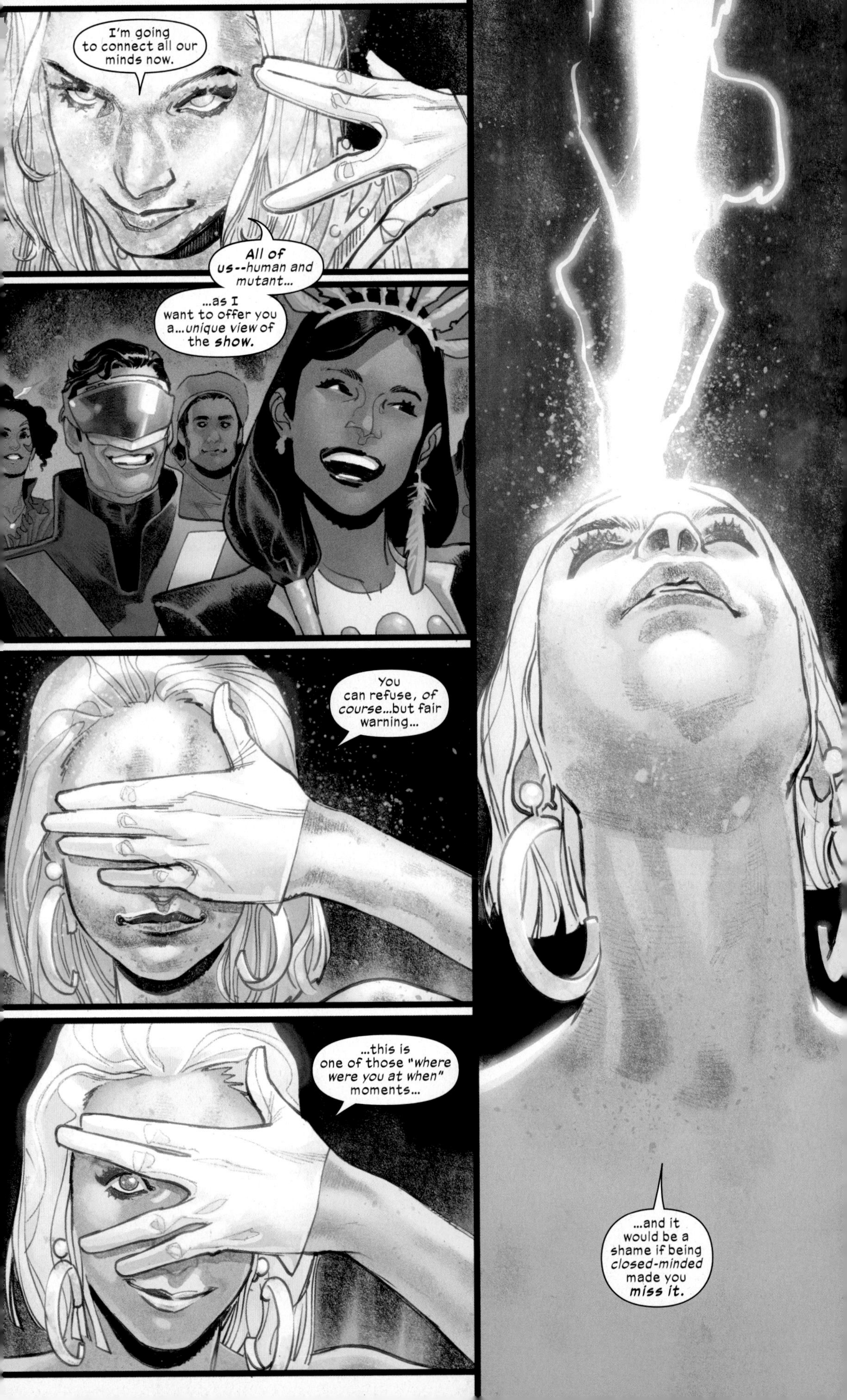
I'm going to connect all our minds now.
All of us--human and mutant...
...as I want to offer you a...unique view of the show.
You can refuse, of course...but fair warning...
...this is one of those "where were you at when" moments...
...and it would be a shame if being closed-minded made you miss it.

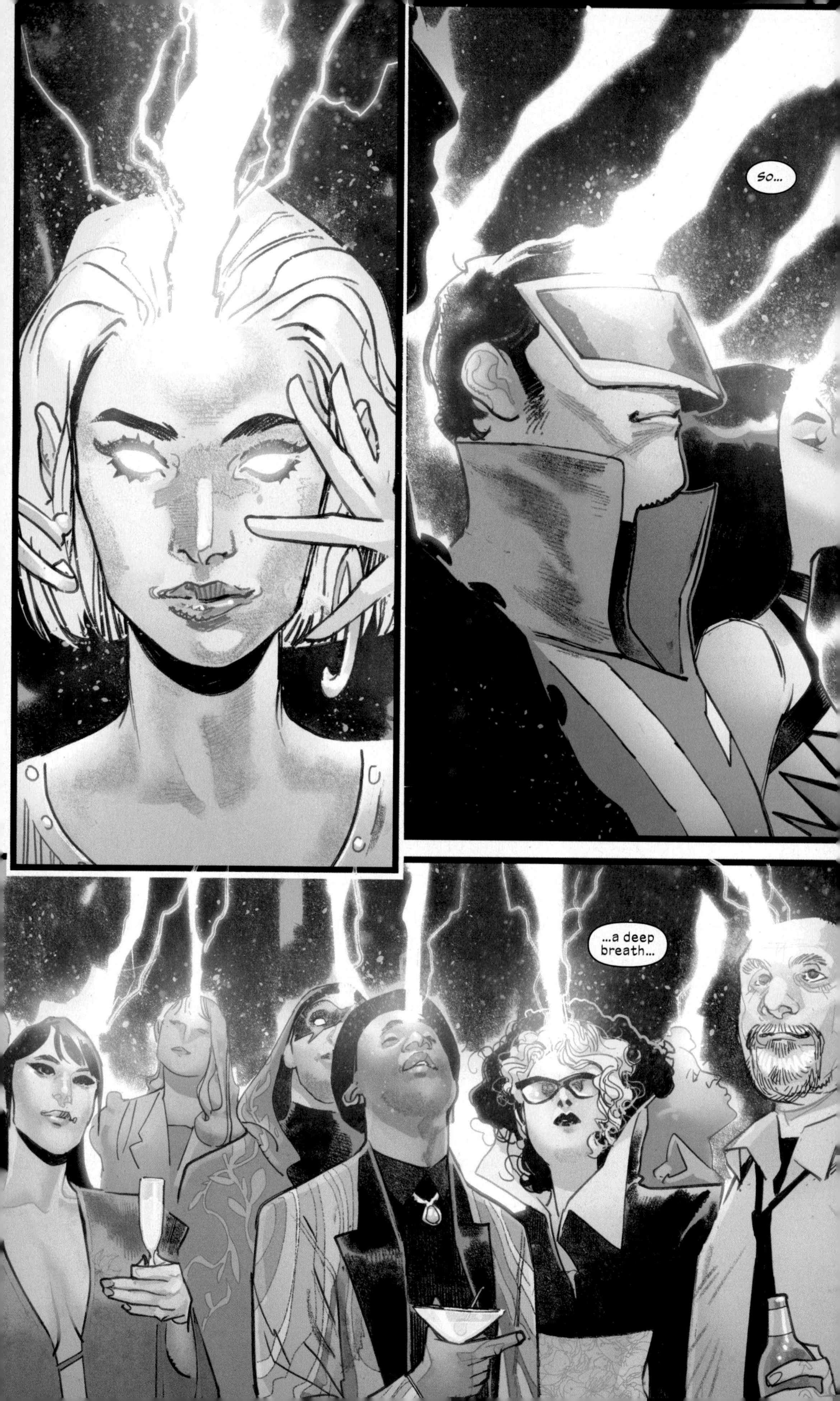
SO...
...a deep breath...

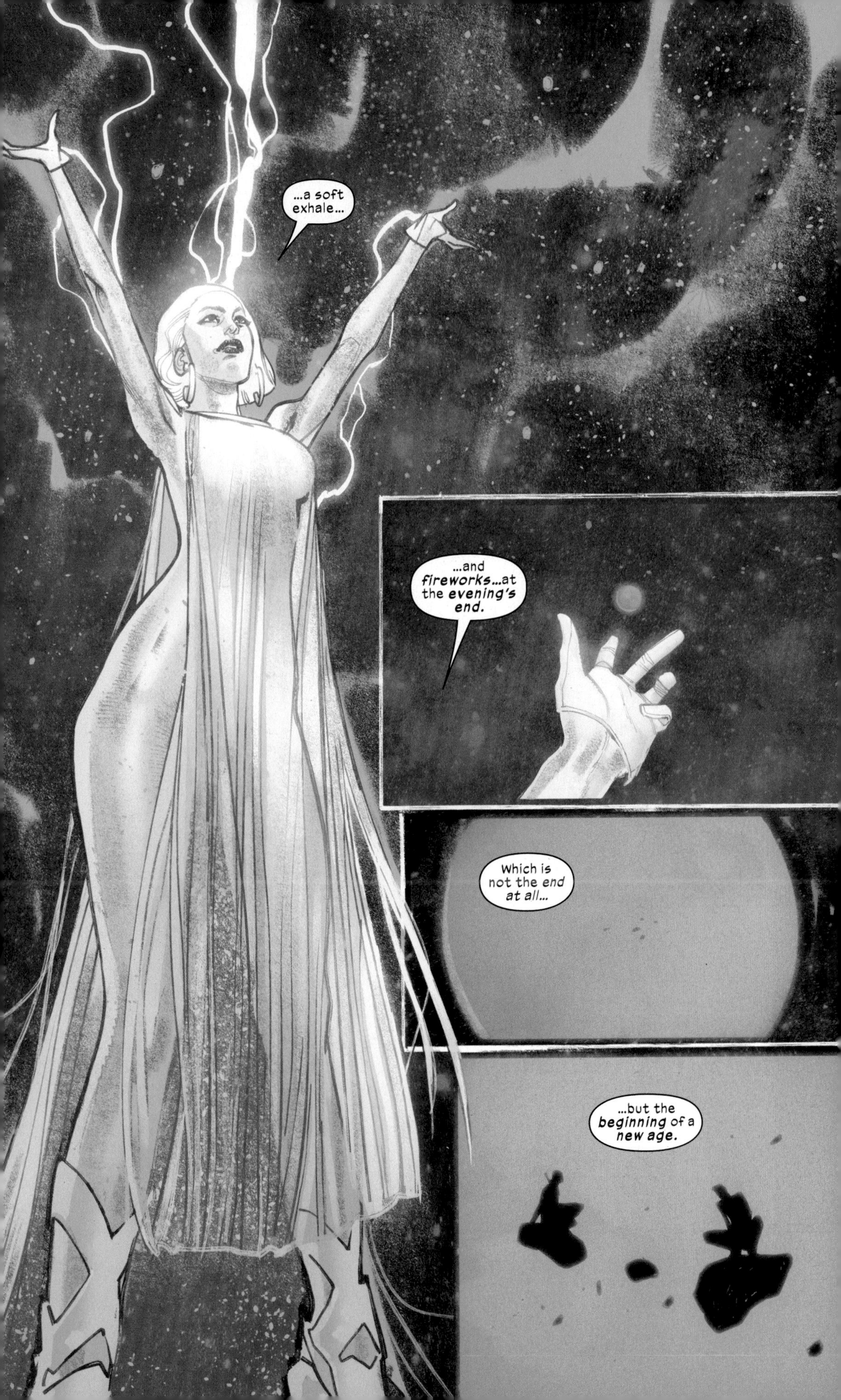

...a soft exhale...
...and fireworks...at the evening's end.
Which is not the end at all...
...but the beginning of a new age.

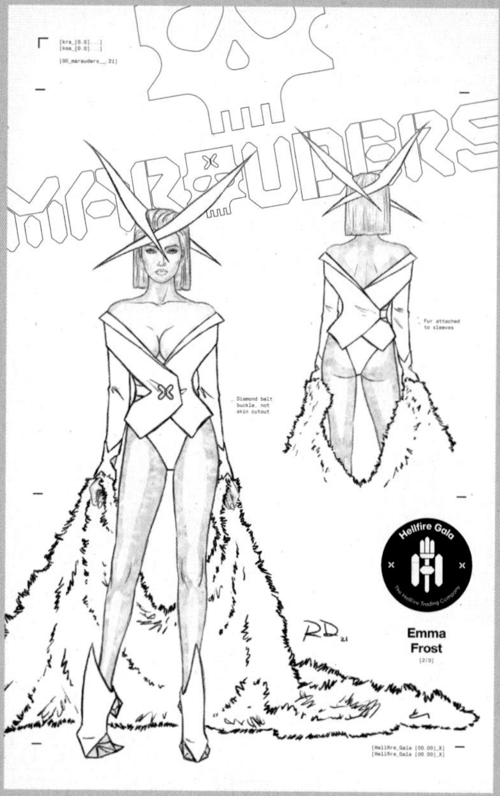
MARAUDERS
Fur attached to sleeves
Diamond belt buckle, not skin cutout
Hellfire Gala
The Hellfire Trading Company
RD 21
Emma Frost
[2/3]

Marauders #21 Design Variant
by Russell Dauterman

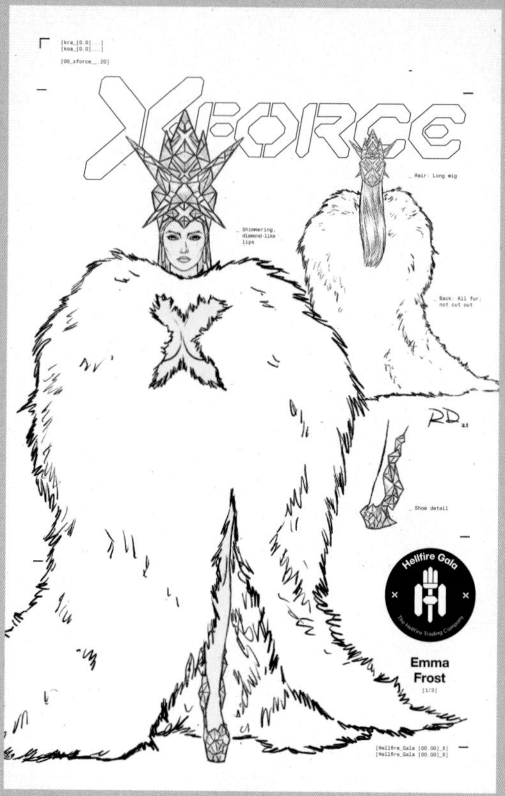
X-FORCE
Hair: Long wig
Shimmering, diamond-like lips
Back: All fur; not cut out
Shoe detail
Hellfire Gala
The Hellfire Trading Company
RD 21
Emma Frost
[1/3]

X-Force #20 Design Variant
by Russell Dauterman

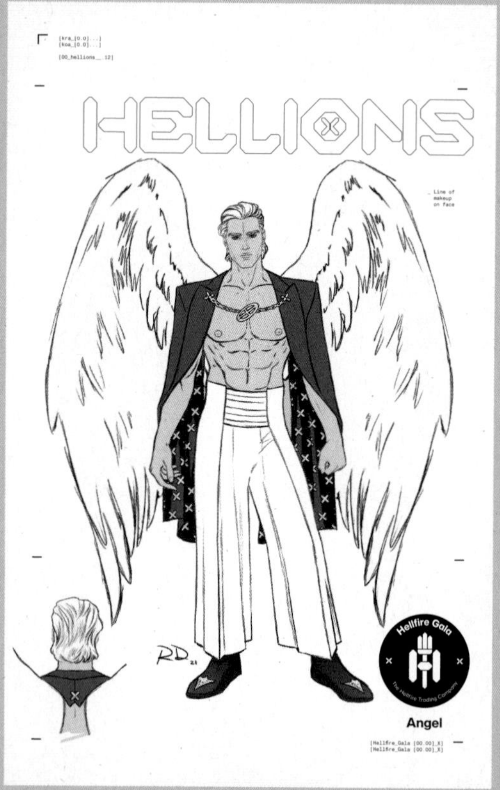
HELLIONS
Line of makeup on face
Hellfire Gala
The Hellfire Trading Company
RD 21
Angel

Hellions #21 Design Variant
by Russell Dauterman

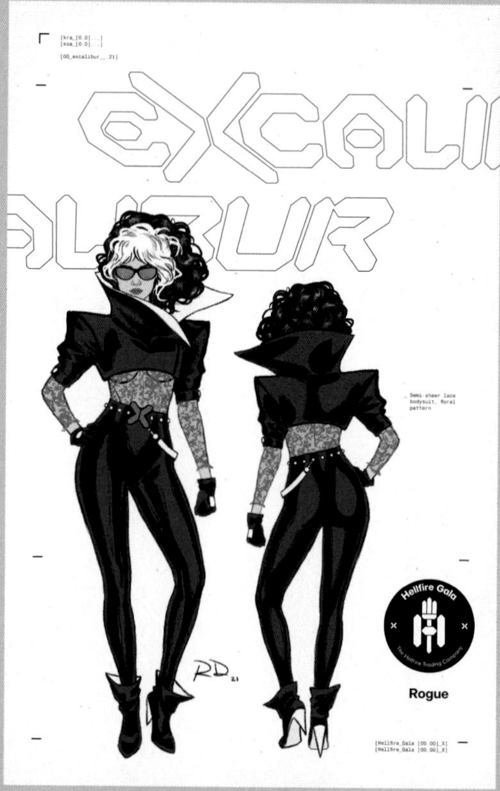
EXCALIBUR
Semi-sheer lace bodysuit, floral pattern
Hellfire Gala
The Hellfire Trading Company
RD 21
Rogue

Excalibur #21 Design Variant
by Russell Dauterman

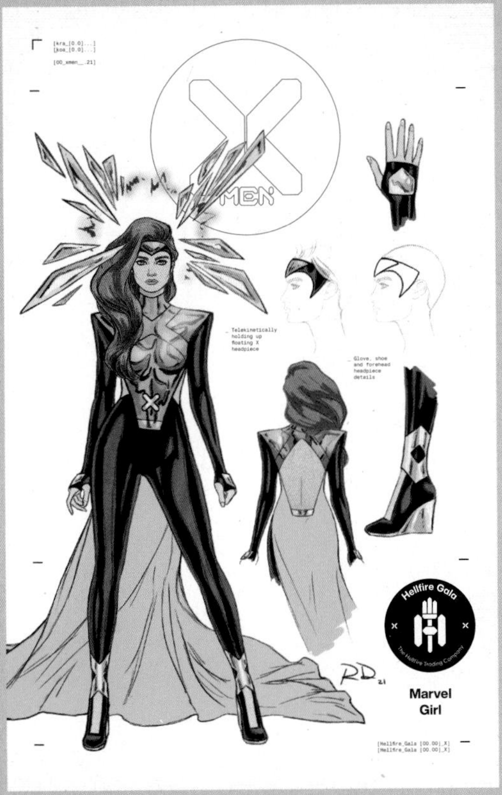
Telekinetically holding up floating X headpiece
Glove, shoe and forehead headpiece details
Hellfire Gala
The Hellfire Trading Company
Marvel Girl

X-Men #21 Design Variant
by Russell Dauterman

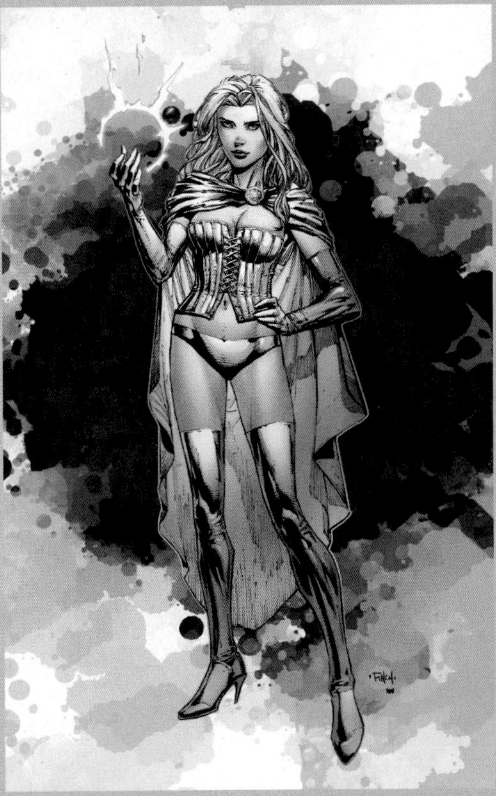

Marauders #21 Variant
by David Finch & Frank D'Armata

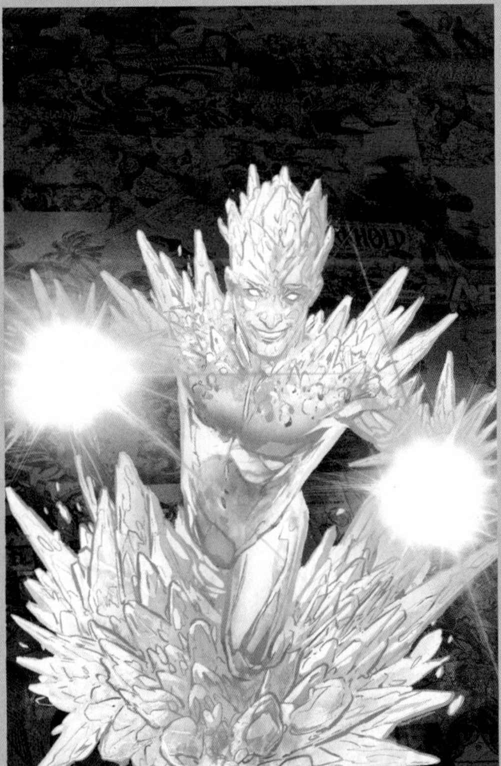

Marauders #21 Pride Month Variant
by Phil Jimenez & Marte Gracia

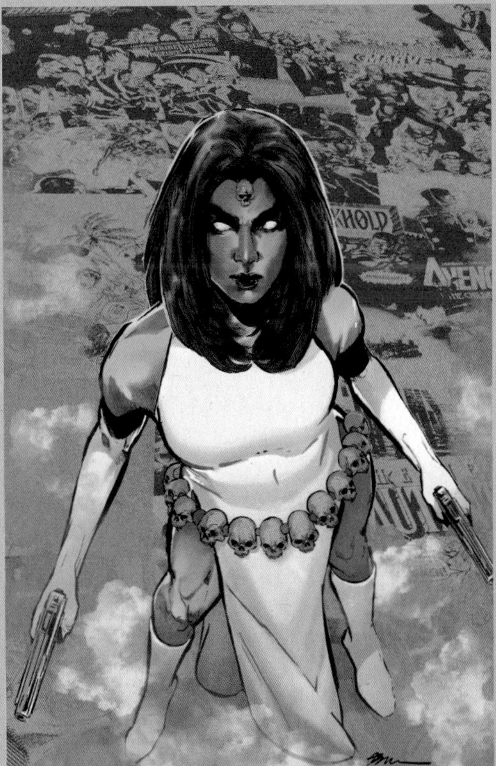

X-Men #21 Pride Month Variant
by Phil Jimenez & Marte Gracia

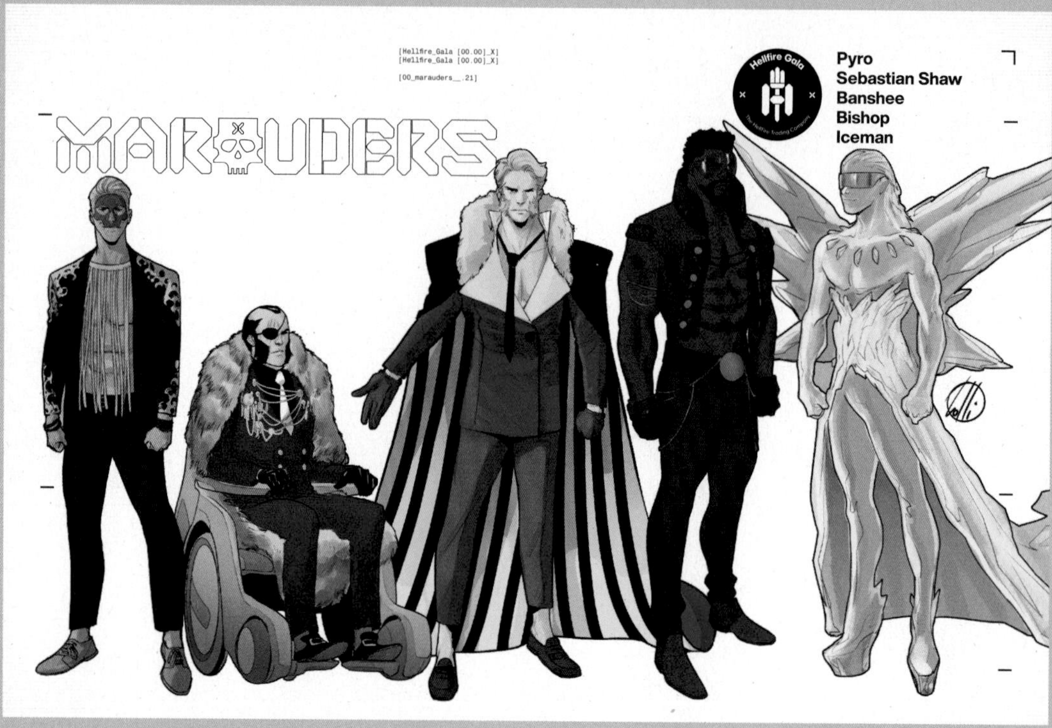

[Hellfire_Gala [00.00]_X]
[Hellfire_Gala [00.00]_X]
[00_marauders__.21]
MARAUDERS
Hellfire Gala
The Hellfire Trading Company
Pyro
Sebastian Shaw
Banshee
Bishop
Iceman

Marauders #21 Design Variant
by Matteo Lolli

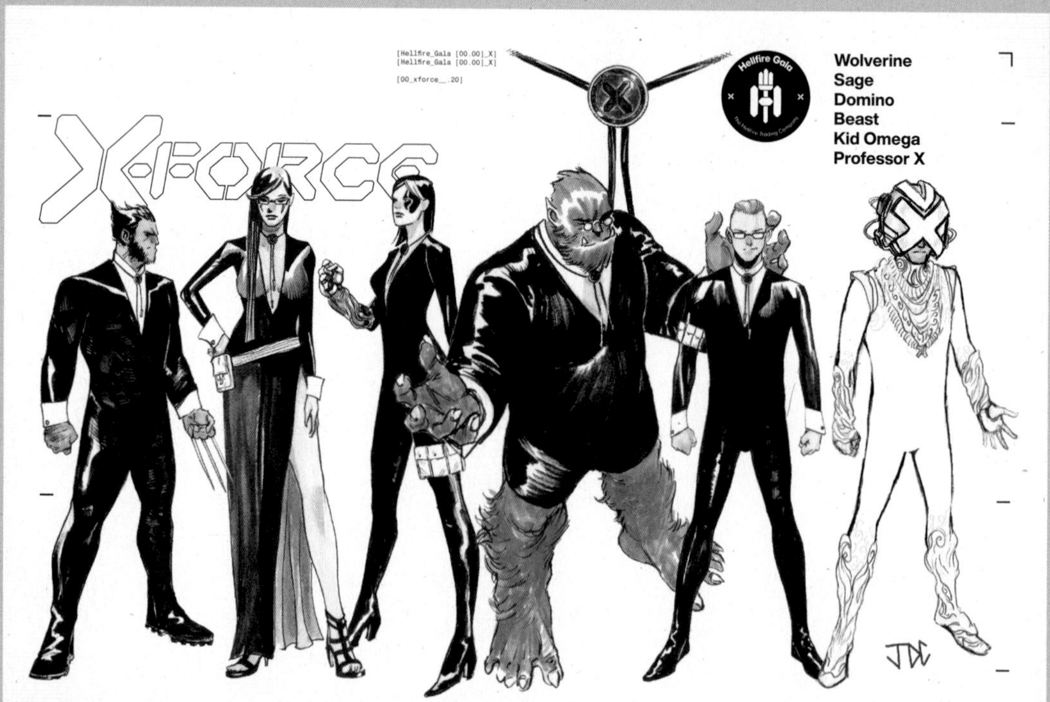

[Hellfire_Gala [00.00]_X]
[Hellfire_Gala [00.00]_X]
[00_xforce__.20]
X-FORCE
Hellfire Gala
The Hellfire Trading Company
Wolverine
Sage
Domino
Beast
Kid Omega
Professor X

Hellions #20 Design Variant
by Joshua Cassara

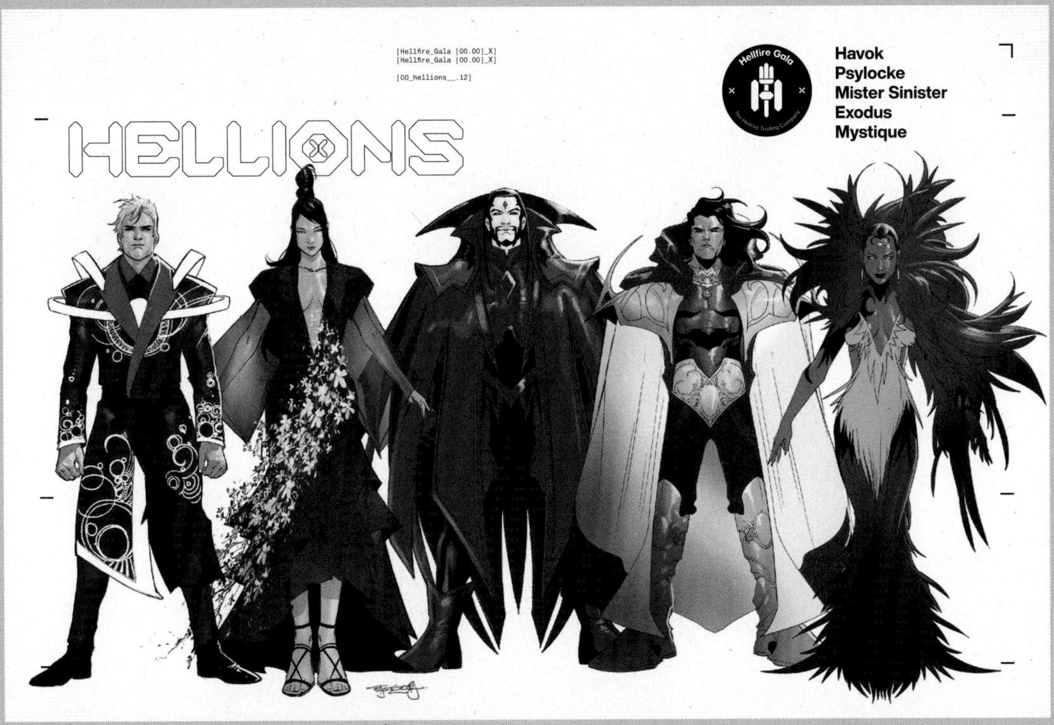
[Hellfire_Gala [00.00]_X]
[Hellfire_Gala [00.00]_X]
[00_hellions__.12]
Hellfire Gala
The Hellfire Trading Company
Havok
Psylocke
Mister Sinister
Exodus
Mystique
HELLIONS

Hellions #12 Design Variant
by Stephen Segovia

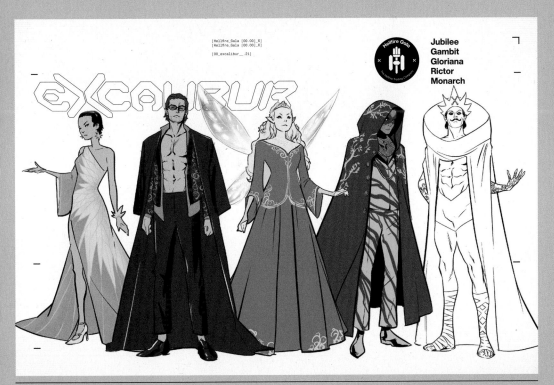

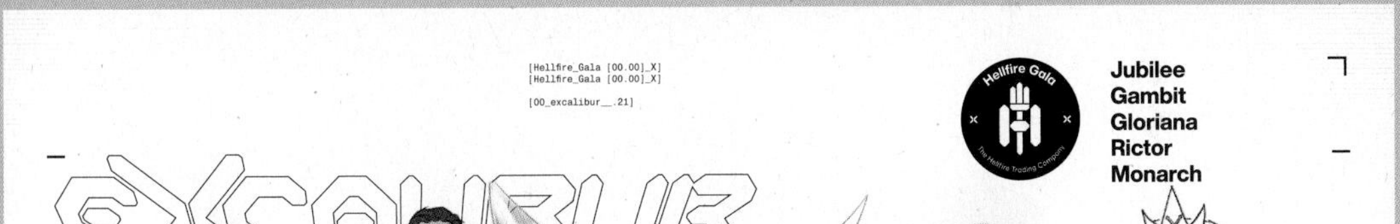
[Hellfire_Gala [00.00]_X]
[Hellfire_Gala [00.00]_X]
[00_excalibur__.21]
Hellfire Gala
The Hellfire Trading Company
Jubilee
Gambit
Gloriana
Rictor
Monarch
EXCALIBUR

Excalibur #21 Design Variant
by Marcus To

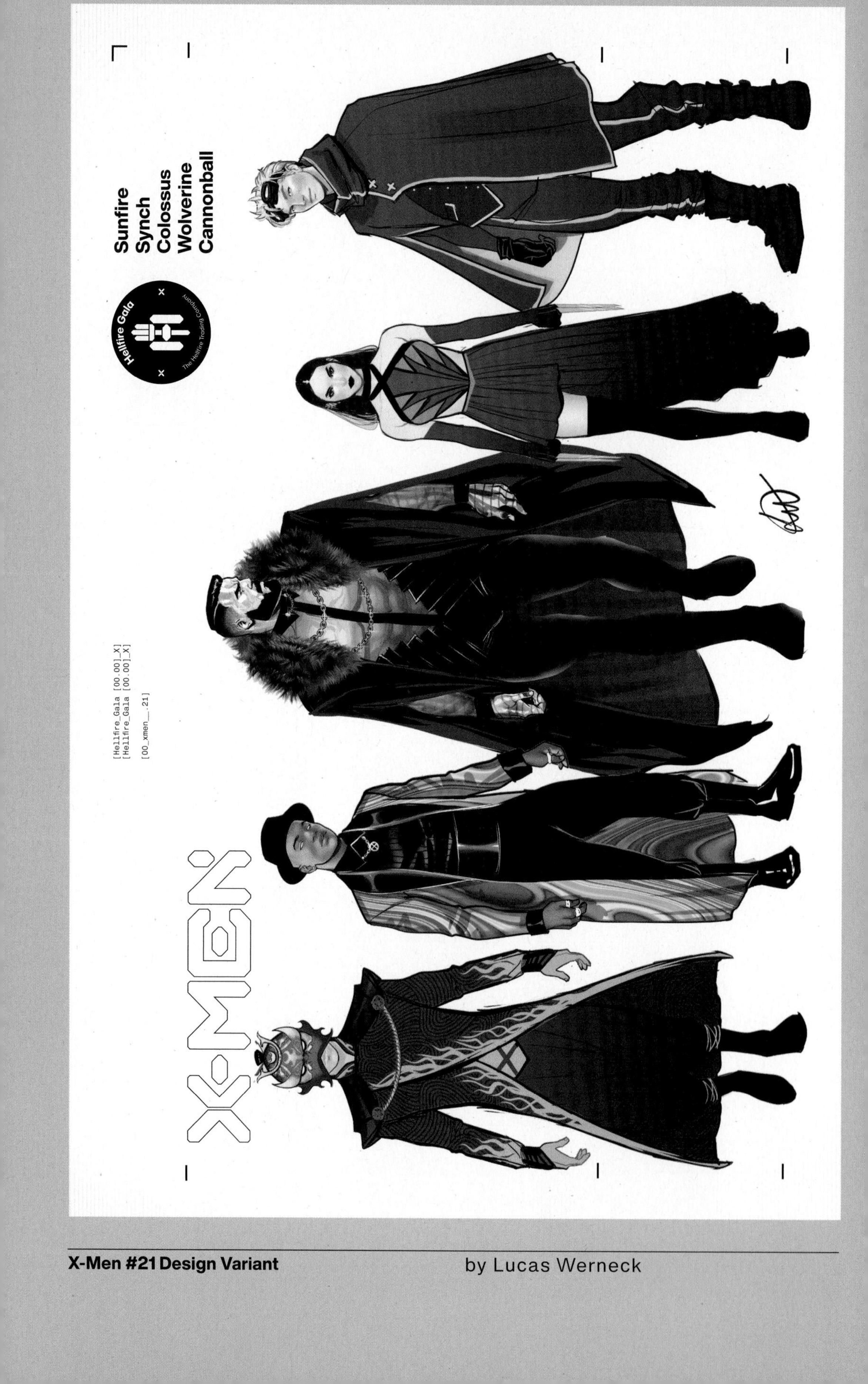
X-MEN
Sunfire
Synch
Colossus
Wolverine
Cannonball
Hellfire Gala
The Hellfire Trading Company
[Hellfire_Gala [00.00]_X]
[Hellfire_Gala [00.00]_X]
[00_xmen__.21]

X-Men #21 Design Variant

by Lucas Werneck

X-Force #20 Connecting Variant
by Russell Dauterman & Matthew Wilson

X-Men #21 Connecting Variant
by Russell Dauterman & Matthew Wilson

Marauders #21 Connecting Variant
by Russell Dauterman & Matthew Wilson

Hellions #12 Connecting Variant
by Russell Dauterman & Matthew Wilson

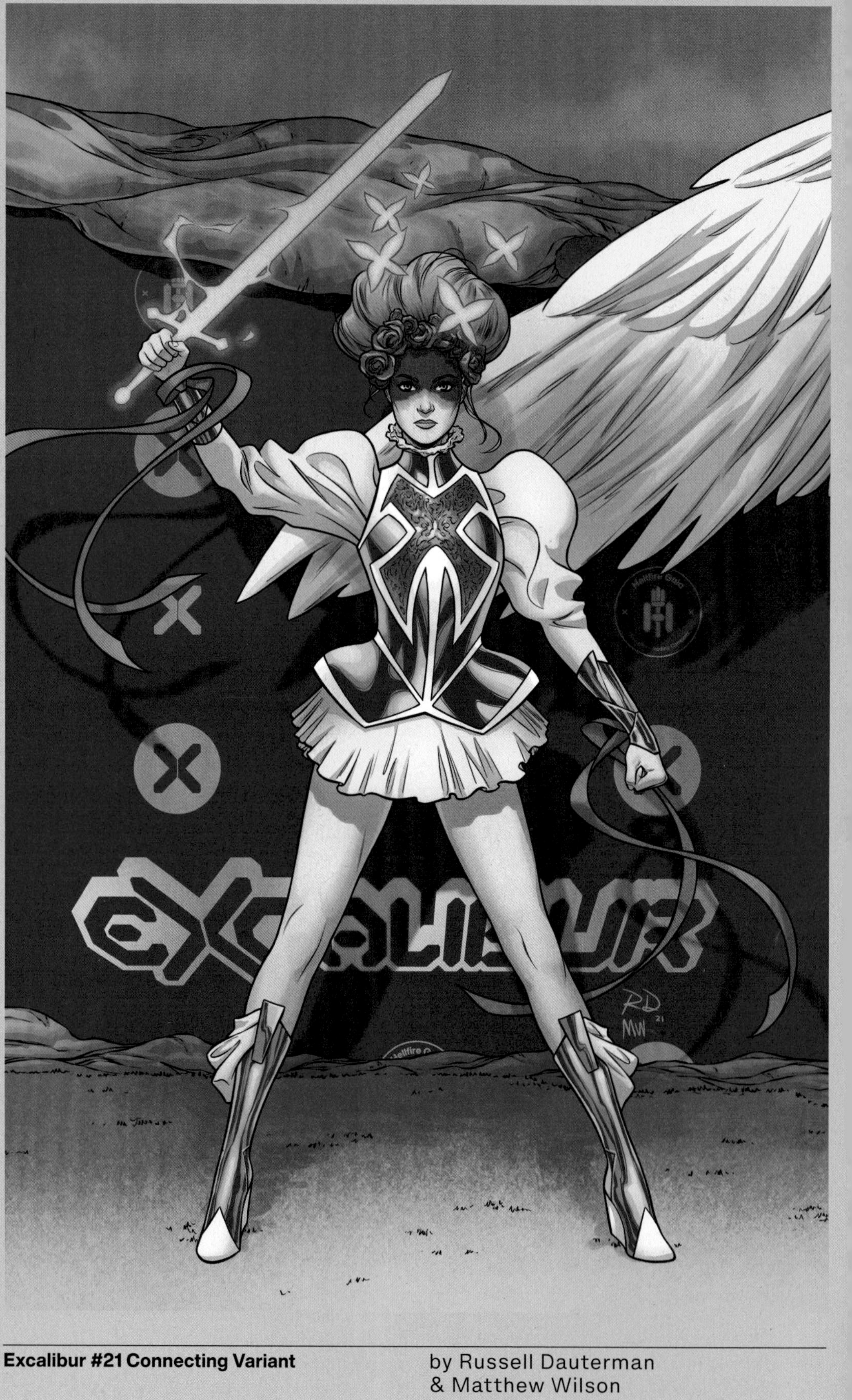
EXCALIBUR

Excalibur #21 Connecting Variant

by Russell Dauterman
& Matthew Wilson